Psychological Therapy in Pr
Other Secure Settings

CW00538905

Psychological Therapy in Prisons and Other Secure Settings

Edited by

Joel Harvey and Kirsty Smedley

Routledge
Taylor & Francis Group

LONDON AND NEW YORK

First Published 2010 by Willan Publishing

Published 2017 by Routledge

2 Park Square, Milton Park, Abingdon, Oxon, OX14 4RN
711 Third Avenue, New York, NY 10017

Routledge is an imprint of the Taylor & Francis Group, an informa business

First published 2010

ISBN   978-1-84392-799-0 paperback
       978-1-84392-800-3 hardback

British Library Cataloguing-in-Publication Data

A catalogue record for this book is available from the British Library

Project managed by Deer Park Productions, Tavistock, Devon
Typeset by GCS, Leighton Buzzard, Bedfordshire

MIX
Paper from
responsible sources
FSC   FSC™ C013985
www.fsc.org

Printed in the United Kingdom
by Henry Ling Limited

Contents

List of figures and tables

Figures

Tables

List of abbreviations

A&E	Accident and Emergency
AAI	Adult Attachment Interview
ADHD	Attention Deficit Hyperactivity Disorder
APA	American Psychological Association
BME	Black and minority ethnic people
CAMHS	Child and adolescent mental health services
CARAT	Counselling, assessment, referral, advice and throughcare
CAT	Cognitive analytic therapy
CBT	Cognitive-behaviour[al] therapy
CMHTs	Community mental health teams
CPA	Care programme approach
CPN	Community psychiatric nurse
CRE	Commission for Racial Equality
CSAP	Correctional Services Accreditation Panel
CSIP	Care Services Improvement Partnership
DBT	Dialectical behavioural therapy
DCSF	Department of Children, Schools and Families
DH	Department of Health
DRE	Delivering Race Equality
DSM-IV-TR	Diagnostic Statistical Manual IV Text Revision
DSPD	Dangerous and Severe Personality Disorder
DTO	Detention and training order
EMDR	Eye movement desensitisation reprocessing
ETS	Enhanced Thinking Skills
FOR	Focus on Resettlement

FWT	Family work team
GBH	Grievous bodily harm
GHQ	General health questionnaire
GP	General practitioner
HMCIP	Her Majesty's Chief Inspector of Prisons
HMP	Her Majesty's Prison
HMPS	Her Majesty's Prison Service
HMSO	Her Majesty's Stationery Office
IAPT	Improving access to psychological therapies
ICD	International Classification of Diseases
IEP	Incentives and earned privileges
IQ	Intelligence quotient
KPIs	Key performance indicators
LASCH	Local authority secure children's home
MAPPA	Multi-agency public protection arrangements
MDT	Multi-disciplinary team
MHA	Mental Health Act
MHIRTs	Mental health in-reach teams
MST	Multi-systemic therapy
NHS	National Health Service
NICE	National Institute for Health and Clinical Excellence
NOMS	National Offender Management Service
NPM	New public management
NSF	National Service Framework
OBPs	Offending behaviour programmes
OBPU	Offending Behaviour Programmes Unit
OMSAS	Offender management and sentencing analytical services
OPB	Offence Paralleling Behaviour
PCTs	Primary Care Trusts
PD	Personality disorder
PORT	Patient Outcomes Research Team
PRT	Prison Reform Trust
PTSD	Post-traumatic stress disorder
RCT	Randomised controlled trial
RNR	Risk-needs responsivity
SC	Supportive counselling
SCMH	Sainsbury Centre for Mental Health
SMI	Severe and enduring mental illness
SoCRATES	The Study of Cognitive Realignment Therapy in Early Schizophrenia

SOTP	Sex Offender Treatment Programme
SST	Strange Situation Test
STC	Secure training centre
TCs	Therapeutic communities
TSCC	Trauma Symptom Checklist for Children
WHO	World Health Organisation
YJB	Youth Justice Board
YOI	Young offender institution
YOT	Youth Offending Team

Acknowledgements

We would like to thank all the authors for taking the time out of their busy jobs to write their chapters. We would also like to thank the team at Willan Publishing for supporting this book. Finally, we would like to thank Deborah Drake, Luke Endersby, Isobel and Tom Harvey, Anna Jack, Heidi Kailipaka, Trudy Potter, Brigitte Squire, Maggie and Sean Smedley, Chrissie Verduyn and Daniel Wakelin for their support, encouragement and guidance, which not only helped us in the compiling of this book also but inspired the self-belief that enabled us to attempt the project in the first place.

Joel Harvey
Kirsty Smedley

Notes on contributors

Danny Clark OBE is Head of Substance Misuse, Cognitive Skills and Motivational Interventions at NOMS. He was previously the Head of the Attitudes, Thinking and Behaviour Interventions Unit at NOMS. Danny was employed as a forensic psychologist working in both the Prison and Probation Services. He was responsible for the research on and development of the Offender Assessment System. He has made a significant contribution to the implementation of accredited cognitive-behavioural programmes for offenders in custodial and community settings. His other interests include psychopathy, violent offending and therapeutic communities, all subjects on which he has publications. He is a member of the Canadian Correctional Services Programmes Accreditation Panel.

Mary Haley is a Principal Adult Psychotherapist with Cambridgeshire and Peterborough NHS Foundation Trust. She has worked with the Trust since 2003 as part of the mental health in-reach teams at two adult men's prisons. Her work involves assessment and therapeutic input to prisoners, contribution to multi-agency case management of prisoners and design and delivery of mental health awareness training for prison staff. Prior to this, she was a prison governor grade for 17 years, working at senior management levels both as a manager in prisons and in numerous policy roles including Head of Operational Training, Head of Prison Management Training and Operational Adviser to the Women's Policy Group.

Joel Harvey is a Clinical Psychologist with Cambridgeshire and Peterborough NHS Foundation Trust, seconded to Cambridgeshire Youth Offending Service. He completed his PhD in criminology at the Institute of Criminology, University of Cambridge and then trained as a clinical psychologist at the University of Manchester. Joel has previously published *Young Men in Prison: Surviving and Adapting to Life Inside* (Willan Publishing). Joel is an Honorary Visiting Fellow at the Department of Criminology, University of Leicester and a Visiting Scholar at Institute of Criminology, University of Cambridge.

Kathleen Kendall received her BA and MA in Sociology from the University of Saskatchewan and PhD in Social Policy from the University of Manchester. She previously worked with the Department of Psychiatry, University of Saskatchewan and the Correctional Service of Canada researching issues related to prisoner mental health. Kathleen is currently a Senior Lecturer in Sociology as Applied to Medicine in the School of Medicine, University of Southampton where she continues to research various topics related to prisoner mental health including an evaluation of HMP Winchester's Mental Health In-Reach Team. She is also currently working on projects related to the history of psychiatry in Canada including a study of the Rockwood Criminal Lunatic Asylum, the first purpose-built institution for individuals considered to be criminally insane.

Heather Law completed an undergraduate degree in Psychology at the University of Manchester in 2006 and since then has worked as a research assistant for the Young Persons' Directorate at Greater Manchester West Mental Health NHS Foundation Trust. Heather is currently also working as an assistant psychologist at HM YOI Hindley as part of the mental health in-reach team, under the supervision of Dr Andrew Rogers, Clinical Psychologist. During her time with the Young Persons' Directorate, Heather has been part of the team commissioned by the Department of Health and the Youth Justice Board to work on the development of a comprehensive health screening and assessment tool for young offenders in custody and to develop a model pathway of care for all young people in the criminal justice system. Heather is about to undertake a PhD at the University of Manchester on the topic of recovery from psychosis. Also, from April 2010 her new role has been as a research programme coordinator for five projects on the topic of recovery from psychosis funded by the National Institute of Health Research.

Frank Lowe works part-time as a Consultant Social Worker and Psychoanalytic Psychotherapist in the Adolescent Department of the Tavistock Clinic. He has worked formerly as a Social Services Inspector with the Social Services Inspectorate at the Department of Health and has been a senior manager of mental health services for a number of local authorities in London. Frank has for many years worked to improve access to psychological therapies for black and minority ethnic communities and currently leads a service at the Tavistock aimed at making therapy more accessible to young black people. He teaches on a number of courses and is the chair of 'Thinking Space', a monthly learning forum at the Tavistock which explores issues of race and culture in therapy. Frank has a private psychotherapy practice, consults to organisations and has published a number of papers on race and psychotherapy.

Alice Mills is a Lecturer in Criminology in the School of Social Sciences at the University of Southampton. Her research interests include healthcare in prisons, women offenders, prisoner resettlement and prisoners' families, and the relationship between prison and healthcare professional cultures. Along with colleagues from the Universities of Manchester, Lincoln, Southampton and the Institute of Psychiatry, King's College London, she has been involved in several research projects to evaluate the operation and effectiveness of the prison mental health in-reach programme in England and Wales. She is currently working on a two-year project to examine the role of the third sector (voluntary and community sector) in criminal justice and prisoner resettlement, funded by the Economic and Social Research Council.

Jules Pearson is a Consultant Clinical Psychologist at the North London Forensic Service, and has considerable experience of working in forensic settings. She has previously been employed sessionally at HMP Holloway, working with mentally ill and personality-disordered female offenders. She has been a lead psychologist on a low-secure women's ward in East London and her clinical experience has extended to consultations within the London Metropolitan Police. Throughout her career she has had a passion for exploring how race, class and gender are thought about in clinical practice and is committed to raising these issues within her forensic lectures on women, personality disorders and risk management at the University of Hertfordshire and UEL clinical psychology training courses.

Andrew Rogers is a Consultant Clinical Psychologist and is employed by the NHS as joint professional lead for clinical psychology provision into an adolescent forensic mental health service. This includes provision of specialist mental health services to a young offender institution. Andrew has worked within a health or social care setting for over 12 years and has a long-standing interest in working with young people who are 'looked after' and/or in contact with the criminal justice system. He has a special interest in attachment theory, trauma and links to youth offending. Andrew has previously led the development and provision of clinical psychology into an innovative NHS multi-disciplinary team providing mental health support for young people who were resident in both local authority secure and open residential provision. He has also worked clinically within a Tier 2 and Tier 3 child and adolescent mental health service and provided clinical psychology input to a local youth offending service. Andrew is a committee member of the British Psychological Society Faculty for Children and Young People (CYP) and a founder member of CPAFFS, a network of the CYP for clinical psychologists working with adolescents in forensic settings.

David Shelton qualified as a clinical psychologist in 1991 and worked initially in a community-based Learning Disability service, before moving into forensic services with, initially, adult offenders in the East Midlands forensic psychiatric services, and latterly with young offenders in west London since 1997. As Head of Psychology Services in the Forensic Adolescent Directorate, his work is divided between HM YOI Feltham and the Wells Unit, a 10-bedded inpatient adolescent secure unit based at the Three Bridges RSU in Ealing. In addition to his work as a psychologist, he works as part of the Family Work Team, a service dedicated to working with families of detained patients within West London Forensic Services. He qualified as a Systemic and Family Psychotherapist in 2004 at the Institute of Family Therapy in London.

John Shine is a Consultant Forensic Psychologist working for the East London NHS Foundation Trust. He has worked as a forensic psychologist for over 25 years in prison, probation and forensic mental health settings, including HMP Grendon and HM Inspectorate of Probation. He has a long-standing interest in the assessment and treatment of personality-disordered offenders and was a member of the NHS Forensic R&D Expert Advisory Committee for several years. He has published articles in many academic journals and edited two books. He is a co-author of the Professional Practice Board Report by the British Psychological Society, *Understanding Personality Disorder*.

Richard Shuker is a Chartered Forensic Psychologist and Head of Psychology and Research at HMP Grendon, a therapeutic community prison for personality-disordered offenders. He has managed cognitive behavioural programmes within adult and young offender prisons and is lead clinician on the assessment unit at HMP Grendon. His special interest is in needs assessment and treatment of high-risk offenders. He is Series Editor for the book series *Issues in Forensic Psychology* and has publications in the areas of risk assessment, treatment outcome and therapeutic communities. He has recently co-edited a book on HMP Grendon.

Kirsty Smedley is a Consultant Clinical Psychologist working for Affinity Healthcare's Young People's Service based at Cheadle Royal Hospital. Prior to this she worked in the Adolescent Forensic Service in Manchester for 10 years, where her work included developing and providing an in-reach clinical psychology service for young men at HMYOI Hindley. Kirsty was the clinical supervisor for a University of Manchester pilot study aimed at delivering CBT to young offenders in secure units and prisons. She also has a background in working with young people who are being looked after in residential care and foster placements. Kirsty has a specialist interest in working psychologically with young people with psychosis and has maintained her interest in the delivery of psychological interventions to young prisoners. She is an Honorary Lecturer at the University of Manchester.

Graham Towl is Professor of Psychology at Durham University. He has a background of working in psychiatric hospitals and prisons. He is a recipient of the British Psychological Society's (BPS) Award for Distinguished Contributions to Professional Practice, for his work in fundamentally restructuring, expanding and placing on a firmer professional footing the work of psychologists in prisons. He was previously Chair of the BPS Division of Forensic Psychology where he led work on professional standards in general and ethical standards in particular. His roles have included the senior civil servant positions of Head of Psychology for Prisons and Probation Services at the Home Office, and subsequently Chief Psychologist at the Ministry of Justice. In 2000 he was made Visiting Professor at Birmingham University.

He has published extensively in the field of forensics. His most recent book, *Forensic Psychology* (2010) was co-edited with Professor David Crighton. In 2008 he was appointed as Professor of Psychology at Durham University and also as the Principal of St Cuthbert's Society which is a college of the university.

Abigail Willis is a Clinical Psychologist with South Staffordshire and Shropshire Healthcare NHS Foundation Trust. She qualified as a practitioner in cognitive analytic therapy in 2003. Since then she has worked with young people presenting risky behaviours in the community, custody and residential care settings. Abigail has recently accepted a new post as Consultant Clinical Psychologist with the North Wales Forensic Adolescent Consultation and Treatment Service (FACTS).

Foreword

Graham J. Towl

Durham University

This is a ground-breaking book. In recent years there have been books on therapeutic communities in prisons, psychology in prisons, psychiatry in prisons, forensic mental health, forensic psychology, forensic psychotherapy and cognitive behavioural interventions designed to reduce reconvictions, but nowhere else have I encountered such a broad-ranging collection of chapters on psychological therapy in prisons and other secure settings. Joel Harvey and Kirsty Smedley should be congratulated on their achievement in drawing together this eclectic range of works.

The quest for 'equivalent' services realised?

Health care in general and psychological services in particular have benefited from very significant increases in funding over the past decade or so in prisons. The move of responsibility for health care from the Prison Service to the National Health Service served to secure greater funding for psychological work in prisons. Politically, it is more attractive to give increased funding to health care than to prisons. The much-vaunted notion of establishing an equivalent level of health care within and beyond prisons is something that a number of the authors from this collection touch on. As a number of contributors comment, there are some distinct challenges to the configuration of health care services within the prison environment. Despite this, prisons and hospitals have much in common. So there are synergies, sometimes positive, sometimes not. Putting aside prisons the National Health Service is very far from perfect. Indeed the very term 'National *Health* Service' can be seen as something of a misnomer. National Illness Service might be deemed a more accurate description, in that it is largely a service led by illness with far more focus on the treatment of ill health than on the development and preservation of good physical and mental health. Hence, a number of significant organisational and structural problems have been transferred to prisons. There is the potential for the worst of both worlds! The dysfunctional parts and processes of the NHS mapped onto the coercive context of prisons can be a toxic mix. It is no surprise that the levels of physical and mental health assessment and treatment in prisons are very variable, given that they are not exempt from the current 'postcode lottery' that accounts for much service delivery in the NHS. In this sense, it can indeed be claimed that services are equivalent, being highly variable independent of clinical need.

Perverse incentives and professional self-interests

Political discourse on the NHS has over the past decade and beyond run in a particular and predictable direction. Doctors and nurses have tended to be viewed as 'good' while other workers remain largely unseen, except 'managers' who are routinely captured as 'bad' or at least not delivering 'frontline' services (and are therefore less worthy!). Periodically some relabelling goes on, whereby some managers who are also nurses or doctors get relabelled using their health professional status – but do the same role. This can give the appearance of a reduction in the number of managers, which can be politically desirable. Such nonsense reflects the perverse interests that can develop from inappropriate target-setting (more of this later, especially in relation to psychological work aimed at reducing the risk of reconvictions).

The perceived 'goodness' of doctors has over recent years been called into question with an increasing focus on how levels of pay have increased very markedly. Survey results indicate that the majority of the public consider general practitioners to be overpaid (at an average pay level of £104,000 in 2010 from the NHS for the services they provide (YouGov 2010 accessed at www.yougov.co.uk). However, cash incentives for individual professionals seem to have driven a range of NHS reforms aimed at changing the behaviour of doctors in order to focus upon the goals of government. The pay of many psychologists has also risen sharply within applied psychological services under, for example, the 'Agenda for Change' pay structures. What is clear is that much of the money invested into improvements in health has gone into staff pay and conditions, particularly for the higher end of experienced professional staff, rather than being sufficiently invested in improved patient outcomes. Pay rises have been similarly marked for psychologists in prisons, particularly for fully qualified staff. There is always a balance to be struck between fair pay awards and the number of staff employed within limited budgets.

Psychologists will be as keen as other professionals appear to be to preserve their market interests in service delivery. To some degree this is simply the nature of professions. But, unacceptably, professional self-interests can, at times, get in the way of providing the best for those who most need it. This can be seen within applied psychology with some forensic psychologists not accepting that clinical, counselling, health and educational psychologists have a role to play in psychological services for prisoners or other forensic patients. It is competence with the accountability of qualification as an applied psychologist, from whatever sub-specialism, which should drive the process, not the tribalism of the British Psychological Society's divisional structures. The alternative is fewer and poorer services with less access for those most in need. Similar problems exist with clinical psychologists sometimes attempting to shut out health, counselling, educational and forensic psychologists from NHS facilities with varying degrees of 'success'.

The regrettable truth is that as psychologists we can sometimes be part of the problem and reduce opportunities for some of the most vulnerable to access much-needed services. In our different ways, we can sometimes, if often inadvertently, effectively be simply putting our own professional interests first.

New public management and targets

As major public services, health and criminal justice have been subject to what has become known as the discipline of New Public Management (NPM). In short, NPM is based upon the questionable assumption that private-sector management methods may be routinely and directly applied to public services, which makes them more efficient and effective. Public managers of the twenty-first century tend to assume that their services will have a 'business plan', despite not being businesses. It is one thing to be businesslike, with an eye to controlling costs and ensuring that public money is well spent, but it is another to pretend that a prison or a hospital is a business. This is not to claim that, however disagreeable to some, patient and prisoner experiences cannot be viewed as 'commodities', insofar as there has been the introduction of pseudo-markets and private-sector providers of public services. Public services are, though, primarily driven by politics and the private sector is driven by markets. Both beget different types of relationships. At a general level there has effectively been a marketisation of service provision with inbuilt elaborate commissioning structures.

The bureaucracy of NPM includes the setting of Key Performance Indicators (KPIs). This is significant in its direct impact upon which therapy is and is not undertaken in prisons. It was the organisational aim of reducing the risk of reconviction as a KPI that effectively institutionalised the running of such 'programmes' of interventions in prisons. In the traditional 'command and control' managerial structures of prisons, such 'completions' would take place. Historically the evidence in support of the efficacy of prisoner 'programmes' has been somewhat overblown. Despite some initially promising results, large-scale UK studies to date have shown no treatment effects. For example, sex offender treatment programmes have been running for over 15 years in prisons and yet there are no Randomised Control Trials (RCTs) demonstrating their effectiveness in reducing the risk of reconvictions for sex offences in the UK. In work to reduce the risk of reconvictions through 'programmes' there remains an overreliance upon international evidence and historical small-scale studies from the UK, often with an undue reliance upon psychometric data of questionable relevance or scientific quality. From a therapeutic perspective what some described as 'standards and accreditation', others viewed merely as manual compliance and effectively deprofessionalisation and 'dumbing down'. The introduction of such a large-scale manual-based approach with annual 'completion' targets to working with prisoners, based upon equivocal evidence, was an act of faith which led to the effective exclusion of some other therapeutic approaches.

It is encouraging to see that things are starting to change, and this book is a tribute to such changes. The institutionalisation of staff compliance through manualisation has its limits, as alluded to by some of this collection of authors. Such compliant responses are challenged in this stimulating volume with a salutary reminder of the need to have an increased emphasis upon 'therapist characteristics'.

The misuse of the vaguely medicalised terms routinely used in the literature and practice of 'prisoner programmes' is potentially misleading, or at best merely inaccurate. Terms such as 'criminogenic' and 'high dosage' which serve to facilitate the process of mistaking some 'behavioural technologies' for science are routinely misused. At very best this is unnecessary jargon.

There is no mention in this entire volume of 'healthogenic needs', and with good reason; that would equally be nonsense. Such terms amount to little more than pseudoscientific terms used as marketing tools for such approaches. This is a shame because this can serve to demean sometimes potentially effective work. The idea of measuring an element of treatment effectiveness in prisons simply by the number of people who have attended an intervention does not stand up to any serious scientific scrutiny.

However, Orwellian, terms such as 'programme compliance' and 'treatment integrity' may well not, arguably, be out of place in health care settings where patients may be routinely referred to as 'non-compliant', 'threatening suicide', 'manipulative' and 'attention seeking' and it is in this way that the cultures of health and criminal justice settings have, worryingly, much in common. Patients and prisoners can become those that we do things to, rather than do things with or, indeed, for. And this is touched upon by some of the authors. There are perceived to be 'deserving' and 'undeserving' prisoners and patients. These cultural barriers to effective work are challenged in this book, in which many contributors recognise the need to work alongside the prisoner or patient to achieve effective meaningful change.

In short, hospitals and prisons have much in common in their cultures and public-sector contexts. Much of this is dysfunctional, as indicated above. However, with significant injections of investment in health services, this book perhaps attests to the fact that there is hope to build on some of the health service improvements for patients who are resident in prisons. This hope is all the stronger if, as professionals, we are bold enough to challenge current orthodoxies and to take a truly evidence-based approach to our work, underpinned by a compassion, consideration and respect for those we serve: our patients.

I hope that readers take the opportunity to reflect critically upon the chapters of this book to inform and improve their understanding of therapeutic work in the challenging environment of prisons.

Chapter 1

Introduction

Joel Harvey and Kirsty Smedley

In 2001, the government document *Changing the Outlook: A Strategy for Developing and Modernising Mental Health Services in Prisons* (DH and HMPS 2001) set out a five-year plan to improve the health care provision of prisoners. This document put forward the principle of 'equivalence', in that 'prisoners should have access to the same range and quality of services appropriate to their needs as are available to the general population through the NHS' (DH and HMPS 2001). In 2006 the transferring of commissioning responsibility from the Prison Service to the NHS was completed. Mental health in-reach teams (MHIRTs) were introduced between 2003 and 2006 in order to support prisoners with severe and enduring mental health problems. In practice, MHIRTs have taken a broader remit and have also attempted to meet the needs of prisoners with a range of mental health difficulties including depression, self-injury and post-traumatic stress disorder (PTSD), to name but a few (see Bradley 2009). However, there still remains a high level of unmet need (Durcan and Knowles 2006; SCMH 2009) and although there are now some primary care services offering psychological therapy (e.g. HMP Liverpool) it is argued that there is still a need for more primary care services within prisons (SCMH 2007; SCMH 2009). In 2009 the Department of Health published the document *Improving Access to Psychological Therapy (IAPT) Offenders Positive Practice*. This document, aimed at commissioners of IAPT services, states that 'IAPT services should be available and effective for both men and women who come into contact with the criminal justice system, as well as those who are at risk of offending' (DH 2009: 4). In recent years there has been a move to set up IAPT services in prisons, as for example in HMP Brixton, but this work is in progress.

At a policy level steps have thus been taken to stress the importance of meeting the needs of prisoners, although how these needs are met in practice is another complex question. It is important to state at the outset of this book that the psychological needs of offenders far exceeds the mental health resources available to meet those needs (Brooker *et al.* 2008). To receive psychological therapy in prison remains a rare occurrence given the number of prisoners who could potentially benefit from a therapeutic intervention (Brooker and Gojkovic 2009). Nevertheless, we must not underestimate the valuable work that is being carried out across prisons in England and Wales. In fact, this book sets out to examine a number of different therapeutic approaches that are used in prisons and other secure settings in England and Wales and to offer insights into the challenges of such work.

Prisons and other secure settings are psychologically demanding environments which require people to draw upon a range of internal and external resources in order to survive. There are 138 prisons in England and Wales and they vary in function, size, architecture, security classification and whether they are run by the public or private sector (see Jewkes 2007; HMPS 2010). There are also four private secure training centres for young people aged between 15 and 17. On 30 June 2009 there were 83,454 people in prison; of these 79,158 were male and 4,292 were female (Ministry of Justice 2009). The rate of imprisonment in England and Wales has almost doubled since January 1993, despite crime rates remaining relatively stable (PRT 2009). Indeed, Jewkes and Johnston (2006) argue that the UK has developed 'a deep cultural attachment to the prison' (p. 284). In addition to over 80,000 prisoners in custody, there are 3,937 'mentally disordered offenders' detained in hospital settings in England and Wales (Ministry of Justice 2010).[1] In 2008 the number of people transferred from prison to hospital was 926 (Ministry of Justice 2010), although it has been recognised that on average there were 262 prisoners waiting to be transferred to an NHS hospital who were still in prison (Bradley 2009). This book also makes reference to therapy provision within these medium- and low-secure hospital settings.[2] Considering secure hospital settings alongside prison helps to tease out the issues that are specific to therapy provision within the prison environment.

The mental health needs of prisoners

It is well documented that people who are in prison have a number of psychological difficulties (Singleton *et al.* 1998; Fazel and Danesh 2002; Rickford and Edgar 2005; HMCIP 2007; Bradley 2009; Corston 2007; Romily and Bartlett 2010). And as well as having mental health needs, and yet related to those needs, many prisoners suffer great social exclusion (Social Exclusion Unit 2002). The Social Exclusion Unit (2002) found that prisoners differed from people in the general community, in that: 27 per cent of prisoners were taken into care as a child (compared to 2 per cent of the general population), 32 per cent were homeless (compared to 0.9 per cent of the general population), 67 per cent were unemployed before coming to prison (compared to 5 per cent of general population), 65 per cent had numeracy difficulties and 48 per cent had reading difficulties (compared to 23 per cent and between 21 per cent and 33 per cent of the general population respectively). It is important that these needs are met, alongside mental health needs, in order to improve prisoners' quality of life and sense of well-being. Indeed, a holistic approach to the care of prisoners is needed in order to bring about psychological change.

Analysing the mental health needs of prisoners in more detail, Singleton *et al.* (1998) found that 90 per cent of prisoners had a diagnosis of at least one mental disorder. These difficulties include depression, anxiety, psychosis, PTSD and personality disorders (see Mills and Kendall, Chapter 2, this book). It has been found that the prevalence rate for psychosis is between 6 per cent and 13 per cent (Singleton *et al.* 1998) among prisoners compared to 0.4 per cent of the general working population (Singleton *et al.* 2000). A prevalence rate of between 40 per cent and 76 per cent was found for neurotic disorders (Singleton *et al.* 1998) compared to 17.3 per cent in the general working population (Singleton *et al.* 2000). Singleton *et al.* (1998) found that between 50 per cent and 78 per cent of prisoners reached the criteria for a personality disorder compared to between 3.4 per cent and 5.4 per cent in the general working population (Singleton *et al.* 2000).

Adams and Ferrandino (2008) state that 'the most common mental illnesses in the inmate population are depression, schizophrenia and bipolar disorder, a finding that applies to prisons in both the United States and the United Kingdom' (p. 914). It has also been found that a high proportion of prisoners have had problems with substance misuse prior to entering prison (Singleton *et al.* 1998; Brooke *et al.* 2000; Liebling *et al.* 2005; Fazel *et al.* 2006). Fazel *et al.* (2006) found that the prevalence rate for alcohol abuse and dependence ranged between 18 and 30 per cent for male prisoners and 10 to 24 per cent for female prisoners. Prevalence rates for drug abuse and dependency ranged from 10 to 48 per cent for male prisoners and 30 to 60 per cent for female prisoners.

Moreover, as mentioned above, many people with mental health difficulties in prison may require hospital treatment but, due to a shortage of hospital beds, experience severe delays in their transfer (see Rickford and Edgar 2005). For these individuals imprisonment is not an appropriate place for treatment, and their needs may not be fully met until they are transferred to a hospital setting.

A large proportion of prisoners experience a high level of psychological distress (Liebling et al. 2005; HMCIP 2007; Harvey 2007). A thematic review by Her Majesty's Chief Inspector of Prisons (HMCIP) found that 65 per cent of women and 52 per cent of men obtained high scores on the GHQ-12, a screening tool for psychological distress (HMIP 2007). Extensive research has also been carried out in relation to self-harm and suicide in prisons (Liebling 1992; Shaw et al. 2004; Jenkins et al. 2005; Leese et al. 2006; Liebling 2007). During 2007 there were 22,459 recorded incidents of self-harm; women accounted for 54 per cent of these incidents (PRT 2009). Over 100 prisoners were resuscitated after serious self-harm and 92 completed suicide (PRT 2009). Fazel et al. (2005) note that the number of prisoners completing suicide has risen between 1978 and 2003; prisoners are five times more likely to complete suicide than people in the general community are.

Dear (2008), in a review of his own research over the past 10 years in Australia, concludes that 'self-harming behaviour occurs in a context of heightened distress and one of our central findings was that prisoners who self-harm report poorer coping responses than do those who do not self-harm' (p. 469). He found that prisoners self-harmed following different precipitating factors. They divided these factors into five main groups: a stressful event within the prison, a consequence of imprisonment (e.g. missing a family member), an event occurring outside prison, psychological symptoms (e.g. PTSD symptoms) and aspects of the wider criminal justice system. The first category, a stressful event occurring within the prison, was the most cited reason for self-harm. Dear (2008) put forward five broad recommendations to prison authorities in order to help prevent self-harm in prison: removing aspects of the prison environment that are associated with high levels of self-harm; screening prisoners for the vulnerability factors to self-harm; enabling prison staff to detect prisoners' distress; providing interventions in order to improve prisoners' ability to cope; and, for the management, focusing on supporting distressed prisoners (rather than focusing solely on physical barriers). The role of psychological therapy in prison is also of relevance to the reduction in suicide and self-harm.

The psychosocial experience of imprisonment

For some people, imprisonment might seem an opportunity for stability and containment away from a difficult and confusing life outside; however, it is sad that imprisonment, with its loss of freedoms, can seem the best opportunity one has. And far more people find imprisonment to be challenging and destabilising. Although prisons differ in their 'quality of life' (see Liebling 2004), and although individuals react and cope differently with being in custody (see Adams 1992; Liebling and Maruna 2005), undoubtedly the prison presents practical, social and psychological challenges to many of them. Indeed, as Liebling and Maruna (2005) state, 'fear, anxiety, loneliness, trauma, depression, injustice, powerlessness, violence and uncertainty are all part of the experience of prison life' (Liebling and Maruna 2005: 3). Bullying is prevalent in custody (see Ireland 2002) and can be a precipitator to self-harm (Liebling 1992; Dear 2008). Rickford and Edgar, in their review of the mental health needs of men in prisons in the UK, concluded that 'prisons cause social isolation, subjecting people to danger and idleness, failing to respect their human dignity, and maintaining them, too often, in inhumane conditions' (Rickford and Edgar 2005: 29).

The pains of imprisonment are pervasive and include the deprivations of liberty, goods and services, heterosexual relationships, autonomy and security (Sykes 1958). Sykes states that 'however painful these frustrations and deprivations may be in the immediate terms of thwarted goals, discomfort, boredom, and loneliness, they carry a more profound hurt as a set of threats or attacks which are directed against the very foundations of the prisoner's being' (Sykes 1958, cited in Jewkes and Johnston 2006: 172). Jamieson and Grounds (2005) remind us that 'the prisoner's time (lost out of a finite life span) is not counted among these pains or losses' (p. 52) and that the pains of imprisonment can extend into the prisoner's life post-sentence through enduring changes in their personality.

Across the period of imprisonment, the entry period has been found to be an acutely painful one, characterised by concerns about

5

separation and loss, a lack of safety, uncertainty, and a loss of freedom (Liebling 1999; Harvey 2007). In a study of young men adapting to their first month in prison, Harvey found that those prisoners who had the most difficulty regulating their emotions and who had higher levels of distress upon entry found it most difficult to adapt to life in prison over time. They had a more painful experience of imprisonment, were more determined by their environment, and found it more difficult to seek and accept any help that might have been on offer.

One of the most extensive studies to be carried out examining this entry period, and prisoners' adaptation subsequently, was carried out by Zamble and Porporino (1988). In their longitudinal study of prisoner adaptation in Canada they interviewed male prisoners a few weeks after their reception into custody and followed up after four and sixteen months. At the first time interval prisoners were having a difficult time and experienced high levels of distress. However, several problems were identified from interviews carried out after a few weeks in prison. These were coded into the following categories: missing their family and friends; missing their freedom; missing a specific object or activity; conflicts with other prisoners; regrets about the past; concern with the future; boredom; cell conditions; medical services; a lack of staff support; a concern with safety; and a lack of programmes or activities. Indeed, being apart from family and friends was cited as the most difficult problem for prisoners during the first two weeks.

The interaction between the individual and the environment is important in determining the prisoners' experience. Toch (1977) argued that in order for an individual to adapt to life inside and to survive psychologically there has to be a match between an individual's needs and the environment. Toch identified seven needs which were the needs for: safety, privacy, structure, emotional feedback, support, activity and freedom. When there is a 'fit' between the individual's needs and the environment's ability to meet these needs then successful adjustment may occur. It could be argued that the provision of psychological therapy may go some way to meeting the emotional needs of prisoners. Moreover, Liebling *et al.* (2005), in their evaluation of the safer locals programme,[3] found that both self-reported levels of pre-existing vulnerability (e.g. previous self-harm, substance misuse, psychiatric problems) *and* also aspects of the quality of the prison environment contributed to levels of prisoner distress. Indeed, 'levels of distress were associated with relational dimensions (including relationships with staff, respect, fairness), dignity, frustration, family contact and participating in offending behaviour programmes and personal development activities' (Liebling *et al.* 2005: 10). The environment thus clearly matters in relation to the experience of imprisonment. Furthermore, it appears that the environment can offset the distress experienced by 'high vulnerability' prisoners. Liebling *et al.* (2005) found that 'high vulnerability' prisoners (that is those with a history of psychiatric difficulties and self-harming behaviour) showed less distress when they had more time out of cell, more employment, fewer cancellations of association, greater opportunities of contact with family members and an opportunity to participate in offending behaviour courses. When specifically considering prisoners with pre-existing mental health difficulties it appears that the prison can either help alleviate, or can contribute further to, their psychological distress through its response as an institution.

Meeting the mental health needs of prisoners through psychological therapy

Many prisoners thus experience mental health problems before arriving at the prison gate and the prison experience may present them with further social and psychological challenges. So how can staff respond to the psychological needs of prisoners? How can prisoners be helped to cope with imprisonment? Or, indeed, how can staff prevent prisoners' psychological difficulties being exacerbated? In this book it is argued that the provision of psychological therapy could, in part, contribute to the alleviation of this distress. It is recognised that prisoners draw upon support from a number of different professionals working in the prison and that mental health support is just one form of support. Indeed, family contact, when available and supportive, is what prisoners yearn for most in order to improve their well-being while in custody (Harvey 2007). However, it is argued that therapy may have a useful role to play in helping prisoners who are experiencing psychological difficulties.

But what is defined as therapy? Roth and Fonagy (2005) in their critical review of psychotherapy in mental health cite Strupp's (1978) definition of psychotherapy as 'an interpersonal process designed to bring about modifications of feelings, cognitions, attitudes and behaviour which have proved troublesome to the person seeking help from a trained professional' (cited in Roth and Fonagy 2005: 5). Roth and Fonagy organise the different therapies that are practised in the general community into seven main areas: psychodynamic; behavioural and cognitive-behavioural; interpersonal; strategic or systemic; supportive and experiential; group; and counselling (see Roth and Fonagy 2005: Ch. 1).

And what types of therapy are practised in prisons? In the US, Boothby and Clements (2000) carried out a survey of correctional psychologists working in state and federal prisons. They found that most psychologists had degrees in clinical psychology (67 per cent in state prisons and 49 per cent in federal prisons). The majority of respondents used cognitive-behavioural therapy (CBT) in their practice but people also used other approaches, including behavioural, rational-emotive, psychodynamic, humanistic, existential and systemic ones. The four most common problems treated were depression, anger, psychosis and anxiety. Kjelseberg *et al.* (2006) carried out a survey examining the provision of therapy in Norwegian prisons, excluding offending behaviour programmes. They found that the therapy offered was of a supportive or cognitive-behavioural modality; psychodynamic approaches were rare. However, in England and Wales, to our knowledge, no such survey exists and therefore the full range of therapeutic practices is not currently known.

This book focuses on four psychological therapies used: attachment-based psychodynamic psychotherapy, cognitive behaviour therapy (CBT), cognitive analytic therapy (CAT) and systemic psychotherapy. The book also considers democratic therapeutic communities. These therapies were chosen based on an 'opportunistic' sample of psychologists and psychotherapists who were willing to write about their practice and therefore by no means should this list be considered exhaustive. There are therapeutic approaches that are used in prisons in England and Wales which are not documented in this book. For example, dialectical behavioural therapy (DBT) has been piloted with women who have been diagnosed with borderline personality disorder (BPD) (Nee and Farman 2005, 2007, 2008). Nee and Farman (2008) summarise the results of two pilots in three prisons in England and conclude that 'we have seen that DBT can statistically significantly reduce psychometric measures of the borderline profile, impulsivity, locus of control, self-esteem and emotion control in the one-year programmes, up to six-month follow-up, and bring about a downturn in self-harm in the prison context' (p. 11). The authors note that the pilot sites did not continue to offer DBT but that the Department of Health and Ministry of Justice was to include DBT within its model of working with very high-risk women.

Other therapeutic approaches used in prison have been researched in other countries. Johnson and Zlotnick (2008) in the US carried out a pilot study of interpersonal therapy for depressed prisoners. They found that 72 per cent no longer met the criteria for depression after completing the therapy. Zlotnick *et al.* (2003) carried out a pilot study in the US examining the effectiveness of CBT with women who had problems with substance misuse and PTSD. They found that, after treatment, 52 per cent of women no longer met criteria for PTSD and 46 per cent no longer did at a three-month follow-up, although they note that they did not include a control group and that therefore the findings are tentative. Among other therapies, Mahoney and Daniel (2006) provide an account of narrative therapy with women in a US prison and conclude that it could 'become a powerful tool for ensuring that the voices of incarcerated women are heard and that their preferred ways of being are taken seriously' (p. 87).

Brooker *et al.* (2002) carried out a systemic of the literature (with inclusion and exclusion criteria) on the evidence of pharmacological and non-pharmacological interventions used to treat 'major mental disorders' among prisoners, whose difficulties included personality disorder, neurotic disorders, alcohol and drug dependency, suicide and self-harm, schizophrenia and other related psychoses. They found that some research had been carried out in relation to 'mental and behavioural disorders due to psychoactive substance abuse', 'schizophrenia, schizotypal and delusional disorders' and 'disorders of adult personality and behaviour'. However, they found no specific research on interventions with prisoners with 'affective disorders' or 'neurotic, stress-related and somatoform disorders'. From this review Brooker *et al.* (2002) concluded that 'the paucity of research on interventions for prisoners with mental disorders is disappointing. What evidence exists is frequently of a poor quality and poorly reported. Only one study was an RCT and only two additional studies presented results from a concurrent control group' (p. 37). More recently, Brooker *et al.* (2007), in their updated review which included literature from 2002 to 2006, found three new trials. However, none of these trials 'compared the efficacy of an intervention with a control condition – so according to our strict criteria should maybe not have been included at all' (Brooker *et al.* 2007: 46). They conclude that 'there is a clear clinical and ethical need to carry out more intervention outcome research with this special population' (Brooker *et al.* 2007: 47).

While there is no documented research or evidence base for using the therapies detailed in this book in prisons in the UK, their exploration marks a step in understanding the potential benefits of their approach. It is hoped that this book may therefore spark an interest in evaluating specific therapy modalities. Moreover, as Yalom (2001) states, '*nonvalidated* therapies are not *invalidated* therapies' (p. 223). It is hoped that an evidence base will accumulate as services develop in prisons over time.

A shift in the role of psychologists in prisons

Prior to the introduction of MHIRTs, the psychologists who were working in prisons – predominantly forensic psychologists – have focused mainly on interventions that aim to reduce reoffending, suicide prevention and on general organisational issues (see Towl 2003). It has been argued that historically this tradition of forensic psychology in prisons has 'taken on a single-paradigmatic approach, little informed by, or integrated with, other paradigms' (Crighton and Towl 2008: 9) with 'an increasingly narrow focus on pre-set output targets (completions), often at the expense of impacts for individuals or for broader outcomes of social utility' (*ibid*: 9). The focus of offending behaviour courses has been to meet the 'criminogenic' needs of offenders, factors found to be associated with reoffending (Andrews and Bonta 2006). Psychologists have drawn upon the principles of risk-need-responsivity. In short, the risk principle 'suggests that offenders being assessed as being at high risk for offending should receive higher levels of intervention, including high-intensity treatment' (Ward and Maruna 2007: 91); the needs principle 'proposes that only variables empirically associated with offending reduction should be targeted in treatment' (*ibid*: 93); and the responsivity principle 'describes the role of treatment-level issues in the match between treatment modality and offender's learning style [and] the individual characteristics of offenders which will make them more or less likely to engage with treatment' (*ibid*: 95). Treatment has therefore become synonymous with reducing criminality. While learning skills through an offending behaviour programme may potentially equip prisoners with skills to deal with the other difficulties in their lives, the focus of the work is on reducing the likelihood that they will engage in offending behaviour. As McGuire (2002) states, 'non-criminogenic needs are important but changing criminogenic needs should be the touchstone in working with offenders' (p. xii).

However, through the introduction of MHIRTs and development of some primary care psychological services the role of psychologists, and the meaning of 'treatment', has the potential to become broader. MHIRTs were created 'in order to address generic mental health problems rather than any link between mental health and offending' (HMCIP 2007:19). This is not to say that such therapeutic work cannot focus on offending behaviour. A prisoner may be motivated to work specifically on understanding why he committed an offence. Moreover, the prisoner may focus on a goal, for example on understanding his emotions and how to regulate them, which may be a contributing factor towards offending behaviour. However, therapy provided in this broader manner has greater scope to work on the problems that prisoners themselves bring to therapy and to develop individual case formulations. These interventions may be more tailored to meeting the needs of specific individuals rather than suited to delivery in a group format. Prisoners have been eager to receive interventions that aim to help them in general, rather than interventions that focus on their offending. Crewe (2009), in his study of a Category C prison, found that prisoners 'were crying out for neutral interventions' and that 'a large proportion expressed concerns about mental health issues and longed for help to deal with deep-rooted personal problems' (p. 120). Psychologists and psychotherapists now have more opportunity to provide a broader range of services in prisons. Mullen (2002) states that 'addressing active [mental health] symptoms is the core task for mental health professionals and it is a bonus if this also reduces the risk of criminal behaviour' (p. 303). He states that the 'time has come to return to a traditional concern with care and treatment of patients' (*ibid.*).

Moreover, it can be argued that non-offence-focused work may be a necessary condition for offence-focused work to take place later. Indeed, as Ward and Maruna (2008) have stated: 'targeting non-criminogenic needs might often be a necessary condition of targeting criminogenic needs by virtue of the fact that any intervention requires that offenders are sufficiently attentive and receptive to the therapeutic content of sessions' (p. 102). Ward and Maruna (2007) argue that non-criminogenic needs, such as 'distress', financial problems or low self-esteem, can impact upon the therapeutic alliance and so they argue that 'therapists should direct attention to some types of non-criminogenic needs, not just because it is ethical and "good" to do so, but because of the value on sustaining a sound therapeutic alliance' (p. 102). They argue that this broader attention is a mandatory, not a discretionary, part of an intervention and will determine whether it is effective or not. Thus, focusing on 'non-criminogenic' needs is not only essential in order to alleviate the distress of someone in prison but might also help an individual engage in offence-focused work.

The main focus on this book is therefore on psychological work that takes place outside the realm of offending behaviour programmes. However, it is also argued that there is a need for better integration of psychological provision from applied psychologists within prisons. A person's needs cannot be divided neatly into 'criminogenic' versus 'non-criminogenic' needs; both sets of needs may be important to improve well-being and reduce reoffending. This book therefore does also discuss offence-related work and in particular has a chapter which focuses exclusively on the development and evaluation of offending behaviour programmes (see Clark, Chapter 11, this book). It has been recognised that there has also been a shift in the manner in which some offending behaviour programmes are provided, as more emphasis has been placed on the therapeutic relationship within offending behaviour programmes (see Clark, Chapter 11).

In order to make progress towards meeting the psychological needs of prisoners, it appears that psychological services predominately focusing on mental health and those services predominately focusing on offending behaviour would benefit from integration. While there is a need for effective multidisciplinary working with other professions, there is also a need for intradisciplinary working within psychology itself, with the sub-specialisms learning from one another.

Outline of chapters

To advance that conversation, this book brings together a collection of papers from academics and practitioners and analyses in detail a range of psychological therapies used with prisoners. It brings them together within one volume and highlights the complexity of providing therapy in prisons. One of the editors of this book interviewed many of the contributors about their work providing psychological therapy in prisons and other secure settings. These interviews were transcribed in order to help them in reflecting on their own practice and in forming the content of their chapters. The breadth of experience of the contributors combines both clinical psychology and forensic psychology, along with psychotherapy and criminology; they have experience too in a range of environments, including juvenile and young offender establishments, local prisons, dispersal prisons and working at HM Prison Service Headquarters. The authors also have experience working in medium- and low-secure settings for male and female offenders and at male adolescent forensic units in England.

Alice Mills and Kathleen Kendall, in Chapter 2, start the book by exploring in more detail the recent changes in policy that have attempted to address the mental health needs of prisoners (Durcan and Knowles 2006; HMCIP 2007). They recognise that despite these changes there still remains a high level of unmet need. Mills and Kendall examine the development of MHIRTs and provide further consideration of the mental health problems of prisoners. Their chapter critically examines the concept of 'equivalent' health care and asks whether it is possible, or indeed desirable, for MHIRTs to provide psychological therapy. They detail four key arguments for the provision of therapy: that prisoners' criminal behaviour may be linked to mental disorder and that, therefore, therapy should be provided to help with the disorder and to reduce re-offending; that because offenders have poor access to mental health services in the community, they should have access while in prison; that even if mental health input does not 'cure' a disorder or reduce reoffending, it gives prisoners the opportunity to talk and to help them in crisis; and that an emphasis on treatment can lead to more humane prison conditions. However, Mills and Kendall also highlight the challenges to therapy provision and the limitations in its delivery. Security lies at the heart of prison management and therapists have to work around these constraints (Adams and Ferrandino 2008). This is a theme that emerges in several chapters of this volume. As Doctor (2001) states, 'the main obstacle in working as a psychotherapist in the prison lies in the prison culture itself' (p. 57). Mills and Kendall also suggest that providing therapy in prison could result in 'therapeutic sentencing', which could make agencies in the criminal justice system less willing to send people to other secure settings which might be more appropriate. Moreover, providing individual therapy might also take the focus off broader structural issues that are implicated in crime and punishment. Here lies a dilemma, because it would not be useful for these arguments to be used to legitimate the decision not to support offenders with mental health difficulties in custody. Mills and Kendall conclude that while they view improvements in prison mental health care as positive, they also question why individuals with serious mental health problems are in custody at all.

The next four chapters in the book focus on different psychological therapies that have been practised in prisons in England and Wales.

Mary Haley in Chapter 3 provides an account of attachment-based psychodynamic psychotherapy in two adult male prisons: a dispersal prison and a category C prison. She details attachment theory, put forward by Bowlby (1969, 1973, 1980). This theory, which stresses the important impact of interpersonal experiences on one's sense of self and one's view of others, has clear links to CAT (described below). Haley outlines the relevance of attachment theory to work with adult offenders and discusses attachment related themes that permeate the prison experience. Attachment has emerged as an important theme throughout this book. The very fact that imprisonment involves separation and loss (which has been noted as one of the 'pains of imprisonment'; Sykes 1958) is of relevance as these themes are prominent in attachment theory. Haley reminds us that some prisoners may have an ambivalent attachment to prisons and that attachment difficulties may be exacerbated by the prison experience.

Haley details her therapeutic work with prisoners who have difficult attachment histories. This work involves helping prisoners make sense of painful and disjointed narratives and she stresses the importance of doing so within a safe therapeutic relationship. Indeed, she argues that feeling safe is a prerequisite to the process of recovering from trauma. She argues that making sense of past experiences may help in reducing psychological distress and reducing violent responses. Therefore, therapeutic work that aims to reduce psychological distress could be argued to help reduce reoffending in turn. Indeed, it may be important for a prisoner to make sense of their own experience of victimisation and to begin to learn to mentalise, before making sense of themselves as a perpetrator of violence. In this chapter Haley also examines what could be considered as markers of progress in therapy. From her reflections, it is evident that therapists (and commissioners) may have to think broadly and creatively when thinking about what demonstrates a positive outcome. Haley also highlights how it is important to think about the ending of therapy, even before the therapy has begun.

In Chapter 4 Kirsty Smedley examines the use of CBT within adolescent secure settings, particularly focusing on a juvenile prison (working with young males aged between 15 and 17). Smedley argues that it is important to take developmental issues in adolescence into account when working therapeutically with young people. In her chapter, Smedley outlines the principles of CBT and provides a case example of a young man who is experiencing psychotic symptoms while in custody. Using the case example, Smedley outlines the process of assessment, formulation and intervention. This chapter also explores in detail the challenges of providing therapy in prison and argues that we need to think about the competing aims of the mental health profession and the prison service. Again, these challenges point to the importance of accounting for context when thinking about the therapy and the barriers to it.

In Chapter 5 Abigail Willis examines using CAT with young adult offenders (aged 18 to 21). She recognises the problems that young adults face in custody and the disruption that imprisonment can have on their self-identity. She points out that engaging young people in psychological therapy is difficult as they have often not wanted to engage in therapy prior to coming into custody. The same can be said for other prisoners and is a key issue to think about when providing therapy in prison. Prisons are low-trust environments (Liebling 2004) and many prisoners have entered prison with abusive experiences which have made it difficult for them to place trust in others. Willis examines the process of reformulation, recognition and revision within CAT and brings the therapy alive through a composite case vignette.[4] Willis also highlights that CAT can be used to support systemic interventions and consultation in prison. Individual therapy, carried out in isolation, without involving prison staff, may have limited impact, given the impact the prison environment can have on an individual's behaviour. Through thinking systemically this allows the therapist to highlight contextual factors rather than developing an individual pathological model of behaviour.

Developing the importance of context in other chapters, David Shelton in Chapter 6 examines the utility of a systemic approach to therapy in prisons. The focus of this chapter is on working with young people in custody, both juveniles and young adults. Shelton provides a brief review of the literature on systemic practice as applied to those in forensic settings and then outlines key systemic concepts that can be applied to prison settings. These include context and multiple perspectives, communication, neutrality/curiosity, connectivity, circularity and collaboration. Shelton provides a composite case example of a young man who was struggling with feelings of anger. This work, which involved reflections in front of the client and his partner, demonstrates how traditional systemic practices, such as the reflective team approach, can be adapted with limited resources.

Having outlined these therapies, the book then turns to specific issues in therapy provision in prisons and other secure settings. In Chapter 7 Andrew Rogers and Heather Law focus on working with traumatised prisoners. As mentioned above, many prisoners enter prisons with trauma-related symptoms and these may be compounded by the experience of imprisonment itself. Having outlined a brief theory of trauma, Rogers and Law examine the relationship between attachment, trauma and brain development (see also Haley in Chapter 3). Rogers and Law state that when children have had abusive earlier life experiences, this impacts on their brain development, attachment style and ability to regulate their emotions. Rogers and Law discuss the diagnosis of PTSD but argue that a diagnosis of PTSD does not capture the psychosocial experience of young people who have more complex presentations. They argue that young people who have experienced long-term repetitive experiences and disrupted attachments may be suffering from 'complex trauma'. They outline the intervention approaches supported by NICE guidance (EMDR (eye movement desensitisation reprocessing) and CBT) but also highlight the importance of taking a systemic approach. They stress that it is fundamental to work alongside the prison system, rather than with the individual in isolation. So, for example, in their composite case example, the intervention entails working with both the system and the individual. They then examine the challenges and ethical considerations of working with traumatised individuals who are in custody and pose the question of when it is 'safe enough' in prison to engage a young person in trauma-related interventions. This is something that a therapist must be mindful of in order not to increase the risk of re-enactment.

Chapter 8 focuses on therapy provision with women in prison and other secure settings. Jules Pearson examines the complex dynamics at play within female forensic settings and considers how these dynamics can be managed. She discusses how many women in prisons and other secure settings have traumatic and neglectful histories and how their psychological distress resulting from these experiences may be expressed through offending behaviours. She reminds us that women enact scenes from the past with those who are attempting to care for them. The chapter focuses on three main areas: the internal worlds of women in prisons and other secure settings; the impact the internal world of women has on service dynamics; and the ways in which staff can respond to disturbing histories and re-enactments of the past.

In Chapter 9 Frank Lowe and Jules Pearson focus on therapy provision with black and minority ethnic (BME) people. BME prisoners are over-represented in the prison population, and indeed at every stage of the criminal justice process (Edgar 2007; Rickford and Edgar 2005). Lowe and Pearson argue that it is essential for therapists and patients to be thoughtful about the experience and meaning of race in order to achieve therapeutic effectiveness. They argue that the main challenge in working therapeutically with BME clients is whether or not therapists can develop to become aware of the impact of racialised practices and assumptions in forensic environments. In particular they stress the importance of recognising and challenging stereotyped thinking when thinking about assessments of risk and dangerousness. Lowe and Pearson examine two case studies, those of Zahid Mubarek and David Bennett, in order to explore the issues delineated in the chapter. Lowe and Pearson acknowledge that considerable progress has been made with the basic understanding of race but argue that more work still needs to be done in order to achieve good clinical practice (see also Edgar 2007).

Richard Shuker and John Shine in Chapter 10 examine the role of therapeutic communities (TCs). Their chapter begins with an outline of the origins and background of the practice in democratic therapeutic communities, documenting such practice within the prison service for half a century. Shuker and Shine then detail therapeutic community interventions with offenders and demonstrate how it has only been within the past five years that TCs have become adequately defined and researched. The chapter outlines a treatment model developed by Shine and Morris (2000) which is based on three therapeutic domains: attachments, criminal behaviour, and behaviour on the unit. They argue that TCs have a number of defining characteristics: the engagement of prisoners and the staff; the opportunities to learn new skills; consistency, structure and an emphasis on therapeutic boundaries. Shuker and Shine also detail future challenges in working in TCs, such as cost effectiveness, the provision for the range of psychological difficulties experienced by prisoners, and possible adaptations to the model.

In the final chapter of the book Danny Clark focuses on the role of offending behaviour programmes within prisons. With the introduction of MHIRTs to prisons it will be important for members of such teams to forge links with forensic psychology departments in order to provide a holistic service. Therefore, while this book's predominant focus is on psychological therapy aimed at non-offence work, this chapter focuses on the development of offending behaviour programmes, and adaptations of them over time. Clark's chapter begins with a history of the development of psychological interventions with prisoners and then describes the standardisation and accreditation of offending behaviour programmes and the evaluation and outcomes of these programmes. Clark discusses the debate about the use of manualised interventions; he argues that manuals are useful but alongside a therapeutic relationship between the client and practitioner. He states that offending behaviour programmes (OBPs) have incorporated recent advances from psychotherapy and clinical psychology and it has been increasingly recognised that the therapeutic relationship between offenders and practitioners delivering interventions is important. The provision of OBPs thus has the potential to move in a direction which is more collaborative and transparent. The extent to which these shifts will affect practice is yet not known. However, it could be argued that if programmes were to place more emphasis on the therapeutic relationship and to focus more on positive adaptive functioning, then prisoners might develop more trust in these programmes and become more motivated to attend them.

Keeping context central to therapy provision

A theme that has emerged throughout this volume is the importance of taking a systemic approach when providing psychological therapy in prisons. Haney (2005) argues that psychological models applied to imprisonment have traditionally been individualistic in nature, despite the contextual revolution that has taken place within the discipline of psychology. However, in this volume therapists see context as central to their work. It is essential that therapists take such a contextual approach to their work in order to engage in a meaningful manner and to increase the chances of meeting the needs of prisoners. There are several reasons why an understanding of the prison world is a prerequisite when delivering psychological therapy.

First, it is necessary for the therapist to understand the experience of imprisonment in order to understand how psychological problems may develop during it or how it may exacerbate or maintain existing problems. The system of the prison itself may appear in psychological formulations and a shared understanding of a problem may need to include the very context in which the therapy is being provided.

Second, when prisoners enter into a therapeutic relationship, an imbalance of power exists and should be reflected upon by the therapist and, where appropriate, discussed with the prisoner too. The prisoner may divulge information, for example, information which reveals that he may be a risk to himself or others, and such information needs to be shared with the prison authorities or other agencies such as MAPPA. At these points in therapy, from the prisoner's perspective 'help may quickly be replaced with punishment' (Donohue and Moore 2009: 331). It also has to be borne in mind that there are consequences for prisoners if they have been referred for psychological therapy but decide that they do not want to participate. Although the therapist may view this decision as the client exercising free will, viewing them similarly to a patient who has been referred by their GP in the general community and who chooses not to attend, there may be additional consequences for the prisoner. For people in custody, non-attendance may be constructed as 'refusal to engage' and could be seen as a marker of them not progressing through a sentence. Indeed, within the HCR-20, an assessment tool for predicting risk of violence, one of the risk factors is 'non-compliance with remediation attempts' (Webster *et al.* 1997). While this is indeed a factor that may heighten an individual's risk of future offending, these dynamics need to be considered in the provision of therapy. So, even when therapists take a collaborative approach to their work, the wider dynamics set up by the system need to be reflected on.

Third, understanding the prison is important in order to be aware of the barriers that the prison environment presents to providing therapy. These include the transient nature of the prison population and the dominant role that security plays. Therapy sessions may be cancelled due to 'lock downs', or prisoners may be deemed too 'at risk' to engage in one-to-one sessions. The therapy may therefore be disrupted or even prevented from taking place.

Fourth, prisons are low-trust environments and this lack of trust has implications for the provision of therapy. Many prisoners enter custody having had experiences which have led them to hold a distrustful view of others, the world and even themselves; the prison environment may exacerbate such concerns and confirm these beliefs. In order to benefit from therapy, an emotive and interpersonal process, the prisoner must develop trust in the therapist. While developing a trusting relationship may be at the core of personal growth, the prisoner is taking a risk in placing trust in another human being who works in the prison. The perceptions prisoners have about the specific role of psychologists in prison are also of relevance here. Crewe (2009) found that prisoners saw psychology as a profession that was there to protect the public and not a profession that was there to help them with their personal problems. Prisoners were aware of the focus on the risk of reoffending and because of this they were cautious about what information to share. Indeed, 'unsure about what fears they could safely divulge, and concerned that they could snag themselves in their own net of risk factors, many prisoners withheld their worries. The identities that they presented to psychologists were more confident and secure than their inner realities' (Crewe

2009: 129–30). It is important that psychologists providing therapy are aware that prisoners might hold certain views about them and (as stated above) might see them as powerful figures, for this might impact upon prisoners' willingness to engage.

Fifth, it is important for therapists to be aware of any key incidents that have occurred within the prison, such as physical altercations, suicide attempts, suicides, changes in the regime, as they may impact upon the well-being of prisoners and their ability to focus on other problems within therapy. Moreover, it is important for therapists to be aware of the impact a therapy session might have on an individual, who might be returning to an isolated prison cell and left to ruminate on his problems. Being aware of a prisoner's ability to cope with imprisonment allows the therapist to work with the client in order to think about the level of emotional processing in which he can engage.

Sixth, it is important for the therapist to be aware of the prison system, because in order for the psychological work in therapy to be effective the therapist also has to work with the broader prison system. Indeed, if an intervention is being developed to improve self-confidence or reduce levels of social anxiety, it is important for staff on the wing to work alongside the prisoner and therapist in order to help the prison in developing alternative means of thinking and behaving. As Rogers and Law argue in Chapter 7, in relation to working with prisoners who are traumatised, it is essential for staff to understand why a prisoner may react the way he does in order for them not to contribute, unthinkingly, to his problems.

Finally, it is argued that a contextual approach to prisoners' needs allows the therapist to depart from a solely pathological model of emotion and behaviour. It frees up the therapist to work more closely with the system and – in theory – places greater responsibility on the system to ensure that it does not have a detrimental impact on those in custody.

Thus, in order for therapists to keep context central to their work with prisoners, it would be important for them to keep in mind the findings from research on the effects of imprisonment in general (Liebling and Maruna 2005) and to understand the 'moral performance' of the particular prison in which they are based (Liebling 2004). It is through understanding the prisoners' experiences that therapists can become more attuned with them and can establish a trusting therapeutic relationship. In order to keep context at the centre of practice in this way, it is important for therapists to know the prison world in which they are working. Just as ethnographic researchers immerse themselves in the prison community, so too therapists need to understand the routines and practices of the prison, to be aware of the interpersonal exchanges that occur on the wings, and to know about the 'moral climate' of the prison in which they work. They need to be informed if there are serious incidents and to have a sense of the care–control balance of the institution in which they are based. This would involve spending time outside one-to-one therapy work – spending time on the wings and in the workshops. It is through spending time with prisoners, and with staff, that therapists can develop an understanding of the prison community and establish meaningful relationships.

Notes

1 These figures pertain only to 'restricted' patients: those patients that are subject to risk management by the Secretary of State for Justice (Ministry of Justice 2010).
2 However, it does not focus on therapy provision within the three high-secure hospitals (Broadmoor, Ashworth and Rampton). Refer to Rutherford and Duggan (2007), McMurran *et al.* (2009) and Bartlett and Kesteven (2010) for an overview of forensic mental health services in England and Wales.
3 The safer locals programme, part of the wider 'safer custody programme' aimed at reducing self-harm and suicide rates in prisons, was piloted in five prisons in England. Changes were made to the built environment, including safer cells, care suites, refurbishing health care centres and creating detoxification units.
4 Composite vignettes are created in these chapters in order to ensure the anonymity of the prisoners. The case examples are based on clinical work but on work with various clients, amalgamated into one case, and with details changed in order to ensure that individuals cannot be identified.

References

Adams, K. (1992) 'Adjusting to prison life', in M. Tonry (ed.), *Crime and Justice: A Review of Research, 16* (pp. 275–361). Chicago, IL: University of Chicago Press.
Adams, K. and Ferrandino, J. (2008) 'Managing mentally ill inmates in prisons', *Criminal Justice and Behavior*, 35(8): 913–27.
Andrews, D.A. and Bonta, J. (2006) *The Psychology of Criminal Conduct*, 4th edition. Cincinnati, OH: Andersen Publishing.

Bartlett, A. and Kesteven, S. (2010) 'Current service provision for mentally disordered offenders', in A. Bartlett and G. McGauley (eds), *Forensic Mental Health: Concepts, Systems and Practice*. Oxford: Oxford University Press, pp. 351–8.

Boothby, J.L. and Clements, C.B. (2000) 'A national survey of correctional psychologists', *Criminal Justice and Behavior*, 27(6): 716–32.

Bowlby, J. (1969) *Attachment and Loss, Vol 1: Attachment*. New York: Basic Books.

Bowlby, J. (1973) *Attachment and Loss, Vol 2: Separation, Anxiety and Anger*. New York: Basic Books.

Bowlby, J. (1980) *Attachment and Loss, Vol 3: Loss, Sadness and Depression*. New York: Basic Books.

Bradley, L. (2009) *The Bradley Report: Lord Bradley's Review of People with Mental Health Problems or Learning Disabilities in the Criminal Justice System*. London: Department of Health.

Brooke, D., Taylor, C., Gunn, J. and Maden. A. (2000) 'Substance abuse as a marker of vulnerability among male prisoners on remand', *British Journal of Psychiatry*, 177: 248–51.

Brooker, C. and Gojkovic, D. (2009) 'The second national survey of mental health in-reach services in prisons', *Journal of Forensic Psychiatry and Psychology*, 20(1): S11–28.

Brooker, C., Duggan, S., Fox, C., Mills, A. and Parsonage, M. (2008) *Short Changed: Spending on Prison Mental Health Care*. London: Sainsbury Centre for Mental Health.

Brooker, C., Repper, J., Beverley, C., Ferriter, M. and Brewer, N. (2002) *Mental Health Services and Prisoners: A Review*. Sheffield: University of Sheffield School of Health and Related Research.

Brooker, C., Sirdifield, C. And Gojkovic, D. (2007) *Mental Health Services and Prisoners: An Updated Review*. Lincoln: University of Lincoln Criminal Justice and Mental Health Research Group.

Corston J. (2007) *The Corston Report: A Review of Women with Particular Vulnerabilities in the Criminal Justice System*. London: Home Office.

Crewe, B. (2009) *The Prisoner Society. Power, Adaptation, and Social Life in an English prison*. Oxford: Oxford University Press.

Crighton, D.A. and Towl. G.J. (2008) *Psychology in Prisons*, 2nd edition. Oxford: BPS Blackwell.

Dear, G.E. (2008) 'Ten years of research into self-harm in the Western Australian prison system: Where to next?', *Psychiatry, Psychology and Law*, 15(3): 469–81.

DH (2009) *Improving Access to Psychological Therapies. Offenders. Positive Practice Guide*. London: Department of Health.

DH and HMPS (2001) *Changing the Outlook: A Strategy for Developing and Modernising Mental Health Services in Prisons*. London: Department of Health.

Doctor, R. (2001) 'Psychotherapy and the prisoner – impasse or progress?', in J.W. Saunders (ed.), *Life Within Hidden Worlds: Psychotherapy in Prisons*. London: Karnac.

Donohue, E. and Moore, D. (2009) 'When is an offender not an offender? Power, the client and shifting penal subjectivities', *Punishment and Society*, 11(3): 319–36.

Durcan, G. and Knowles, K. (2006) *London's Prison Mental Health Services: A Review*. London: Sainsbury Centre for Mental Health.

Edgar, K. (2007) 'Black and minority ethnic prisoners', in Y. Jewkes (ed.), *Handbook on prisons*. Cullompton: Willan Publishing, pp. 268–92.

Fazel, S. and Danesh, J. (2002) 'Serious mental disorder in 23,000 prisoners: a systematic review of 62 surveys', *The Lancet*, 359: 545–50.

Fazel, S., Bains, P. and Doll, H. (2006) 'Substance abuse and dependence in prisoners: A systematic review', *Addiction*, 101: 181–91.

Fazel, S., Benning, R. and Danesh, J. (2005) 'Suicide in male prisoners in England and Wales, 1978–2003', *The Lancet*, 366: 1301–2.

Haney, C. (2005) 'The contextual revolution in psychology and the question of prison effects', in A. Liebling and S. Maruna (eds), *The Effects of Imprisonment*. Cullompton: Willan Publishing, pp. 66–93.

Harvey, J. (2007) *Young Men in Prison: Surviving and Adapting to Life Inside*. Cullompton: Willan Publishing.

HMCIP (2007) *The Mental Health of Prisoners: A Thematic Review of the Care and Support of Prisoners with Mental Health Needs*. London: HM Inspectorate of Prisons.

HMPS (2010) *List of Prisons and Contact Details*. Available at: www. hmprisonservice.gov.uk/prisoninformation/locateaprison/

Ireland, J. (2002) *Bullying Among Prisoners: Evidence, Research and Intervention Strategies*. Hove: Brunner-Routledge.

Jamieson, R. and Grounds, A. (2005) 'Release and adjustment: Perspectives from studies of wrongly convicted and politically motivated prisoners', in A. Liebling and S. Maruna (eds), *The Effects of Imprisonment*. Cullompton: Willan Publishing, pp. 33–65.

Jenkins, R., Bhugra, D., Meltzer, H., Singleton, N., Bebbington, P., Brugha, T., Coid, J., Farrell, M., Lewis, G. and Paton, J. (2005) 'Psychiatric and social aspects of suicidal behaviour in prisons', *Psychological Medicine*, 35: 257–69.

Jewkes, Y. (ed.) (2007) *Handbook on Prisons*. Cullompton: Willan Publishing.

Jewkes, Y. and Johnston, H. (eds) (2006) *Prison Readings: A Critical Introduction to Prisons and Imprisonment*. Cullompton: Willan Publishing.

Johnson, J.E. and Zlotnick, C. (2008) 'A pilot study of group interpersonal psychotherapy for depression in substance abusing female prisoners', *Journal of Substance Abuse Treatment*, 34: 371–7.

Kjelseberg, E., Hartvig, P., Bowtiz, H., Kuisma, I., Norbech, P., Rustad, A., Seem, M. and Vik, T. (2006) 'Mental health consultations in a prison population: A descriptive study', *BMC Psychiatry*, 6(27): 1–9.

Leese, M., Stuart, T. and Snow, L. (2006) 'An ecological study of factors associated with rates of self-inflicted death in prisons in England and Wales', *International Journal of Law and Psychiatry*, 29: 355–60.

Liebling, A. (1992) *Suicides in Prison*. London: Routledge.

Liebling, A. (1999) 'Prison suicide and prisoner coping', in M. Tonry and J. Petersilia (eds), *Crime and Justice: A Review of Research*, Vol. 26. Chicago, IL: University of Chicago Press, pp. 283–360.

Liebling, A. (2007) 'Prison suicide and its prevention', in Y. Jewkes (ed.), *Handbook on Prisons*. Cullompton: Willan Publishing, pp. 423–46.

Liebling, A., assisted by Arnold, H. (2004) *Prisons and Their Moral Performance. A Study of Values, Quality and Prison Life*. Oxford: Oxford University Press.

Liebling. A. and Maruna, S. (eds) (2005) *The Effects of Imprisonment*. Cullompton: Willan Publishing.

Liebling, A., Tait, S., Durie, L., Stiles, A. and Harvey, J. (2005) *An Evaluation of the Safer Locals Programme*. Cambridge Institute of Criminology: unpublished report.

Mahoney, A.M. and Daniel, C. (2006) 'Bridging the power gap: Narrative therapy with incarcerated women', *The Prison Journal*, 86(1): 75–88.

McGruck, B.J., Thornton, D.M. and Williams, M. (eds) (1987) *Applying Psychology to Imprisonment: Theory and practice*. London: HMSO.

McGuire, J. (2002) 'Preface', in J. McGuire (ed.), *Offender Rehabilitation and Treatment: Effective Programmes and Policies to Reduce Re-offending*. Chichester: John Wiley & Sons.

McMurran, M., Khalifa, N. And Gibbon, S. (2009) *Forensic Mental Health*. Cullompton: Willan Publishing.

Ministry of Justice (2009) *Population in Custody Monthly Tables June 2009. Ministry of Justice Statistical Bulletin*. London: Ministry of Justice.

Ministry of Justice (2010) *Statistics of Mentally Disordered Offenders 2008 England and Wales. Ministry of Justice Statistics Bulletin*. London: Ministry of Justice.

Mullen, P.E. (2002) 'Serious mental disorder and offending behaviours', in J. McGuire (ed.), *Offender Rehabilitation and Treatment: Effective Programmes and Policies to Reduce Re-offending*. Chichester: Wiley, pp. 289–305.

Nee, C. and Farman, S. (2005) 'Female prisoners with borderline personality disorder: Some promising treatment developments', *Criminal Behaviour and Mental Health*, 15(1): 2–16.

Nee, C. and Farman, S. (2007) 'Dialectical behaviour therapy as a treatment for borderline personality disorder in prisons: Three illustrative case studies', *The Journal of Forensic Psychiatry and Psychology*, 18(2): 160–80.

Nee, C. and Farman, S. (2008) 'Treatment of borderline personality disorder in prisons: Findings from the two dialectical behaviour therapy pilots in the UK', in J.C. Hagen and E.I. Jensen (eds), *Personality Disorders: New Research*. New York: Nova Science Publishers, Inc.

PRT (2009) *Bromley Briefings Prison Factfile*. London: Prison Reform Trust.

Rickford, D. and Edgar, K. (2005) *Troubled Inside: Responding to the Mental Health Needs of Men in Prison*. London: Prison Reform Trust.

Romily, C. And Bartlett, A. (2010) 'Prison mental health care', in A. Bartlett and G. McGauley (eds), *Forensic Mental Health: Concepts, Systems and Practice*. Oxford: Oxford University Press, pp. 339–50.

Roth, A. and Fonagy, P. (2005) *What Works For Whom? A Critical Review of Psychotherapy Research*. London: The Guilford Press.

Rutherford, M. and Duggan, S. (2007) *Forensic Mental Health Services: Facts and Figures on Current Provision*. London: Sainsbury Centre for Mental Health.

SCMH (2007) *Getting the Basics Right: Developing a Primary Care Mental Health Service in Prisons*. London: Sainsbury Centre for Mental Health.

SCMH (2009) *Mental Health Care and the Criminal Justice System: Briefing 39*. London: Sainsbury Centre for Mental Health.

Shaw, J., Baker, D., Hunt, I.M., Moloney, A. and Appleby, L. (2004) 'Suicide by prisoners: National clinical survey', *British Journal of Psychiatry*, 184: 263–7.

Shine, J. and Morris, M. (2000) 'Addressing criminogenic needs in a prison therapeutic community', *Therapeutic Communities*, 21(3): 197–219.

Singleton, N., Bumpstead, R., O'Brien, M., Lee A. and Meltzer, A. (2000) *Psychiatric Morbidity Among Adults Living in Private Households 2000*. London: Office for National Statistics.

Singleton, N., Meltzer, H. and Gatward, R. (1998) *Psychiatric Morbidity Among Prisoners*. London: Office for National Statistics.

Social Exclusion Unit (2002) *Reducing Re-offending by Ex-prisoners*. London: Office of the Deputy Prime Minister.

Strupp, H.H. (1978) 'Psychotherapy research and practice: An overview', in A.E. Bergin and S.L. Garfield (eds), *Handbook of Psychotherapy and Behavior Change*, 2nd edition. New York: Wiley, pp. 3–22.

Sykes, G. (1958) *The Society of Captives*. Princeton, NJ: Princeton University Press.

Toch, H. (1977/1992) *Living in Prison: The Ecology of Survival*. Washington, DC: American Psychological Association.

Towl, G.J. (ed.) (2003) *Psychology in Prisons*. Oxford: BPS Blackwell.

Ward, T. and Maruna, S. (2007) *Rehabilitation: Beyond the Risk Paradigm*. Abingdon: Routledge.

Webster, C.D., Douglas, K.S., Eaves, D. and Hart, S. (1997) *HCR-20 Version 2*. Simon Fraser University, BC: Mental Health Law and Policy Institute.

Yalom, I.D. (2001) *The Gift of Therapy: Reflections on Being a Therapist*. London: Piatkus Books.

Zamble, E. and Porporino, J. (1988) *Coping, Behavior and Adaptation in Prison*. New York: Springer-Verlag.

Zlotnick, C., Najavits, L.M., Rohsenow, D.J. and Johnson, D.M. (2003) 'A cognitive-behavioral treatment for incarcerated women with substance abuse disorder and posttraumatic stress disorder: findings from a pilot study', *Journal of Substance Abuse*, 25: 99–105.

25

Chapter 2

Therapy and mental health in-reach teams

Alice Mills and Kathleen Kendall

Introduction

Within the past decade, the provision of mental health care in prisons has changed considerably from highly patchy and often inadequate care to mental health in-reach teams (MHIRTs) now working in most prisons. Such teams seek to offer prisoners access to the same range and quality of services as patients receive in the community. Providing such equivalent care has, however, proved to be challenging within the prison environment, particularly in relation to the provision of various therapies. This chapter will first examine the development and aims of MHIRTs in the context of high levels of mental health problems and wider debates about the provision of prison health care. It will then discuss the challenges that MHIRTs have faced in seeking to provide equivalent care, and will critically discuss whether it is possible or desirable for MHIRTs to provide therapeutic interventions in prisons.

The context of the prison mental health in-reach programme

Levels of mental health need

Before discussing the development of MHIRTs, it is useful to examine the reasons why such provision has emerged, notably the demand for mental health services. The prevalence of mental disorder among prisoners is considered to be high and substantially higher than in the general population. The most recent comprehensive prevalence study, conducted in 1997, found that over 90 per cent of prisoners had one or more of the five psychiatric disorders measured, which were psychosis, neurosis, personality disorder, drug dependence and hazardous drinking (Singleton *et al.* 1998), which is four times the corresponding rate in the wider community (Brooker *et al.* 2008). Rates of psychosis varied between 7 per cent in the male sentenced population and 14 per cent in female prisoners, compared to a prevalence of 0.4 per cent in the general population. Seventy-eight per cent of male remand prisoners, 64 per cent of male sentenced prisoners and 50 per cent of female prisoners were found to have a personality disorder. Women were considerably more likely to suffer from neurotic disorders, which affected 76 per cent of female remand prisoners and 63 per cent of female sentenced prisoners; the corresponding figures for men being 59 per cent and 40 per cent (Singleton *et al.* 1998). The mental health problems of prisoners also tend to be complex and are often associated with a combination of need unmet by primary mental health care, substance misuse, learning difficulties, multiple disadvantages and social exclusion (HMCIP 2007). Co-morbidity is the norm (Gunn *et al.* 1991; Birmingham *et al.* 1996; Birmingham 2001), with approximately a fifth of remand prisoners and one in seven sentenced prisoners having four or more psychiatric disorders (Singleton *et al.* 1998). The prison population also has high levels of suicidal and deliberate self-harming behaviours, with prisoners approximately seven times more likely to commit suicide than people in the community (Mental Health Foundation 1999).

Research suggests that specific groups of prisoners have higher levels of complex need than others. The above figures for women prisoners indicate higher rates of mental disorder than men, but they also have higher rates of suicide and self-harm (WHO 2009), with half of all self-harm incidents in prison carried out by women, even though they make up only 6 per cent of the population (Fawcett Society 2009). The higher prevalence of mental health problems is often explained by the 'multiplicity of disadvantage and damage' (Medlicott 2007: 250) that women prisoners are said to experience, notably high levels of physical and sexual abuse and bereavement (O'Brien *et al.* 2001; Corston 2007) and greater use of harmful substances (Borrill *et al.* 2003). Women are also thought to be more vulnerable to the 'pains of imprisonment' (Giallombardo 1966; Carlen and Worrall 2004), notably separation from and concerns about their family and children, with a consequent effect on their mental health

(CSIP 2006; Corston 2007; Royal College of Psychiatrists 2007). This is particularly the case because they are considerably more likely to be held away from their home area, which makes contact with family members difficult (HMCIP 2007; Fawcett Society 2009).

Studies have shown that the prevalence of mental disorder is even higher among young offenders and juveniles, with 95 per cent suffering from at least one psychiatric disorder and 80 per cent experiencing more than one (Lader et al. 2000). The growing number of older people behind bars has also been of considerable concern in recent years (PRT 2003; HMCIP 2004a; Crawley 2007). Rates of depressive illness among older prisoners are five times greater than that found among young adult prisoners or in a matched community sample (Fazel et al. 2001), although prison mental health care tends to be aimed at a younger, more vocal population (HMCIP 2004a).

Mental health services in prison

Historically, despite the high levels of mental health problems, adequate and competent mental health services have not been provided in prisons. Broadly, there are four main reasons for this. First, many mental health problems have gone, and continue to go, undetected when prisoners first come into prison and can remain untreated throughout their stay. The initial reception screen is often rushed and not carried out by a trained mental health professional; it is estimated to pick up only between 25 per cent and 33 per cent of prisoners with serious mental illness (Brooker et al. 2002), meaning that the opportunity to treat individuals, who often do not engage with services in the community or who are regarded as difficult and unpopular patients, may be lost (Birmingham 2001).

Second, until recently, even where mental health needs were detected, they often went untreated. Singleton et al.'s (1998) study found that only between 15 per cent and 30 per cent of prisoners had received any help for their problems, with the most frequently cited source being the prison doctor. One in seven prisoners had been refused help. At the time, the provision of psychiatric services in prisons was patchy and dependent on localised arrangements between the prison and local psychiatric providers. In a review of 19 prison inspections, Reed and Lyne (1997) ascertained that although all but two prisons had visits from local psychiatrists, they were predominantly to facilitate transfers. None had arrangements for mentally disordered inpatients to be under the care of a consultant psychiatrist nor had they a full multidisciplinary mental health team.

Continuity of care, both between prisons and between the prison and the wider community, was also lacking, despite the contribution this can make to reducing the risk of reoffending (HMCIP 1996; DH and HMPS 1999; Social Exclusion Unit 2002).

Third, for those prisoners deemed suitable, transfers to outside psychiatric care were painfully slow. Reed (2003) estimated that up to 500 patients in prison were sufficiently ill as to require admission to outside NHS care, but they could be waiting for months for an initial psychiatric assessment. Even with agreement about the individual's suitability for such care, long delays could occur due to a shortage of beds and disputes over the necessary level of security, funding, dual diagnosis issues and the 'treatability' of the offender (Gunn et al. 1991; Reed 2003; Mills 2005).

Finally, people diagnosed with serious mental illness awaiting transfer or not deemed eligible for transfer to NHS facilities were often placed in prison health care centres, which rarely provided adequate levels of support or stimulation (Reed and Lyne 1997, 2000; HMCIP 2004b), due to few opportunities to participate in constructive activities such as work or education (Mills 2002, 2005).

Until recently, health care services in prisons were the sole responsibility of the Prison Service (HMPS). They were constantly criticised for being inadequate and substandard in comparison to the NHS (Birmingham et al. 1996; Smith 1999) and for being more concerned with control and custody than care (Sim 1990, 2002; Woolf 1991). Since 1964, professional bodies, academics, penal reform groups and prisoner campaign groups have all called for prison health care services to be integrated with the NHS in order to ensure equivalence of care with that of the general population (Gostin and Staunton 1985; Gunn et al. 1991; Grounds 1994; HMCIP 1996; Reed and Lyne 1997; Birmingham 2003). Perhaps the most influential of these demands was put forward by the Chief Inspector of Prisons who, in a 1996 discussion paper, highlighted the limitations of prison health care and reviewed possible solutions, with a view to ensuring that prisoners have access to the same quality and range of health care services as the general public receives from the NHS. The paper recommended that, in order to ensure equivalence and continuity of care, the NHS should assume 'responsibility for the delivery of all healthcare by the introduction of a purchaser/provider relationship that acknowledges the full and peculiar needs of the Prison Service' (HMCIP 1996: Foreword).

A joint Prison Service and NHS Executive working group was established to address the Chief Inspector's recommendations. While the resulting report acknowledged the poor standard of health care in some establishments and endorsed the aim of providing equivalent care to that in the community, it was felt that this could best be done through a partnership between the Prison Service and the NHS. The Prison Service remained responsible for primary care but the NHS became responsible for secondary care, community mental health and visiting NHS specialist support. In relation to mental health, the report recognised that many of the more specialist services such as occupational therapy and community mental health teams were lacking in prisons. It thus proposed that care of mentally disordered prisoners should develop in line with NHS mental health policy, including the development of community mental health outreach work on prison wings (DH and HMPS 1999).

In 2001, the prison mental health strategy, *Changing the Outlook*, set out a vision for the development and modernisation of prison mental health services for the following three to five years (DH and HMPS 2001). It aimed to meet the requirements of the National Service Framework for Mental Health and the NHS plan, the latter of which stated: 'by 2004, 5,000 prisoners at any time should be receiving more comprehensive mental health services in prison. All people with severe mental illness will be in receipt of treatment, and no prisoners with serious mental illness will leave prison without a care plan and a care co-ordinator' (DH 2000: para. 14.36).

To do this, multidisciplinary mental health in-reach teams (MHIRTs), funded by local primary care trusts (PCTs), were to be introduced. They were to provide specialist mental health services to prisoners in the same way as community mental health teams (CMHTs) do to patients in the wider community. To reduce the number of prisoners accommodated in health care centres, mental health care services were to be provided to prisoners on prison wings, and the number of day care places increased. To ensure continuity of care, it was recommended that MHIRTs should implement the care programme approach (CPA), so that those on a CPA before they came into prison would be able to continue their treatment as far as possible within the prison; and it was recommended that MHIRTs should liaise with community-based care coordinators on the prisoner's release. Additionally, it was hoped that these proposals would lead to quicker and more effective arrangements for transferring seriously ill prisoners between NHS facilities and prisons, would improve integration between Prison Service and NHS staff, and would facilitate the exchange of information (DH and HMPS 2001).

Yet *Changing the Outlook* did not give specific guidance on how such proposals were to be implemented. Instead, prisons and their local NHS partners were to be jointly responsible for identifying, planning and managing the delivery of the services needed in each prison, including measures to address the needs of specific groups of prisoners such as women, young prisoners and those from black and minority ethnic (BME) groups. Although it was anticipated that all prisoners would eventually benefit from the introduction of in-reach services, it was suggested that the early focus should be on those with severe and enduring mental illness (SMI), in line with the NHS Plan (DH and HMPS 2001). The in-reach programme was initially piloted at 16 prisons in 2001–02 and has now recruited over 360 members of staff, with MHIRTs providing services in over 100 prisons (HMPS 2007).

The realities of the in-reach programme

Improving mental health care

The proposals made in *Changing the Outlook* could be seen as monumental, finally putting in place a programme of comprehensive, nationwide mental health services and committing the NHS and PCTs to the principle of equivalence. There is no doubt that the introduction of MHIRTs has led to considerable improvements in mental health care, both in direct benefits for patients, and also indirectly in increased awareness of mental health problems among prison staff (HMCIP 2007). Prisoners in receipt of MHIRT services are largely positive about the care that they receive (HMCIP 2007; Durcan 2008). In a qualitative evaluation study of a MHIRT in a local prison in southern England, which involved focus groups and interviews with prisoners, in-reach team members and staff from all parts of the prison, we found that clients highly valued the input of in-reach staff, feeling that they were being listened to and that their difficulties were being taken seriously (Kendall and Mills, forthcoming). Prisoners on MHIRT caseloads in Durcan's (2008) study reported finding 'talking therapies' helpful and appreciated guidance given on symptom recognition, medication and its possible side effects. MHIRT staff can also act as advocates for prisoners, liaising with other agencies inside and outside prison, leaving prisoners feeling more confident about the support that will be available to them when they leave custody (Durcan 2008). Additionally, prison

31

staff have displayed positive attitudes towards MHIRTs, feeling that they help to stabilise prisoners and speed up assessments and care (Kendall and Mills, forthcoming).

Barriers and challenges

Nevertheless, MHIRTs have come across a range of barriers which have challenged their ability to reach their full potential. Prisoners' often chaotic lifestyles and their perceived 'undesirability' as clients in the community means that imprisonment can provide opportunities for prisoners with mental health problems to engage with services (Reed and Lyne 2000). However, such opportunities may be hampered by the sizeable pressure on in-reach services due to the high levels of mental health need in the prison population. Unsurprisingly, MHIRTs have struggled to meet the high demand for services, with approximately four out of five feeling unable to respond adequately to the range of need (HMCIP 2007). On average, MHIRTs have five whole-time-equivalent members of staff, an increase from four in 2004 (Brooker and Gojkovic 2009), but the demand for in-reach services has also increased during this time with caseloads rising by 32 per cent. At the same time, many teams have suffered from staff recruitment and retention problems, meaning that they rarely operate to their full capacity. Brooker and Gojkovic (2009) found that 70 per cent of teams had at least one vacant post in the previous year, with 46 per cent of teams having two or more and 16 per cent of teams being unable to recruit a team leader. Working in prison may be perceived as less attractive and more dangerous than community settings, and retaining staff can also be challenging (Kendall *et al.* 2006; Brooker and Gojkovic 2009). The high demand for services and staffing difficulties have also influenced the kinds of services MHIRTs are able to provide, with assessment, liaison and support dominating their time and tasks, particularly in local prisons which have a high turnover of prisoners. In such circumstances, teams may feel that they offer a crisis management service rather than a mental health service (Brooker and Gojkovic 2009), while wing-based services, day care and talking therapies have remained considerably underdeveloped (see below).

Despite the introduction of MHIRTs, many serious mental health needs still go unrecognised and untreated in prison. The national evaluation of in-reach services followed a cohort of prisoners with severe and enduring mental illness (SMI) from reception into prison for six months or until they were released or transferred, whichever one of these was sooner. It found that only 23 per cent were assessed by in-reach services and only 14 per cent were taken onto in-reach caseloads (Shaw *et al.* 2008). A variety of factors may explain why these figures are so low. Triage by primary care may be poor due to a fundamental lack of expertise and inadequate funding for primary mental health care (Brooker and Gojkovic 2009). Specialist mental health practitioners rarely attend reception screening, which still essentially relies on prisoners to tell staff about their mental health problems. Prisoners may be reluctant to disclose mental health issues, particularly if they do not wish to reveal any signs of vulnerability, and those who are unaware of their own mental health problems can easily be missed (Brooker and Ullman 2008). HMCIP (2007) found that even when prisoners do reveal a history of mental health treatment, only just over half of these cases were referred to an MHIRT, despite guidance suggesting that previous mental health contact should lead to an automatic referral.

'Mission creep' and primary mental health care
The low proportion of prisoners with SMI who were in receipt of in-reach services may also be explained by the changing and uncertain role of MHIRTs. In-reach services have developed using 'limited and idiosyncratic models of care' (Steel *et al.* 2007: 374), possibly due to the lack of guidance on their development and operation. Originally they were intended to be targeted at those with SMI, but national policy has since been broadened to include all prisoners with any mental disorder (Brooker *et al.* 2005). Such 'mission creep' has partly been driven by the need to provide joined-up mental health care in prisons, although the degree of integration and care coordination with primary mental health services varies considerably (Brooker and Gojkovic 2009), as does the quality of primary mental health care. Not all prisons employ primary mental health care staff, and when they do, they often deploy primary mental health care nurses in generic nursing roles, with any specialist services they provide vulnerable to staff shortages (All-Party Parliamentary Group on Prison Health 2006; HMCIP 2007; Durcan 2008). In such circumstances, there may be considerable confusion about the role of MHIRTs and they may be treated as the resource for all those with mental health problems (All-Party Parliamentary Group on Prison Health 2006). As Brooker and Gojkovic (2009: 23) suggest, this obviously raises 'issues around the adequacy of the resources available' as MHIRTs are likely to struggle to manage such diverse caseloads. Given the inadequacy of primary mental health care and high demand for in-reach services, the recent

Bradley review of services for offenders with mental health problems has recommended the improvement of primary mental health care services in prisons to enable the role of MHIRTs to be refocused on those with SMI (Bradley 2009).

Mission creep and confusion about their role can lead to MHIRTs receiving many perceived inappropriate referrals, putting them under additional strain (SCMH 2007a), and can lead to disputes with custodial staff as to who is suitable for mental health in-reach care. At HMP Gloucester, Meiklejohn *et al.* (2004) found that prisoners referred to the MHIRT often had complex mental health problems rather than SMI, but were the prisoners who were more able to communicate their problems to prison staff or who presented with disciplinary issues that drew attention to them, while their quieter counterparts with SMI were often overlooked in their cells. Prison staff have reported frustration at stringent entry criteria, feeling that MHIRTs should be dealing with all mental health problems (HMCIP 2007; Durcan 2008), but MHIRTs should not be seen as a panacea for the problem of prisoners who are seen as difficult to manage (Armitage *et al.* 2003). Good communication between prison staff and MHIRTs is thus necessary to identify more appropriate referrals. Mental health awareness training for prison officers may assist in this process but, although offered in some prisons and desired by many officers (HMCIP 2007), it is not mandatory and it is not yet clear what proportion of staff have received it.

Practical issues

In-reach teams have also faced various practical difficulties in trying to carry out their role within prisons. Unlike CMHTs outside prison, MHIRTs do not have direct admission rights to inpatient NHS beds (Royal College of Psychiatrists 2007). Arranging transfers to outside care can monopolise their time, thus reducing their availability to perform other tasks (Edgar and Rickford 2009). Despite recent measures to try and expedite transfers within 14 days of a psychiatric assessment (HMPS 2006), they can still be subject to serious delays and in some cases, prisoners can still be waiting over 100 days from the time of being referred to being transferred (Forrester *et al.* 2009). During this time, no treatment can be enforced without the patient's consent, unless under common law (Wilson and Forrester 2002), as prison health care centres do not count as hospitals under the Mental Health Act. Care planning in prison can also be challenging due to the rapid movement of prisoners around the system, particularly in the current climate of overcrowding, where prisoners are moved wherever there is space for them. As a consequence, they may have to endure several different assessments of their mental state, but may not be in any one prison long enough to receive any effective treatment. Such experiences can make prisoners reluctant to build up trust with staff again, particularly if they have disclosed traumatic events such as child sex abuse (Durcan 2008). Even when prisoners are offered support from MHIRTs, a shortage of staff to escort them to appointments may mean not only that they will not receive the help they need, but also that in-reach staff waste considerable time waiting for prisoners who are unable to attend, or assume that they have actively decided to refuse treatment (Kendall and Mills, forthcoming).

Difficulties working with other agencies
Brooker and Birmingham (2009) argue that providing a good standard of mental health care and continuity of care requires input not just from mental health professionals, but also from various agencies such as probation, offender management, prison psychology departments, teachers and prison officers, who should all be encouraged to make relevant contributions to prisoners' individual care plans. In reality, however, integrated multi-agency working is rare. Despite high levels of co-morbidity, guidance as to how mental health and substance misuse services should work together has not been issued (HMCIP 2007). Joint working seems to be largely limited to in-reach teams and CARAT (counselling, assessment, referral, advice and throughcare) services referring clients to each other if they see a prisoner's problems as being predominantly the concern of the other service (HMCIP 2007; Durcan 2008; Edgar and Rickford 2009). More formal collaboration between mental health and CARAT services is thus needed to develop specialist dual-diagnosis services (Steel *et al.* 2007). According to Department of Health guidance, residential staff should also be involved in the CPA, but again such input is uncommon and may be hampered by a widespread belief among clinical and non-clinical staff that medical information should not be shared (HMCIP 2007). Only half of MHIRTs have a procedure for briefing staff when an inpatient returns to a residential wing (HMCIP 2007), despite the fact that residential staff effectively act as primary carers for MHIRT patients.

In trying to ensure continuity of care when a patient is released from prison, in-reach teams should ideally be working with offender management and resettlement departments in order to ensure the prisoner is adequately prepared and able to engage with appropriate mental health intervention. In some cases this may lead to resettlement issues being addressed much earlier because, as noted above, MHIRTs can act as advocates for prisoners with agencies inside and outside the prison, including probation (Durcan 2008). However, in general few resettlement teams receive input from MHIRTs or are invited to attend care planning reviews (HMCIP 2007). This is despite the fact that obtaining suitable accommodation can be crucial in trying to secure continuity of care, as prisoners may be unable to register with a GP or may be rejected by community mental health services unless they have an address in their local area (Mills 2002). Outside services may be reluctant to engage with ex-prisoners, particularly if they have co-morbid substance misuse problems, or where the potential client wishes to resettle outside the prison's local area (Mills 2002; Birmingham 2003; Meiklejohn *et al.* 2004; HMCIP 2007). Continuing care in prisons may also be hard to plan if prisoners are released or transferred with little or no notice, particularly if their medical notes do not accompany them (Durcan 2008). Yet multi-agency working and information sharing can be successfully achieved, as exemplified by the multi-agency public protection arrangements (MAPPA) process which involves various agencies, including probation, police and prison services and health, sharing information to support, coordinate and review risk management plans for high-risk offenders when they leave prison or secure psychiatric care.

Difficulties meeting the needs of diverse groups

Concerns have also been raised that in-reach services have neglected the needs of particular groups. As noted above, mental health services may target prisoners who appear visibly to need attention to the neglect of those with hidden needs such as quieter, older prisoners suffering from depression (HMCIP 2004a). For women prisoners, who tend to experience high levels of emotional and psychological distress, primary mental health care and counselling are likely to be of greater significance than the secondary care provided by most MHIRTs, and this has led to calls for MHIRTs in women's prisons to be much larger and more multidisciplinary, with wider remits, including counselling services (CSIP 2006). At HMP New Hall, the MHIRT has taken the specific needs of women on board and alongside full-time psychiatric and dual-diagnosis nurses, services include sessional input from specialists in self-harm, substance misuse, anger management, trauma and abuse (CSIP 2006).

Despite their over-representation in the prison population, BME prisoners are less likely to receive mental health services in prison than their white counterparts. This may be due to lower rates of referral, as illustrated by the finding of the Chief Inspector of Prisons that fewer BME prisoners (49 per cent) had needs identified at the reception screen followed up in comparison to white prisoners (68 per cent). BME prisoners are also less likely to have had previous contact with mental health services in the community, to have a care plan or a key worker, or to be aware of their medication's potential side effects. MHIRTs showed little awareness of the health needs of different ethnic groups and in only 30 per cent of cases was patients' ethnicity recorded, despite NHS requirements to do so (HMCIP 2007).

Equivalence: Achievable? Realistic? Desirable?

One of the key aims of the prison mental health in-reach programme is to provide prisoners with 'access to the same range and quality of services appropriate to their needs as are available to the general population through the NHS' (DH and HMPS 2001: 5), but the efficacy and appropriateness of this aim are open to debate. Seeking to provide equivalent care suggests that community mental health services are the gold standard against which MHIRTs should be measured. This shrouds huge problems and inequalities within community provision, which are illustrated by the long histories of transcarceration of many prisoners on MHIRT caseloads. In short, prison is where a considerable number of patients for whom community care has failed end up (Kupers 1999). The meaning of equivalence is also unclear in this context. The minimal guidance provided in *Changing the Outlook* suggests that in-reach services should be provided 'as far as possible in the same way as they are in the wider community' (DH and HMPS 2001: 26). Yet doubts have been raised as to whether this approach can adequately address the high and complex levels of multiple need in the prison population (Durcan 2008), particularly in relation to co-morbidity. Rather, it has been argued that services should be tailored to the specific needs of the prison population but should be provided 'of a range and quality which deliver the same *outcomes* for prisoners as they do for the general population' (SCMH 2007b: 6).

Providing care of the same range and quality as that available in the community is also currently simply unachievable within prisons. In the community, CMHTs work alongside other services such as assertive outreach and crisis resolution teams, which have not yet been introduced into prisons (Brooker *et al.* 2008), and primary mental health care for those with common mental illness. The lack of these services in prison suggests that this cannot amount to equivalent provision, and in striving to provide equivalence, in-reach teams may be expected to take on board these other roles, thus placing further demands on their already scarce resources. Prison MHIRTs also do not have the full complement of staff equivalent to community standards to meet the prevalence and severity of psychiatric morbidity in prisons. To offer an equivalent service to a CMHT, a typical men's prison of 550 prisoners would require 11 whole-time-equivalent practitioners (Boardman and Parsonage 2007), over double the current level of provision (Brooker and Gojkovic 2009). Per capita spending on prison mental health care would also have to rise from the current level, which is between 3.9 and 7.3 times higher per head than spending in the general population to about 20 times higher (Brooker *et al.* 2008).

Although the original intention was for MHIRTs to be multidisciplinary like CMHTs, in practice the majority of staff are psychiatric nurses, and there is variable and often limited input from other disciplines such as social work, occupational therapy, clinical psychology, and support work (Brooker and Gojkovic 2009). Consequently, despite the high levels of traumatic events experienced by the prison population, such as childhood and domestic abuse, torture, bereavement, military combat and family breakdown, prisoners are unlikely to have the same access to psychological therapies as their counterparts in the community. Although theoretically 62 per cent of MHIRTs offer cognitive behavioural therapy (CBT) (HMCIP 2007), in actuality in-reach teams conduct on average fewer than four sessions per week of psychological interventions (Brooker and Gojkovic 2009), consisting predominantly of individual CBT or anxiety management sessions (Brooker and Gojkovic 2009). Only 36 per cent of teams offer some form of counselling, and although other interventions such as art therapy, groupwork, psychotherapy, anger management and coping strategies are available, their use is far from widespread, with female prisoners having better access to such interventions, largely due to greater input from a range of non-statutory organisations (HMCIP 2007). Several research studies have found that MHIRT patients would most like 'someone to talk to' about their problems (Mills *et al.* 2005; HMCIP 2007; Durcan 2008; Kendall and Mills, forthcoming). In our qualitative evaluation of the MHIRT in a local prison, it was suggested that, without this provision prisoners' mental health may deteriorate, leading them to require more input than was initially needed (Kendall *et al.* 2006).

Finally, it must be questioned how realistic and achievable it is to provide equivalent mental health care in a closed, restrictive, punitive and essentially 'anti-therapeutic' setting. Although for some people prison may act as a 'stabiliser' (Durcan 2008: 31), allowing a break from chaotic lifestyles outside and potentially providing the opportunity to engage with mental health treatment, the prison, with its rules and regimes governing daily life, can be seriously detrimental to mental health (Birmingham 2003; Nurse *et al.* 2003). For Niveau (2007) equivalence of mental health care in prisons is unachievable because a doctor simply cannot give prisoners what they most need to improve their mental health, such as stable family relations, fulfilling work and liberty. He further argues: 'From a clinical point of view, the principle of equivalence is often insufficient to take account of the adaptations necessary for the organization of care in a correctional setting' (Niveau 2007: 610).

Some treatments may be impractical in prisons with no scope to monitor them effectively or time to deliver them properly before the prisoner is released or transferred. The key priority of the prison is to maintain order, control and discipline (Sim 2002), rather than to provide health care or welfare. Due to limited resources and high demand, prison psychiatrists tend to concentrate on the most urgent situations such as high risk of suicide, acute psychosis and major behavioural disorders (Niveau 2007), thus potentially serving the needs of the prison rather than the needs of the prisoners. In such a context, prisoners may not feel free to refuse treatment for fear that it will have an impact on their future care in prison or parole opportunities, and may have little autonomy, for example, to choose which doctor they see or to ask for a second opinion about their diagnosis (Birmingham *et al.* 2006). Furthermore, it has been suggested that the prison officer culture with its stress on the punitive degradation of prisoners (Sim 2009) can lead to prisoners being 'constructed by staff as less eligible subjects whose criminality has placed them beyond the contractual pale of respectable society' (Sim 2002: 317). Any attempts to engage in therapeutic work may thus be viewed as 'disturbing the normative equilibrium of the punitive culture' (2002: 316), although it should be noted that not all officers will share this disdainful approach. In our study of a MHIRT, team members reported open hostility and animosity from prison staff who perceived them to be 'do-gooders' whose clients were to be controlled and managed, rather than treated (Mills *et al.* 2005). Until both the formal and informal networks of penal power are addressed, any hopes for providing equivalent care are unlikely to be realised (Sim 2002).

39

Prison therapy: a contradiction in terms?

It is also worth questioning whether it is possible or even desirable to offer therapy in prisons. There are four key arguments for the provision of therapeutic interventions. First, it is argued that prisoners' criminal behaviour may be linked to mental disorder. Treatment should therefore be provided, not only in order to address the underlying disorder, but also to reduce the likelihood of recidivism. Second, since offenders' use of mental health services while in the community still lags behind that of the rest of the population, it is only fair that they have access to such services while incarcerated. Key barriers to service utilisation in the community include poor access to mental health facilities and resources due to lack of access to a GP, but also the fact that such services may not be offered to offenders by health professionals because they do not feel they have the necessary skills to deal with their needs (DH 2009). In addition, distrust of doctors and other authority figures, fear of stigma and chaotic lifestyles can all inhibit help-seeking for mental health problems among this group (Howerton *et al.* 2007). Third, even if mental health services do not 'cure' a disorder or reduce recidivism, they allow prisoners to speak to someone about their experiences and feelings, assist them in a crisis, provide advocacy and simply help to pass the time (Durcan 2008). Finally, an emphasis on treatment and rehabilitation can contribute to more humane prison conditions (Haney 2006). As mentioned earlier in this chapter, our study of a MHIRT found that prisoners highly valued the in-reach team and their services. In addition, both prisoners and staff credited the team with making the prison more humane (Kendall and Mills, forthcoming).

Despite strong arguments for the provision of therapeutic interventions, there are serious limitations to their delivery within prison, including the practical and time constraints noted above, and there is tension in offering mental health services in an 'anti-therapeutic' environment. As the fundamental purpose of prison is to punish people by confining them against their will, security will always remain the primary concern. Carlen (2002) has argued that anything that appears to challenge or erode this security will always be suppressed or transformed, a process that she names 'carceral clawback'. Prisoners with mental health problems may be more likely than others to experience such 'clawback', as they are often seen to pose an increased risk to prison security (Kupers 1999). In our study, for example, some prisoners perceived to be dangerous were often not seen by the team due to a lack of the required number of staff thought necessary to unlock their cell. Attempts to establish therapeutic group work were also thwarted by security concerns, as frequently the team were informed that there were not enough officers available to escort prisoners to group sessions or that there were no suitable rooms to safely hold a number of prisoners together.

'Carceral clawback' is further evident where progressive policies and practices which challenge the punitive nature of prison, including therapeutic interventions, are neutralised or destroyed. Efforts in Canada to introduce radical prison reforms, which operationalised a feminist-inspired and culturally sensitive prison regime were undermined by processes of co-optation, in which feminist and Aboriginal organisations were co-opted by the Correctional Service of Canada, and by encroachment, where reforms were gradually eroded away and replaced with conventional correctional methods (Hannah-Moffat 2002). Where good therapeutic practice has been established in the UK, it has tended to remain isolated and unrecognised or to be terminated, as was the case with the Barlinnie Special Unit, the Max Glatt Annexe (Sim 2009) or with C wing at HMP Parkhurst, which was closed down in the security clampdown following the 1995 escapes. At HMP Dovegate, efforts to replicate the therapeutic community approach pioneered at HMP Grendon have also encountered difficulties, as a high number of prisoners have dropped out of therapy and are said to be affecting the progress of those who remain; yet they cannot be moved to other establishments due to overcrowding pressures (HMCIP 2008).

Given these serious practical and political barriers to successful prison rehabilitative efforts, why does therapy continue to proliferate? Carlen and Tombs (2006: 341) argue that 'because [prison] so nearly violates so many human rights and is so painful', any claims that it can rehabilitate prisoners and reduce crime through therapy or other means provide prison with legitimacy and obfuscate the pains of imprisonment. Such claims may encourage 'therapeutic sentencing' whereby sentencers send people to prison believing that prisoners' needs will be met there (see also Peay 2002) and justify longer prison sentences on the grounds that they are necessary for therapy to be effective. The promise that prison can be both therapeutic and punitive, or 'therapunitive', has, according to Carlen and Tombs (2006), resulted in material resources being transferred from the community into the prison. This was recently confirmed by the Bradley review of services for offenders with mental health problems, which worryingly reported that, in some cases, funding for diversion and liaison schemes has been re-routed to finance mental health in-reach services (Bradley 2009).

Finally, by suggesting that the causes of crime and their treatment lie within the minds or psychology of individual prisoners, the 'therapunitive' prison also serves to individualise crime and to deflect attention away from structural issues, such as poverty, racism, sexism, violence and poor educational attainment, involved in both crime and punishment. Nevertheless, such criticisms of prison therapy present something of a dilemma due to the real danger that they may be used to reduce or eliminate mental health services, leaving prisoners with no support for their distress and mental health problems.

Conclusion

Since they were first proposed, MHIRTs have faced high expectations of the quantity and type of mental health services they should provide. Yet it has become increasingly clear that they cannot meet such expectations due to the high demand for their services, staffing and resource constraints and the various practical and political barriers to providing both equivalent care and therapy in prisons. Such difficulties have been compounded by 'mission creep', by confusion over their role and by the lack of integrated working with other agencies. It is also apparent that for the mental health problems of prisoners to be meaningfully addressed, primary mental health care in prisons needs to be substantially improved to help to identify serious mental health issues and to deal with common mental health problems such as mild depression and anxiety. Brooker and Ullman (2008) have recently recommended that all mental health staff should be integrated into multidisciplinary mental health teams in order to improve the quality of care and coordination of services, but without substantial commitment and investment in primary mental health care, such comprehensive services are unlikely to materialise.

The provision of mental health care in prisons in the future may also be affected by wider public and political pressures. In April 2003 the responsibility for funding and commissioning all health services in public sector prisons in England was transferred to the Department of Health, and PCTs now have to weigh up the competing demands of prison health care against care for patients in the wider community, which may lead to funding for prison-based services being placed in jeopardy (Mason 2006), particularly if prisoners are seen as less eligible patients.

More fundamentally, while improved provision of prison mental health care is generally regarded as a positive development, the fact that individuals with serious mental health problems are in prison at all should be seriously questioned. Until more compassionate ways of responding to deviant and troublesome behaviour by people with mental health problems are developed, need will always remain greater than capacity (HMCIP 2007). Indeed, given the potential psychological, emotional and physical harm caused by incarceration, we must consider alternatives to imprisonment for all.

References

All-Party Parliamentary Group on Prison Health (2006) *The Mental Health Problem in UK HM Prisons*. London: House of Commons.

Armitage, C., Fitzgerald, C. and Cheong, P. (2003) 'Prison in-reach mental health nursing', *Nursing Standard*, 17(26): 40–2.

Birmingham, L. (2001) 'Screening prisoners for psychiatric illness: who benefits?', *Psychiatric Bulletin*, 25: 462–4.

Birmingham, L. (2003) 'The mental health of prisoners', *Advances in Psychiatric Treatment*, 9(3): 191–201.

Birmingham, L., Mason, D. and Grubin, D. (1996) 'Prevalence of mental disorder in remand prisoners: consecutive case study', *British Medical Journal*, 313: 1521–4.

Birmingham, L., Wilson, S. and Adshead, G. (2006) 'Prison medicine: ethics and equivalence, *British Journal of Psychiatry*, 188: 4–6.

Boardman, J. and Parsonage, M. (2007) *Delivering the Government's Mental Health Policies: Services, Staffing and Costs*. London: Sainsbury Centre for Mental Health.

Borrill, J., Maden, A., Martin, A., Weaver, T., Stimson, G., Farrell, M. and Barnes, T. (2003) *Differential Substance Misuse Treatment Needs of Women, Ethnic Minorities and Young Offenders in Prison: Prevalence of Substance Misuse and Treatment Needs*. London: Home Office.

Bradley, L. (2009) *The Bradley Report: Lord Bradley's Review of People with Mental Health Problems or Learning Disabilities in the Criminal Justice System*. London: Department of Health.

Brooker, C., Repper, J., Beverley, C., Ferriter, M. and Brewer, N. (2002) *Mental Health Services and Prisoners: A Review*. Sheffield: University of Sheffield School of Health and Related Research.

Brooker, C., Ricketts, T., Lemme, F., Dent-Brown, K. and Hibbert, C. (2005) *An Evaluation of the Prison In-Reach Collaborative*. Sheffield: University of Sheffield School of Health and Related Research.

Brooker, C., Duggan, S., Fox, C., Mills, A. and Parsonage, M. (2008) *Short Changed: Spending on Prison Mental Health Care*. London: Sainsbury Centre for Mental Health.

Brooker, C. and Ullman, B. (2008) *Out of Sight, Out of Mind: The State of Mental Healthcare in Prison*. London: Policy Exchange.

Brooker, C. and Birmingham, L. (2009) 'The psychiatric aspects of imprisonment revisited', *Journal of Forensic Psychiatry and Psychology*, 20(1): S1–4.

Brooker, C. and Gojkovic, D. (2009) 'The second national survey of mental health in-reach services in prisons', *Journal of Forensic Psychiatry and Psychology*, 20(1): S11–28.

Care Services Improvement Partnership (CSIP) (2006) *Women at Risk: The Mental Health of Women in Contact with the Judicial System*. London: Department of Health.

Carlen, P. (2002) 'Carceral clawback: the case of women's imprisonment in Canada', *Punishment and Society*, 4(1): 115–21.

Carlen, P. and Worrall, A. (2004) *Analysing Women's Imprisonment*. Cullompton: Willan Publishing.

Carlen, P. and Tombs, J. (2006) 'Reconfigurations of penality: the ongoing case of women's imprisonment and reintegration industries', *Theoretical Criminology*, 10(3): 337–60.

Corston J. (2007) *The Corston Report: A Review of Women with Particular Vulnerabilities in the Criminal Justice System*. London: Home Office.

Crawley, E. (2007) 'Imprisonment in old age', in Y. Jewkes (ed.), *Handbook on Prisons*. Cullompton: Willan Publishing, pp. 224–44.

DH (2000) *The NHS Plan: A Plan for Investment, A Plan for Reform*. London: Department of Health.

DH (2009) *Improving Access to Psychological Therapies. Offenders. Positive Practice Guide*. London: Department of Health.

DH and HMPS (1999) *The Future Organisation of Prison Healthcare*. London: Department of Health.

DH and HMPS (2001) *Changing the Outlook: A Strategy for Developing and Modernising Mental Health Services in Prisons*. London: Department of Health.

Durcan, G. (2008) *From the Inside: Experiences of Prison Mental Health Care*. London: Sainsbury Centre for Mental Health.

Edgar, K. and Rickford, D. (2009) *Too Little Too Late: An Independent Review of Unmet Mental Health Need in Prison*. London: Prison Reform Trust.

Fawcett Society (2009) *Engendering Justice: From Policy to Practice*. London: Fawcett Society.

Fazel, S., Hope, T., O'Donnell, I., and Jacoby, R. (2001) 'Hidden psychiatric morbidity in elderly prisoners', *British Journal of Psychiatry*, 179: 535–9.

Forrester, A., Henderson, C., Wilson, S., Cumming, I., Spyrou, M. and Parrott, J. (2009) 'A suitable waiting room?: Hospital transfer outcomes and delays from two London prisons', *The Psychiatrist*, 33: 409–12.

Giallombardo, R. (1966) *Society of Women*. New York: Wiley.

Gostin, L. and Staunton, M. (1985) 'The case for prison standards: conditions of confinement, segregation, and medical treatment', in J. Vagg, R. Morgan and M. Maguire (eds), *Accountability and Prisons: Opening Up a Closed World*. London: Tavistock.

Grounds, A. (1994) 'Mentally disordered prisoners', in E. Player and M. Jenkins (eds), *Prisons After Woolf*. London: Routledge, pp. 178–89.

Gunn, J., Maden, A. and Swinton, M. (1991) *Mentally Disordered Prisoners*. London: Home Office.

Haney, C. (2006) *Reforming Punishment: Psychological Limits to the Pains of Imprisonment*. Washington, DC: American Psychological Association.

Hannah-Moffat, K. (2002) 'Creating choices, reflecting on choices', in P. Carlen (ed.), *Women and Punishment: The Struggle for Justice*. Cullompton: Willan Publishing.

HMCIP (1996) *Patient or Prisoner: A New Strategy for Healthcare in Prisons*. London: Home Office.

HMCIP (2004a) *'No Problems – Old and Quiet': Older Prisoners in England and Wales*. London: HM Inspectorate of Prisons.

HMCIP (2004b) *Annual Report of HM Chief Inspector of Prisons for England and Wales 2002–2003*. London: HM Inspectorate of Prisons.

HMCIP (2007) *The Mental Health of Prisoners: A Thematic Review of the Care and Support of Prisoners with Mental Health Needs*. London: HM Inspectorate of Prisons.

HMCIP (2008) *Report on an Unannounced Inspection of HMP Dovegate Therapeutic Community, 16–20 June 2008*. London: HM Inspectorate of Prisons.

HMPS (2006) *Transfer of Prisoners to and from Hospital under Sections 47 and 48 of the Mental Health Act 1983*, Prison Service Instruction 03/2006.

HMPS (2007) *Annual Reports and Accounts 2005–2006*, London: Prison Service.

Howerton, A., Byng, R., Campbell, J., Hess, D., Owens, C. and Aitken, P. (2007) 'Understanding help seeking behaviour among male offenders: Qualitative interview study', *British Medical Journal*, 334: 303–6.

Kendall, K. and Mills, A. (forthcoming) *An Evaluation of the New Mental Health In-Reach Service at HMP Winchester*. Research report to HOPE, Wessex Medical Research.

Kendall, K., Mills, A. and Birmingham, L. (2006) 'Equivalence of Care: Lessons from the HMP Winchester Mental Health In-Reach Service', British Society of Criminology Annual Conference, Universities of Glasgow and Strathclyde and Glasgow Caledonian University, 5–7 July 2006.

Kupers, T. (1999) *Prison Madness: The Mental Health Crisis Behind Bars and What We Can Do About It*. San Francisco, CA: Jossey-Bass Publishers.

Lader, D., Singleton, N. and Meltzer, H. (2000) *Psychiatric Morbidity among Young Offenders in England and Wales*. London: Office for National Statistics.

Mason, P. (2006) 'Prison healthcare at a crossroads', *Prison Health Innovation Network Bulletin* 3:1. Available at http://www.healthcareinside.org.uk/documents/PHINBulletin3.pdf

Medlicott, D. (2007) 'Women in prison', in Y. Jewkes (ed.), *Handbook on Prisons*. Cullompton: Willan Publishing, pp. 245–67.

Meiklejohn, C., Hodges, K. and Capon, D. (2004) 'In-reach work with prisoners', *Mental Health Nursing*, 24: 8–10.

Mental Health Foundation (1999) *The Fundamental Facts*. London: Mental Health Foundation.

Mills, A. (2002) 'Mental health in-reach: the way forward for prison?', *Probation Journal*, 49(2): 107–19.

Mills, A. (2005) 'Mentally vulnerable adults in prison: specialist resources and practice', in B. Littlechild and D. Fearns (eds), *Mental Disorder and Criminal Justice: Policy, Practice and Provision*. Lyme Regis: Russell House Publishing.

Mills, A., Kendall, K., Birmingham, L. and Morton, D. (2005) 'Prison mental health in-reach services: care versus custody revisited', British Society of Criminology Annual Conference, University of Leeds, 12–14 July.

Niveau, G. (2007) 'Relevance and limits of the principle of "equivalence of care" in prison medicine', *Journal of Medical Ethics*, 33: 610–13.

Nurse, J., Woodcock, P. and Ormsby, J. (2003) 'Influence of environmental factors on mental health within prisons: focus group study', *British Medical Journal*, 327: 480–5.

O'Brien, M., Mortimer, L., Singleton, N. and Meltzer, H. (2001) *Psychiatric Morbidity amongst Women Prisoners in England and Wales*. London: Office for National Statistics.

Peay, J. (2002) 'Mentally disordered offenders, mental health, and crime', in M. Maguire, R. Morgan and R. Reiner (eds), *The Oxford Handbook of Criminology*, 3rd edition. Oxford: Oxford University Press, pp. 496–527.

Prison Reform Trust (2003) *Growing Old in Prison: A Scoping Study on Older Prisoners*. London: Centre for Policy on Ageing and Prison Reform Trust.

Reed, J. (2003) 'Mental health care in prisons', *British Journal of Psychiatry*, 182: 287–8.

Reed, J. and Lyne, M. (1997) 'The quality of health care in prison: results of a year's programme of semi-structured inspections', *British Medical Journal*, 315: 1420–24.

Reed, J. and Lyne, M. (2000) 'Inpatient care of mentally ill people in prison: results of a year's programme of semi structured inspections', *British Medical Journal*, 320: 1031–4.

Royal College of Psychiatrists (2007) *Prison Psychiatry: Adult Prisons in England and Wales*. London: Royal College of Psychiatrists.

SCMH (2007a) *Mental Health Care in Prisons*. London: Sainsbury Centre for Mental Health.

SCMH (2007b) *Getting the Basics Right: Developing a Primary Care Mental Health Service in Prisons*. London: Sainsbury Centre for Mental Health.

Shaw, J., Birmingham, L., Brooker, C., Harty, M., Kendall, K., Lathlean, J., Lowthian, C., Mills, A., Senior, J., and Thornicroft, G. (2008) *A National Evaluation of Prison Mental Health In-Reach Services*. Unpublished final research report to the National Institute for Health Research.

Sim, J. (1990) *Medical Power in Prisons*. Buckingham: Open University Press.

Sim, J. (2002) 'The future of prison health care: a critical analysis', *Critical Social Policy*, 22(2): 300–23.

Sim, J. (2009) *Punishment and Prisons*. London: Sage.

Singleton, N., Meltzer, H., Gatward, R., Coid, J. and Deasy, D. (1998) *Psychiatric Morbidity among Prisoners*. London: Office for National Statistics.

Smith, R. (1999) 'Prisoners: an end to second-class healthcare?', *British Medical Journal*, 318: 954–5.

Social Exclusion Unit (2002) *Reducing Re-offending by Ex-prisoners*. London: Office of the Deputy Prime Minister.

Steel, J., Thornicroft, G., Birmingham, L., Brooker, C., Mills, A., Harty, M. and Shaw, J. (2007) 'Prison mental health in-reach services', *British Journal of Psychiatry*, 190: 373–4.

Wilson, S. and Forrester, A. (2002) 'Too little, too late? The treatment of mentally incapacitated prisoners', *Journal of Forensic Psychiatry*, 13(1): 1–8.

Woolf, L.J. (1991) *Prison Disturbances April 1990: Report of an Inquiry by the Rt Hon. Lord Justice Woolf (Parts I and II) and His Honour Stephen Tumin (Part II)*. London: HMSO.

World Health Organisation (2009) *Women's Health in Prison: Correcting Gender Inequality in Health*. Copenhagen: WHO Regional Office for Europe.

Chapter 3

Attachment-based psychodynamic psychotherapy

Mary Haley

Introduction

This chapter provides a detailed account of attachment–based psychodynamic psychotherapy and draws upon therapeutic work taking place in two adult male prisons in the UK: a category A (maximum security) prison and a category C prison. Both of these prisons hold life-sentenced prisoners. Those in the category A prison range from people at the beginning of their sentence to people long past their early release date. Those prisoners in the category C prison who have moved from higher secure conditions may be aiming to move to open prison conditions. However, they could also be returned to higher secure conditions if their security classification were to be changed.

The crimes committed by men in these prisons vary and include rape, other sexual offences, robbery, murder and other physical violence. Many of these crimes are drug and/or alcohol related; most of the people entering therapy started misusing substances at a very early age, often before leaving primary education. Of particular pertinence to this chapter is the fact that many prisoners have experienced extremely dysfunctional childhoods. Their histories include parental neglect and violence, sexual abuse, physical abuse, witnessing violence against a person they love and having a parent with mental health problems. Unsurprisingly, these problems have often unfolded against a background of personally disruptive lifestyles and early contact with mental health services.

Men entering therapy have stated that the prison environment can offer the most stable period of their lives; yet this environment also embodies their worst nightmares. It is paradoxical that, for some, their most stable and secure experiences are those which are also their most feared and despised. Many of the men entering therapy have been recidivist prisoners and have only spent a few weeks of their adult life in the general community.

The work detailed in this chapter involves providing individual, weekly psychotherapy to prisoners. Mainly, this is long-term therapeutic work, but sometimes there is a need for brief focal therapy if a prisoner is due for release or transfer in a few weeks or months and is able to work on specific issues.

Key theoretical concepts

The therapeutic approach discussed in this chapter links attachment theory to psychodynamic principles. It is argued that the relevance of this approach to forensic populations is strong. The author worked as a governor grade in the Prison Service for 17 years prior to completing psychotherapy training. The knowledge gained from training in psychotherapy would have made understanding prisoners easier, including understanding the likely aetiology of violent acts both prior to, and during, imprisonment.

Psychodynamic psychotherapy is a descendant of Freudian psychoanalysis and at its heart is the premise that unconscious internal conflict, which includes conflict affecting how a person relates to others, is at the core of psychological distress (Bateman *et al.* 1991; Gomez 1997). Further, it is posited that various defence mechanisms, again unconscious, are developed to help a person manage these conflicts: these include projection, repression, denial, reaction formation and rationalisation. For example, in 'projection' we might criticise another for doing something, not realising that this is a trait other people identify in us. One psychodynamic school arising from psychoanalysis is object relations, which emphasises the impact of external relationships on the developing mind (see Gomez 1997). Within this school of thought, Melanie Klein proposed that an infant views the world first in a split way (the paranoid/schizoid position), with good and bad being total states (see Gomez 1997); but later understanding of the world shows that this prior understanding is flawed and that the reality is that there are good and bad aspects to all things. This she called the 'depressive condition', as the infant

49

recognised that it might have hurt or destroyed something good which it had seen as all bad. This model of splitting is useful in the forensic context, as clients who have suffered very difficult childhoods often find it difficult to see shades of grey in interpersonal relationships.

Like object relations theory, attachment theory is also based on the impact of interrelationships on our world view. Attachment theory was put forward by Bowlby in his trilogy *Attachment* (Bowlby 1969), *Separation* (Bowlby 1973) and *Loss* (Bowlby 1980). Since this time there has been a vast quantity of research on attachment theory, some of which links it with psychodynamic theories and cognitive science. Knox (2003) suggests that attachment theory can be seen as a bridge between these two other approaches. Bowlby (1988) describes the development of 'enduring attachments that children and other individuals make to particular others' (p. 29) and observable behaviours associated with these attachments. From these relationships people develop ideas of what the world is like, ideas which Bowlby called Internal Working Models (IWMs) (Bretherton and Munholland 1999). IWMs are the mental maps of 'how the world is' which we develop through our experiences. Thus, if a caregiver is responsive to an infant's needs, the infant may conclude that the world is a place in which his needs are met; from this 'map', the infant can predict what is likely to happen in the future, based on similar past experiences; and this prediction in turn allows him to amend or adjust behaviours to achieve a particular outcome. Our actions follow these IWMs, adopting approaches which can best facilitate our survival and success.

Marvin and Britner (1999) describe Bowlby's research as a 'general systems perspective' (p. 46), which considers human beings as biological systems which have interactive sub-systems that keep the dominant 'system' alive. They note that when a single 'system' (person) is unable to carry out the task of survival alone it will interact with another for assistance. In attachment theory this is the arrangement of infant and caregiver, whereby the infant of the species interacts with a more mature member to keep itself alive. The mature figure becomes a 'secure base' for the younger one. From the caregiver the child receives nurture and protection from threat. Marvin and Britner (1999) note, however, that such a biological interaction also aims to increase the dependent's self-reliance, and therefore a secondary function of the attachment system is to facilitate the infant's ability to 'explore and learn – that is, to develop the skills necessary for self protection through autonomous integration with the larger group'

(Marvin and Britner 1999: 46). Attachment behaviour is activated when a child perceives a threat to its safety; once this threat has passed, the child will continue to explore and develop autonomy.

Attachment theory proposes that infants always attach to their caregivers, although how effective this bond is depends substantially on the quality of this care. Research by Ainsworth (1991) examined how children attached to their caregivers, mainly mothers, but later research shows different attachment styles develop with different people (see also Cassidy 1999). Ainsworth (1991) first observed children and caregivers in their natural surroundings, but then devised the Strange Situation Test (SST): in the SST, children aged between 12 and 20 months were in a room at various times with their mothers, left alone, or were with a responsive stranger. She classified the resulting behaviour into three types of attachment styles: secure, insecure-avoidant and insecure-ambivalent.

Those who were classified as 'secure' were able to use their mother as a secure base, because they explored their surroundings and also relied on her in times of perceived threat. Those classified as 'insecure-avoidant' were able to explore their surroundings, but did not use their mother as a secure base; on separation they displayed little distress, although their heart rate did increase; and on reunion they actively avoided their mothers and often rejected her if she tried to re-establish contact. Finally, those classified as 'insecure-ambivalent' showed distress on entering a new situation and clung to their mothers, failing to explore; on separation, their distress worsened; and on reunion they would either seek contact but not be comforted easily, or would fight against their mothers by kicking and turning away – often alternating both types of behaviours. It was also noted that some children were difficult to classify. Main and Soloman (cited in Ainsworth and Eichberg 1991) examined this classification further and devised a fourth category, 'disorganized/disorientated'. This category included those children who showed no coherent behaviours, obvious goals or intentions. They found that these children were present in much greater numbers in high-risk populations in which children had suffered extreme neglect and/or emotional, physical and sexual abuse. They may 'freeze', engage in strange or unfinished behaviours[1] or show signs of fear towards their mothers. They seemed to have no particular attachment style available to them.

Later work has shown that children's attachment styles develop in response to the type of parenting and caring they receive; and this care is in turn related very strongly to the parents' own style of attaching (see Hesse 1999). Children develop these different styles in order to gain optimum levels of care from their parents or caregivers. For example, for children whose attachment is of the disorganised/ disorientated style, parenting has usually been frightening and generally highly dysfunctional.

A way of relating adult attachment styles to the SST is the Adult Attachment Interview (AAI). This was devised by George, Kaplan and Main in 1985. Hesse (1999) noted that the introduction of this protocol allowed the therapist to investigate parental behaviours, which in turn allowed the therapist to consider these parental behaviours in relation to the attachment style the child develops – that is, to see whether a parent's attachment style is 'passed on' to their offspring. It is argued that a securely attached parent is able to reflect on their experiences, make sense of them and choose how they now wish to act. As van IJzendoorn and Bakermans-Kranenburg (1997) note, it is not the quality of the parents' own early attachment experiences that is important, but whether at some stage in their lives, the parents received a good enough attachment experience to allow a healthy representation of attachment to develop. Even if early attachment was poor, a militating positive experience with, say, a teacher, friend, partner or therapist, can facilitate a later development of a 'secure base' which develops the ability to offer better parenting themselves.

To assess attachment styles, the AAI questions the interviewee about their early relationships with parents and other caregivers, but focuses not only on the content but also on the quality of the narrative. In this way it aims to 'surprise the unconscious' (Main 1991: 141), by giving the interviewee considerable opportunity to contradict themselves or be overly lengthy or short in their answers. The security style is assessed from analysis of the coherence and rationality of the answers they give. The idea behind this assessment of quality is that the coherence of a narrative is an important indicator that the interviewee is able to make sense of what happened to them and is able to consider it in a logical, rational manner without being bound or controlled by the emotions which were present at the time.

The AAI has four attachment styles corresponding with the SST styles. The first is 'secure/autonomous', in which the interviewee gives a coherent account of attachment experiences without idealising or demonising caregivers and in which the interviewee gives rational responses to questions, which allows appropriate interaction between the interviewer and the interviewee without excessive or insufficient detail in response. (This style is linked to the SST style 'secure'.)

The second style is 'dismissing/detached', in which the interviewee appears to minimise childhood events, often giving short, insufficient answers; they usually idealise parents in broad terms but give little evidence to support this, and are more likely to give contradictory detail. (This style is linked to the SST style 'avoidant'.) The third style is 'preoccupied', in which the interviewee gives frequently lengthy responses while often losing track of the original question, in monologues mostly about the wrongs which parents have perpetrated and which still seem to worry the individual intensely; frequent use of present tense is often found, as are conflicting views of parents; sometimes conflicting even within the same sentence. (This style is linked to SST style 'ambivalent'.) Fourth, in line with the SST, a further group has also been noted who do not appear to have any specific secure style. These people were classified as 'unresolved/disorganised' and were interviewees who demonstrated incoherence with regard to emotional issues (including trauma and/or abuse); their narratives were confused and confusing, often appearing irrational and difficult to follow. (See Hesse 1999 for a fuller discussion of these styles.)

Attachment theory and its relevance to adult offenders

Attachment theory offers much to the area of forensic psychotherapy. Its origins include Bowlby's (1944) work on '44 juvenile thieves' and it has been a continued area of interest in attachment research. The occurrence of difficult attachment histories in violent forensic populations has been evidenced in the research literature (Van IJzendoorn et al. 1997; Frodi et al. 2001; Fonagy 2004). These authors have noted that in violent offender populations and violent psychiatric populations there are overwhelmingly higher numbers of people with disorganised/disoriented attachment styles than there are in non-clinical populations.

Attachment research explores why this should be the case. De Zulueta (2001) noted that the absence, including the emotional absence, of good caregivers actually produces physiological changes which increase propensity to violent behaviour. Moreover, she argues that when caregivers are emotionally absent, this can result in the child not developing the ability to empathise and therefore not being able to recognise the impact of pain on another person, as empathy is an extension of our understanding of 'self and other'. She noted that 'they are essentially egocentric and this predisposes them to maladaptive behaviour with others' (p. 184).

Weinfield *et al.* (1999) suggest that empathy is 'the counterpoint to aggression' (p. 78): that empathy reflects experiences of connectedness to others whereas aggression reflects experiences of alienation. Thus, abusive or neglectful early experiences will likely lead not only to feeling insecure (and therefore developing insecure attachment styles) but also to defending oneself against this insecurity through aggressive behaviours.

De Zulueta (2001) brings into focus the link between childhood abuse and later violence perpetrated by an abuse 'survivor'. She states that 'the links between psychological trauma and violence are often denied or minimized, particularly in relation to childhood abuse' (p. 184). She adds that high levels of chronic arousal reduce the individual's capacity 'to use symbols and fantasy to cope with stress' (de Zulueta 2001: 192) Thus, a child who is frequently and regularly exposed to stress is less likely to be able to understand their high emotions as abstract concepts such as 'I am angry' (that is, experiencing an emotion they might learn to control) and are more likely to simply experience angry feelings and equate them with an external trigger, rather than an internal state which can be regulated.

Adshead and Van Velsen (1996) highlighted that research on the impact of trauma is divided between that which emphasises the stressor (that is; trauma) as the main determinant of how well the trauma is dealt with, and that which emphasises an individual's ability to cope with it. They also noted that more recent studies integrated these approaches and showed how early influences impacted on an individual's ability to manage stress. Herman (1997) and de Zulueta (2001) noted that trauma inflicted on people by other human beings has more tenacious and damaging effects than trauma caused by natural disasters; this abuse, trauma deliberately inflicted on one person by another, is a particularly difficult form of trauma to overcome. If the abuse is perpetrated by a person to whom we have formed an attachment, this difficulty is worsened, as the paradoxical nature of a threat coming from one to whom we need to provide care is likely to be confusing and even more frightening.

Fonagy *et al.* (1997), Fonagy and Target (1996) and Fonagy (2004) list several related factors which might predispose a person towards violent crime. They suggest that violent individuals do not possess the mental capacity to understand that their behaviours are driven by mental states (such as anger), beliefs and desires. They suggest that this lack of understanding is part of normal development and call it 'psychic equivalence', a sense that what is felt emotionally is in fact an accurate representation of the world. This early distorted view also makes such individuals more vulnerable to actual brutality, as they are less able to draw on inner resources to withstand it. The child's thoughts, fears and feelings are given a 'concrete' status – but with the child being unaware of this distortion.

In normative development it is suggested that the child learns to integrate inner states and outer reality – learns that they are related but not dependent. As one client said, 'I get it! Sometimes when I feel bad, I hit someone and then I feel OK, but it's only for a few minutes. It's in me, isn't it? It's not about hitting them; it's about changing how I feel inside.' This insight began some very useful therapeutic work.

Fonagy (2004) suggests that where responsive parenting is unavailable, regression to psychic equivalence occurs. This makes the person more vulnerable to violence, as suspicious or other threatening feelings are mistaken for the physical reality. He adds that ensuing acts of violence serve to confirm this erroneous belief – that a physical act can eradicate an unwanted mental state. Additionally, such a view is often met with hostility from others, affirming the view of the world as violent.

It can therefore be seen how pertinent attachment theory is to psychotherapy in a forensic context, particularly in relation to violent offences. It is not, however, only the actual events of a dysfunctional or abusive childhood that are relevant here but the ways in which we remember events. Indeed, trauma also damages the ability of memory to make sense of the traumatic events (Herman 1997). In addition, the 'structure' of our memories makes very early trauma even more difficult to process (Rothschild 2000). We have both explicit and implicit types of memory: explicit memory is conscious and descriptive, using our verbal and cognitive abilities, and is active from about three years of age; implicit memory is active from birth and the information it stores is unconscious and emotional and it forms our conditioned responses to things. Because this early implicit memory is pre-verbal, consequently early abuse or neglect is often stored unconsciously and accessible only as feelings, often in response to stimuli which are not recognised consciously (Rothschild 2000). Thus, not only does trauma, at any age, hinder conscious understanding because memory of it is impaired by the nature of the event(s), but early trauma may leave victims without access to explicit memory. It is relevant to forensic work that memories of traumatic early life experiences might not be available to us consciously, so that we are more vulnerable to feelings which appear overwhelming and have no idea of why these feelings are occurring.

Attachment-related themes in the prison environment

Attachment theory is relevant to adult offenders not only because of the disrupted attachments which they import with themselves into prison, but also because the prison environment itself generates concerns with attachment. Prisoners' ability to cope with threats, whether perceived or real, is frequently challenged by not having good problem-solving and self-soothing strategies. We have seen that early experiences of the world as a threatening place lead to fearful feelings and behaviours designed to avoid perceived threats. This occurs not only at the family level but also, as people become adult members of society, at the level of the wider societal group, with its pressure to conform to its norms and values. We have also seen that prisoner populations are likely to include high numbers of people who have experienced this sort of childhood threatening (van IJzendoorn *et al.* 1997; Frodi *et al.* 2001).

The prison environment also impacts significantly on prisoners' experiences of attachment, because of the very design of the buildings and regimes imposed. Also because being imprisoned involves being separated from one's family and other figures to whom one has attachments. These things are not conducive to reducing anxiety and indeed may even stimulate it. Thus, it is likely that prisoners will experience high levels of threat when living within them. It would seem likely, therefore, that simply being in prison can easily trigger attachment anxiety, and the attachment system works (as we have noted), by individuals seeking protection when feeling threatened. Prisoners have spoken to the author about feeling profound loss when in prison. For some, that loss may be a new and frightening experience; for others, it may serve to confirm a familiar experience of separation and re-inforce their belief that they are unwanted or unacceptable to society. One person described feeling as though he were on a stage with hundreds of dancers, all being watched and applauded by the audience; he was the only one who did not know the steps and was constantly being pushed by the other dancers and 'booed' by the audience.

It has been noted that prisoners are often less able than many other people to manage stress and that admission to prison itself is stressful, involving separation from attachment figures and being in captivity (Adshead 2004). The likely regression to past attachment behaviours causes many prisoners to make what Adshead, (*ibid.*) describes as 'toxic attachments'. These can involve dismissing their emotional needs or alternatively clinging to unhelpful alternative attachments 'often combined with the experience of personal deadness' (Adshead 2004: 154). Adshead relates these 'toxic attachments' not only to prisoners' likely 'acute sensitivities to discrepancies of power and control' (p. 155), but also to the way that the prison experience can remind prisoners of previous difficulties with attachment such as neglect and abuse, perhaps in other institutions in the past. Compounding all of this, Adshead (*ibid.*) adds the fact that the very regimes, processes and physical environment of prisons can lead to attachment difficulties. Some examples given include abrupt terminations of treatment, such as when a staff member leaves, or the need for a prisoner to transfer to another prison, when they wish to remain where they feel 'safe'. Some prison procedures such as adjudications (a court-like system for addressing breaches of prison rules) and segregation (mentioned below) intensify the difficulties of the prison experience.

Among physical features which can lead to attachment difficulties, there are locks; because of all the locks, the staff of course carry keys; these keys are attached to the member of staff with a long chain and a constant background noise in prison is the sound of clanging doors and jingling of keys. It is easy for a member of staff to become used to carrying keys and to see it as a normal part of his or her role. However, this is a clear distinguishing feature for prisoners: it emphasises the imbalance of power and often aids a transference relationship to staff, involving early caregivers. If, as has been discussed, this early attachment was traumatic, the transference relationship is likely therefore to have several difficulties, as prisoners can project their abusive experiences of caregivers in early childhood onto the prison staff.

Yet, for other clients, prison is itself so familiar that they describe it as the only place in which they feel accepted. For example, some prisons have mother and baby units where babies born to mothers in prison might stay for between nine and 18 months. Moreover, some mothers in these units were themselves born in such units, and some of these women have described to the author how they have felt that the unit was the main place of safety throughout their lives. This idea of prison as a 'secure base' recurs in talking to clients: they describe different but analogous stories of feeling rejected by society and their families, but feeling safe in the prison, where they can contain their strongest rages. Many talk about a sense of relief when they are sentenced, as they know that they have to stop acting on their impulses and hope that they perhaps now, in prison, can.

That is not to say that prison is described as a pleasant experience – far from it. It is just that many clients have recognised that, tragically, although the prison is the last place they want to be, it also gives them something which is often unobtainable outside the prison walls: a place in which they feel they belong. The fact that this feeling is obtainable only in prison is usually a cause for deep sorrow, but clients have talked not only about how much sadness they feel but also about how much anger. They have often considered their crimes to be justifiable responses to a society which has rejected them.

For some, however, prison does not seem to be a safe place: some are in physical danger from other prisoners; others perceive themselves to be in such danger; while others feel unsafe psychologically because something else has disturbed them (for example, an anniversary of a traumatic experience), or because they feel that they do not 'fit in' in prison. The feeling of threat can be conscious, for example because of a verbalised threat from a specific person, or unconscious, as for example, when somebody sabotages their own release on temporary licence because (it seems) of fears about going out that are not recognised. For similar reasons, the possibility of recategorisation to a lower security prison can often trigger a return to anti-social behaviour; the authorities often then recategorise such people as 'high' and the prisoners feel justified in complaining about how harshly they are judged; such chains of events of course also hinder good relationships.

It is not uncommon for people in this position to take the strategy of causing a disturbance on the wing, so that they then get placed in the segregation unit. One person told the therapist that he sometimes 'smashed up' his cell in order to hide his self-harm – that is, he would ensure that he cut himself when he was damaging his cell, to hide the other cuts – and in order to get removed from the wing, without other prisoners knowing what he was doing as, he said, he felt that he had to look strong in front of other prisoners. Other clients have said they have used this strategy to obtain the peace they needed; one said that he did this in order to get the quietness he needed in order to revise for a forthcoming examination.

Although some prisoners at some times seek segregation as a respite from the crowded wings, for other prisoners, or at other times, the segregation unit can be highly stressful. In these cases, separation limits severely the opportunities to use defences such as distraction, sublimation or humour, often leaving prisoners with less helpful defences such as splitting or acting out. Segregation can also lead to cycles of distress, as increased feelings of isolation can initiate further acting out, which can in turn increase the staff's feelings of threat and thus distance staff and prisoner further, creating direct hostility. A prisoner can also be segregated because he is considered to be such a threat to himself (through a suicide attempt or deliberate self- harm) can be located in a 'gated cell' where he is under constant supervision from a member of staff who sits outside and looks in; in this situation, there is no privacy nor respite, and it is often difficult, for both prisoner and staff member, to make the best of this situation by useful interaction.

However, these two responses to prison – as a place of security, or as a place of danger – are not mutually exclusive; this is not usually an 'either/or' situation. Rather, most prisoners have described their experiences of prison to the author in ambivalent terms, as a place both familiar and safe, yet also threatening and hostile. This highlights the paradox of prisons as places suitable to address the causes of violent offending. This is not to suggest that the Prison Service is uninterested in rehabilitation or that it does not strive to achieve it. Rather, the dual tasks of custody and rehabilitation are, to a great extent, mutually exclusive, and compromise is inevitable. Yet this tension between two differing goals does not mean that one should not aim for progress; indeed, the fact that the world is not perfect but can still be acceptable is a good model in therapy.

Providing therapy in prison

Providing therapy in prisons is challenging. Therapy and the therapeutic frame are often affected by prison procedures and security restrictions, sometimes to an almost unmanageable degree. These include wing lockdowns when no-one is allowed out of their cell, delays and restrictions of movements which prevent a prisoner being brought to the therapy session in time, cell searches at the time of a session, or simply a room not being available. As stated above, can even mean the sudden transfer of a prisoner, bringing therapy to an abrupt end when it has not been worked through. In addition, therapy usually takes place on the wing in a room with large windows. Also, the therapist is known to many in the prison and so the fact that someone is having therapy is usually common knowledge, thus compromising confidentiality.

Despite these difficulties, prisoners have noted progress with their problems, and have noted that this progress was possible without therapy needing to be fully protected. In many instances, clients have previously employed a kind of Kleinian 'splitting' approach both to their offending and to being in prison (them versus us). The forced compromises and therapeutic benefits despite these problems serve as metaphors for the changes they are seeking to make in their lives. In a similar way, the inevitable ruptures and repairs of the therapeutic relationship, which are also often exacerbated in prison due to such factors as the therapist carrying keys, are a very practical example of how something can be valued even when not perfect.

That said, one obviously aims for as uninterrupted a process as possible and devises a treatment plan. This plan recognises the need for extreme flexibility at times. Prisoners referred for therapy have usually already been assessed by either psychiatrists or psychiatric nurses with regard to any diagnosable mental illness; they are then assessed with regard to their suitability for psychotherapy. This assessment includes recognising individual responsibility, self-curiosity, and the motivation and ability to make changes; it involves meeting the person referred on a number of occasions (at least two) and talking about their histories. The aim of the assessment is to make links between the past and current thoughts, feelings and behaviours, and often to make very early comments about these areas to see how the client is able to respond to them.

The author's caseload almost exclusively includes clients with very difficult attachment histories and whose crimes have involved extreme violence. Part of the psychotherapeutic assessment includes exploring early experiences and current attachments. This is carried out not only by listening to what is said about various aspects of their lives – violence, neglect, physical and sexual abuse, the stability of home life, school experiences, substance misuse, the quality of relationships and offending histories – but also, as is required in attachment-based psychotherapy, by exploring the *quality* of their narratives. As in the AAI (but by no means a substitute for such a full assessment), this exploration involves looking at the paradoxes and contradictions of what is being said in balance with the coherence of it, particularly with regard to the emotional aspects of their lives. It also considers the level of detail given about emotional issues: too little or too much, whether it is balanced or seen only from their own point of experience. While the level of depth achieved in these assessments is nowhere near the degree involved in a full AAI, it does give a good indication of some of the main areas of difficulty.

Unsurprisingly, a major part of therapeutic work involves building trust and trying to help people whose backgrounds and current life experiences have been very unsafe, to feel at least safe enough to begin to explore themselves and their histories. This is probably the most difficult and most important part of the task. Bloom (1997) and Herman (1997) note that feeling safe is the first requisite for the beginning of trauma recovery; this is understandable when one considers that the nature of trauma is a threat to the person. It would follow that recovery must include some confidence in one's current safety. Feeling confident enough to rely on others also seems to be a general requirement for rebuilding confidence in a trauma victim. Sufferers with a good social support network have been found to recover from trauma more quickly than those without such support (Bloom 1997; Herman 1997), and even those who have suffered long-term trauma, such as child abuse, have been found to be able to move some way towards overcoming it with the introduction of a reparative relationship, including a relationship in psychotherapy (Bloom 1997; Herman 1997). As noted above, prisons by their nature can trigger attachment anxiety, and therefore engendering a feeling of safety is made even more difficult when providing therapy in prison. Because of this difficulty, the approach to offering therapy needs to model the view that compromise can be acceptable. From the outset, the therapist accepts that the environment is difficult for both therapist and client and that one has to be pragmatic about what is possible. As noted above, while this is regrettable, it also serves as a useful therapeutic tool.

Beyond this acceptance, then, it is also necessary to demonstrate motivation, concern and, very importantly, honesty. Probably equally important is to demonstrate tenacity – to demonstrate that the therapist both wants to continue working with a person despite the difficulties and is capable of bearing the violent and emotionally draining experiences about which they want to talk. Typically this is a new experience for violent offenders; they are more used to being rejected and can feel more comfortable with that response. This means that their belief in therapy continuing is very fragile. If therapy can withstand the interruptions of prison regimes in these circumstances, it stands a good chance of helping clients make, at least some, beneficial changes.

Within this compromised therapeutic alliance, the main tasks of the therapist's work are to help clients make sense of the very painful, disjointed and confusing narratives they bring. Often these experiences, as both victim and perpetrator, have served to increase the feelings of separation and isolation from others described above, made empathy more difficult and made violent offending easier. Breaking this cycle is pivotal both to decreasing clients' distress and to reducing their propensity towards violent crime. For this reason, another important part of therapy involves helping clients validate their own emotional responses to their experiences: to recognise that it is natural to feel rage and despair at some of the things they have endured. From this recognition, the aim is to help them locate these feelings appropriately and to deal with them by other means, for example talking, rather than acting out or turning to substance misuse to numb them. Frequently this is a very difficult task – for both the therapist and the client – as it is pitted against long histories of severe abuse, violence and rejection, often exacerbated by the client's own violence.

The difficulties of therapy in prison are also compounded by the fact that client confidentiality is compromised in a forensic setting. The 'contract' between client and therapist can never be simply between the two; there is always a third party, who may be considered as providing the therapy. This 'paymaster' may be seen as the Government, the Ministry of Justice, the Prison Service or the public. The 'public' can be further broken down into victims, the prisoners' and victims' families, formal and informal pressure groups (including vigilantes) as well as a general public. This involvement of a third party complicates the therapeutic alliance, as one is always aware of an extra dimension beyond it. While in practice that can be worked with, it nonetheless changes the usual dynamics of therapy and can impinge on what may be brought to the sessions – and indeed what can be kept confidential.

However, as with the difficulties in maintaining the therapeutic frame, this can also be a therapeutic opportunity. Confronting the fact that some things have to be disclosed to the prison authorities has often proved the beginning of very important work with clients, enabling them to see others' points of view and so to begin to mentalise. It has also helped some people to discover that therapy can continue in these circumstances, thus beginning to dismantle the 'splitting' defence.

Case example

The following composite vignette gives an idea of how all this might look in practice. This vignette draws on the experiences of a number of individuals who have been in therapy and uses some fictitious issues, typical of the type of problems seen. Therefore no one individual can be identified.

Richard, a man in his mid-thirties, was referred to the in-reach team following his attendance on a drugs course which had caused him to explore some problems of his earlier childhood and adolescence. These thoughts were now becoming intrusive and he was angry at the Prison Service for 'making' him look at them. He did not see his history as extraordinary; he thought he had 'just a few problems' that he had long since 'got over'. His parents had separated when he was very young but he had seen his father from time to time. He recalled his mother as being very unpredictable and often sleeping through the day following drunken nights, leaving him and his older sister alone. He recalled a number of men in his mother's life, all of whom he remembered as being violent to his mother, himself and his sister. He described being furious once as a young child at seeing his mother's boyfriend threaten her with coals from the fire in the living room. He was terrified and angry both with the man and with his mother for 'allowing' this to happen. He idealised his absent father and blamed his mother for all that had gone wrong in his life.

He began drinking aged 10 and stealing aged about 12. By 14, he was placed in a children's home and here he was sexually abused both by older boys and by the deputy headteacher (who had since been convicted of these offences). He had tried to tell the authorities and his family about these events at the time but had not been believed.

By 17 years of age Richard was a 'successful' burglar and enjoyed a materially good life. He found this life empty though, and money slipped easily in and out of his hand. He had several short-term relationships, but they always ended as he felt tied down. He had two children by different women but did not see them as he felt that they were better off without him. The index offence was grievous bodily harm (GBH); he had burgled a house he thought was empty, but it was not. The occupier had tackled him in the kitchen; Richard grabbed a knife and stabbed the victim several times. He ran from the scene, terrified by what he had done. He had never been violent before. He went home and drank copious amounts of alcohol before telephoning the police and waiting for them to arrest him. He said he did not know whether he would be arrested for GBH or murder and, for the moment, he said he did not care which it was; he felt so numbed by what he had done. On remand he had tried to hang himself, but had been saved by his cellmate raising the alarm.

The quality of Richard's narrative was disjointed. He moved rapidly between subjects and found it hard to recall events. His memory of childhood was almost non-existent; only traumatic incidents were clear, but even they were only clear fragments rather than a cohesive whole. He was very angry with his mother and with society as a whole. This was most recently replayed by his view of the criminal justice system. He had seen his burglary victims as 'fair game' until the index offence which had frightened him.

The early sessions mainly involved Richard talking about this anger. He did not talk about the sexual abuse other than to say it happened – and he fought tears as he said this. At this stage, the therapist's main aim was to provide a 'safe space' for Richard to express these fears and hurts and a 'secure base' for him to use until he felt able to explore things for himself. After almost a year, Richard began to talk about the index offence. At first he spoke only of his own emotions, but was later able to express concern for the victim and to feel remorse for his actions. At first when he spoke about the index offence he spoke only of his own fears and numbness. Later there was a shift as he began to recognise what his actions might have been like for his victim and the victim's family and to recognise the ongoing effects which they might be experiencing.

In total, Richard was in therapy for about three years. During that period he began to recognise the splitting in which he had engaged and became able to mentalise, and then to empathise with other people's (mainly his victims') situations. He began to build a relationship with his mother and to see the flaws in his father, forging a more balanced relationship with him. He was also able to talk about the sexual abuse and to work through this trauma.

The early part was the most difficult, as it was in this period that Richard took the risk of building a therapeutic alliance. For example, at first he clearly found it difficult to trust the therapist and 'tested things out' by talking graphically about very violent things he had experienced or done. He also ridiculed the therapy, once writing to the in-reach team saying that he wanted nothing more to do with it. Two weeks later he retracted this and therapy recommenced. He also found breaks in the therapy (for example, for the therapist's holidays) extremely difficult and would often be more hostile and less engaged in his therapy on the therapist's return. At such times he would also frequently kick against the prison regime by refusing orders or being aggressive to others. These were clear indications of attachment separation anxiety and of reversion to defensive behaviours which had worked for him in the past. Only when he was able to do this could he use this 'secure base' as a starting point from which to begin to explore and accept himself and make sense of his actions.

Markers of progress in therapy

Despite the many difficulties, it is possible to discern progress in therapy. Outside what might be said in the therapy sessions themselves, there are various indicators of progress. These include a reduction in the number of adjudications, better interaction between the client and prison staff, increased self-confidence – for example, leading to people undertaking educational courses not previously thought attainable – the reduction or cessation of substance misuse, increased quantity and quality of family relationships, and positive comments from prison staff. Increased self-esteem is also seen in how, in sessions, clients talk about themselves, their relationships and interactions with others. These events are described with more depth and insight; sometimes new, very distressing material is brought which could not previously be explored. Often the most telling change is in how someone views their offences. Unlike therapy in the community, where one often tries to help people understand how sometimes their distress is a metaphor for rage they might be feeling and do not act upon, often therapy in prison is almost a reversal of that: it can involve helping someone to see that their violence or other crimes are an 'acting out' of rage they have suppressed. Progress in therapy can be seen when this suddenly becomes clear to a client, and the quality of their narrative changes to reflect it. The narrative becomes more coherent and organised. In other words, the client demonstrates that he is making sense of his own story. One can discern change from a client locating all of their problems externally, to a client understanding their own – and often others' – feelings and understanding how their actions have been influenced by them. In other words their narrative shows how they have moved from a point of 'psychic equivalence' to being able to mentalise.

However, progress can be difficult and confusing for clients. The author has often been told that, while clients can see how the insights they now have into their motivations and behaviours are helpful – and make them want change – their past has also given them friends, a way of 'earning' and a way to achieve status within their peer group. Others have talked about being pleased to make the changes they sought, but have felt the need to hide them from family, friends, staff and other prisoners for fear of ridicule or other pressures to avoid change.

Sometimes, a transfer to a lower-security prison or to hospital can also be indicative of progress in therapy. This of course also marks the end of the therapy.

Endings

The ending of therapy can be one of the most difficult aspects of long-term psychotherapy in prisons. From assessment, one has to be aware that therapy can end abruptly and to make this clear to potential clients from the start. This is sometimes a barrier to prisoners feeling confident enough to embark on therapy. Therapy in prison is always vulnerable to unplanned endings. As with most other aspects of prison life, whilst it is disruptive, it also demonstrates that there can be value in something even if it is not able to reach a preferred outcome. This is, however, something which must be considered carefully in the assessment as, for some clients, premature ending might be counterproductive. Ending therapy after beginning to look at some very difficult issues might leave a client feeling fragile, abandoned or rejected, and that could confirm fears and increase rather than decrease distress.

Jones (1997) carried out one of the few studies into therapy and reconviction rates. He showed that terminating therapy before a minimum of 12 months led to an increase in offending rather than a decrease and he recommended that 12 months should be a prerequisite for accepting somebody into therapy. The practice at HMP Grendon at the time of Jones' writing, was to have a minimum period of two years before a prisoner is accepted for therapy. (See Shuker and Shine in Chapter 10 of this book.) Holding this as a guide, the assessment of a potential client for long-term psychotherapy includes looking realistically at how long therapy is likely to be able to continue, given not only what external pressures might be exerted to end therapy, but also the likelihood of the prisoner 'dropping out'. It is usual, therefore, to aim for there to be a strong likelihood of therapy being able to continue for at least two years if a person is to be accepted and if this is not possible, to consider carefully if therapy would still be beneficial.

The importance of clinical supervision

Working in prisons is an interesting and challenging area of psychotherapy. The rewards are potentially huge, but the pressures are also great. One is confronted daily by a prison population that is largely a product of brutal and/or neglectful childhoods and at times the distress feels almost tangible. For this reason, among others, supervision is vitally important. Supervision is always important, of course, in any context: it allows one to reflect in a safe environment on one's work, to receive advice and assistance from an experienced professional(s) and to rebalance what can sometimes feel overwhelming; but in working in prison this need seems even greater, given the particular difficulties. These difficulties include the 'third-party' considerations (discussed above), the operational interruptions to therapeutic work, the attempt to work for one organisation (the NHS) while located in another's premises (HM Prison Service) and the difficulties that this juxtaposition engenders, the dual role of therapist/custodian, the violent nature of many clients' narratives and the often hostile nature of the environment itself.

It is absolutely vital to have good supervision which allows space to process the often draining effects of such work. These can include misgivings about adequacy and competency, feelings of intense sadness, fear and feelings of hopelessness. One may even be unsure whether hope should be promoted in sometimes seemingly hopeless conditions. Supervision is essential to looking after oneself as well as to enable one to provide the level of service that is needed. Additionally, the author has found that the requirement to have therapy oneself for at least the duration of psychotherapy training has been invaluable. One learns about one's own vulnerabilities and triggers. This seems especially important during the early part of therapy when clients may 'test out' the therapist's resilience in the face of what clients themselves find unbearable about themselves and 'need' the therapist to contain their (the client's) overwhelming feelings. Supervision is also relevant here and supervision and therapy often overlap.

Conclusion

The beginnings of attachment-based therapy were in studying the behaviours of offenders. As attachment research continues and as advances in neuroscience demonstrate more about the workings of the brain (in particular the emotions), the importance of attachment relationships is understood more clearly. Attachment-based psychotherapy applies these research findings to clinical work, which appears highly relevant to forensic clients, particularly those living in prisons. This is because it not only considers how early relationships affect thoughts, feelings and behaviours in later life, and thus helps clients to understand some of their offending, but it also helps them to understand some of the feelings they experience in prison itself. By developing an understanding that their actions (including their offences) can be related directly to their early emotional experience, prisoners can understand what seemed previously to be random, overwhelming emotions over which they had no control; this therefore puts the possibility of controlling these emotions within their grasp. It also means that these offences might not be something which makes them 'different' from others in society, but rather things which attest to a common response to a highly disruptive childhood. This understanding has, in the author's experience, been a very reassuring experience for many clients, for it reconnects them to society. A basic tenet of attachment theory is that people need to attach to survive; and therapy based on attachment theory helps offender clients to do this – a fundamental requirement for healing.

Note

1 These included: approaching a parent then turning away; high levels of distress accompanied by turning away from the mother rather than going towards her; and slowed movements or disorientated wandering around (see Lyons-Ruth and Jacobvitz 1999).

References

Adshead, G. (2004) 'Three degrees of security: Attachment and forensic institutions', in G. Adshead and F. Pfäfflin (eds), *A Matter of Security: The Application of Attachment Theory to Forensic Psychiatry and Psychotherapy*. London: Jessica Kingsley Publishers, pp. 147–66.

Adshead, G. and van Velsen, C. (1996) 'Psychotherapeutic work with victims of trauma', in C. Cordess and M. Cox (eds), *Forensic Psychotherapy: Crime, Psychodynamics and the Offender Patient*. London: Jessica Kingsley Publishers, pp. 359–65.

Ainsworth, M. (1991) 'Attachments and other affectional bonds across the life cycle', in C.M. Parkes, J. Stevenson-Hindle and P. Marris (eds), *Attachment Across the Life Cycle*. London: Routledge, pp. 33–51.

Ainsworth, M. and Eichberg, C. (1991) 'Effects on infant–mother attachment of mother's unresolved loss of an attachment figure or other traumatic experience', in C.M. Parkes, J. Stevenson-Hindle and P. Marris (eds), *Attachment Across the Life Cycle*. London: Routledge, pp. 160–83.

Bateman, A., Brown, D. and Pedder, J. (1991) *Introduction to Psychotherapy: An Outline of Psychodynamic Principles and Practice*, 2nd edition. London: Routledge.

Bloom, S. (1997) *Creating Sanctuary: Toward the Evolution of Sane Societies.* London: Routledge.

Bowlby, J. (1944) 'Forty-four juvenile thieves: Their characters and their home lives', *International Journal of Psychoanalysis*, 25: 19–52.

Bowlby, J. (1969) *Attachment and Loss, Vol 1: Attachment.* New York: Basic Books.

Bowlby, J. (1973) *Attachment and Loss, Vol 2: Separation, Anxiety and Anger.* New York: Basic Books.

Bowlby, J. (1979) *The Making and Breaking of Affectional Bonds.* London: Tavistock.

Bowlby, J. (1980) *Attachment and Loss, Vol 3: Loss, Sadness and Depression.* New York: Basic Books.

Bowlby, J. (1988) *A Secure Base.* New York: Basic Books.

Bretherton, I. and Munholland, K.A. (1999) 'Internal working models in attachment relationships: A construct revisited', in J. Cassidy and P.R. Shaver (eds), *Handbook of Attachment: Theory, Research and Clinical Applications.* London: The Guilford Press, pp. 89–111.

Cassidy (1999) 'The nature of the child's ties', in J. Cassidy and P.R. Shaver (eds), *Handbook of Attachment: Theory, Research and Clinical Applications.* London: The Guilford Press, pp. 3–20.

de Zulueta, F. (2001) *From Pain to Violence: The Traumatic Roots of Destructiveness.* London: Whurr Publishers.

Fonagy, P. (2004) 'The developmental roots of violence in the failure to mentalize', in G. Adshead and F. Pfäfflin (eds), *A Matter of Security: The Application of Attachment Theory to Forensic Psychiatry and Psychotherapy.* London: Jessica Kingsley Publishers, pp. 13–56.

Fonagy, P. and Target, M. (1996) 'Personality and sexual development, psychopathology and offending', in C. Cordess and M. Cox (eds), *Forensic Psychotherapy: Crime, Psychodynamics and the Offender Patient.* London: Jessica Kingsley Publishers, pp. 117–51.

Fonagy, P., Target, M., Steele, H., Leigh, T., Levinson, A. and Kennedy, R. (1997) 'Morality, disruptive behaviour, borderline personality disorder, crime and their relationship to security in attachment', in L. Atkinson and K.J. Zucker (eds), *Attachment and psychopathology.* New York: The Guilford Press.

Frodi, A., Dernevik, M., Sepa, A., Phillipson, J. and Bragesjo, M. (2001) 'Current attachment representations of incarcerated offenders varying in degree of psychopathy', *Attachment and Human Development*, 3(3): 269–83.

George, C., Kaplan, M. and Main, M. (1985) *Adult Attachment Interview.* Unpublished Manuscript, University of California, Berkeley.

Gomez, L. (1997) *An Introduction to Object Relations.* London: Free Association Books.

Herman, J.L. (1997) *Trauma and Recovery: The Aftermath of Violence: From Domestic Abuse to Political Terror.* New York: Basic Books.

Hesse, E. (1999) 'Attachment in adolescence and adulthood', in J. Cassidy and P.R. Shaver (eds), *Handbook of Attachment: Theory, Research and Clinical Applications.* London: The Guilford Press, pp. 395–433.

Jones, L. (1997) 'Developing models for managing treatment integrity and efficacy in a prison-based TC: The Max Glatt Centre', in E. Cullen, L. Jones and R. Woodward (eds), *Therapeutic Communities for Offenders.* Chichester: John Wiley & Sons Publishers, pp. 121–57.

Knox, J. (2003) 'Attachment theory as a bridge between cognitive science and psychodynamic theory', in M. Cortina and M. Marrone (eds), *Attachment Theory and the Psychoanalytic Process.* London: Whurr Publishers, pp. 307 –34.

Lyons-Ruth, K. and Jacobvitz, D. (1999) 'Attachment disorganization: Unresolved loss, relational violence, and lapses in behavioural and attentional strategies', in J. Cassidy and P.R. Shaver (eds), *Handbook of Attachment: Theory, Research and Clinical Applications.* London: The Guilford Press, pp. 520–54.

Main, M. (1991) 'Metacognitive knowledge, metacognitive monitoring and singular (coherent) vs. multiple (incoherent) model of attachment: findings and directions for future research', in C.M. Parkes, J. Stevenson-Hindle and P. Marris (eds), *Attachment Across the Life Cycle.* London: Routledge.

Marvin, R.S. and Britner, P.A. (1999) 'The ontogeny of attachment', in J. Cassidy and P.R. Shaver (eds), *Handbook of Attachment: Theory, Research and Clinical Applications.* London: The Guilford Press, pp. 44–67.

Rothschild, B. (2000) *The Body Remembers: The Psychophysiology of Trauma and Trauma Treatment.* New York: W.W. Norton and Company Publishers.

van IJzendoorn, M.H. and Bakermans-Kranenburg, M.J. (1997) 'Inter-generational transmission of attachment: A move to the contextual level', in L. Atkinson and K.J. Zucker (eds), *Attachment and psychopathology.* New York: The Guilford Press.

van IJzendoorn, M.H., Feldbrugge, J.T.T.M., Derks, F.C.H., de Ruiter, C., Verhagen, M.A., Philipse, M.W.G., van der Stask, C.P.F. and Riksen-Walraven, J.M.A. (1997) 'Attachment representations of personality disordered criminal offenders', *American Journal of Orthopsychiatry,* 67: 449–59.

Weinfield, N.S., Sroufe, L.A. Egeland, B. and Carlson, E.A. (1999) 'The nature of individual differences in infant–caregiver attachment', in J. Cassidy and P.R. Shaver (eds), *Handbook of Attachment: Theory, Research and Clinical Applications.* London: The Guilford Press.

Chapter 4

Cognitive behaviour therapy with adolescents in secure settings

Kirsty Smedley

Over the past decade a number of policy documents have been published which have focused on the mental health needs of children and adolescents. In 2004, for example, the Department of Health (DH) set out a vision within the National Service Framework (NSF) for a comprehensive child and adolescent mental health service (CAMHS). Voicing similar aspirations to those in the document *Changing the Outlook* (DH and HMPS 2001), the NSF argued that children and young people in custody should have the same right to access this comprehensive CAMHS service as do those in the general population. More recently a cross-department government strategy document, *Healthy Children, Safer Communities* (DH, DCSF and Ministry of Justice 2009), has highlighted the need for children and young people in contact with the criminal justice system to be viewed holistically. This document argues for the early identification of their mental health difficulties, whether they are directly related to their offending behaviour or not. This represents a shift away from previous thinking that only mental health difficulties directly related to offending behaviour should be the subject of psychological interventions in custody. *Healthy Children, Safer Communities* aims 'to help tackle youth crime and anti-social behaviour, and contribute to community safety in England'. The strategy notes that the health needs of children and young people in the secure estate are noticeably higher than for those in contact with the youth justice system in the community. The document also discusses the opportunity provided by time in custody to attend to children's unmet needs. It recognises, however, that while there are promising developments in the provision of health care, there are also huge challenges. Those challenges include the need for a balance between providing an appropriate secure setting and yet also meeting the therapeutic needs of vulnerable children and young people.

This chapter examines the use of cognitive behaviour therapy (CBT) with adolescents and draws on the author's experience working with young people in both medium- and low-secure hospital settings, as well as in a young offender institution (YOI). The chapter will outline the secure estate for young people and will then consider the mental health and developmental needs of this population. It will then give a brief overview of CBT, with the evidence base for this approach, and will consider the relevance of this approach to working with young people in prison. Before outlining a case example of using CBT with a young person in custody with first-episode psychosis, the chapter will describe what is meant by psychosis and will look at the evidence base of psychological interventions for psychosis. The chapter will end by considering some of the challenges of providing therapy in prison more generally and will contrast the main differences between providing therapy in prisons and other secure hospital settings.

The secure estate for young people

Each year, the Youth Justice Board (YJB) for England and Wales commissions approximately 3,000 custodial places for young people under the age of 18 (Bailey and Kerslake 2008). These places can be in the Prison Service's YOIs, local authority secure children's homes (LASCHs) or private sector secure training centres (STCs) (Morgan and Newburn 2007). In January 2010 there were 2,096 people under 18 in custody (YJB 2010). Of those 104 were girls and 1,192 were boys. 1,712 young people were in prison, 143 in LASCHs and 241 in STCs (YJB 2010). Although there has been a slight decrease recently, the number of young people held in custody has been steadily increasing since the introduction of the Crime and Disorder Act 1998. Solomon and Garside (2008), in their review *Ten Years of Labour's Justice Reforms: An Independent Audit*, argue that additional funding in youth justice has led to a 'net-widening' effect. Goldson (2006) also has commented on the increased use of custody for children in England and Wales and has argued that 'the expansionist drive bears virtually no relation to either the incidence or the seriousness of youth crime' (Goldson 2006: 146).

In England and Wales there are also a number of dedicated adolescent forensic units for young people who have offended but who are detained under the Mental Health Act (MHA 1983, 2007). Young people may be transferred under Section 47 of the MHA from prison to a secure hospital. This process is used for young people whose mental health difficulties are deemed to be so complex, severe or persistent that they require treatment in hospital, often for psychotic disorders but also for severe depression and other diagnoses.

Prevalence rates of mental health difficulties in young offenders

The mental health needs of children and young people in the secure estate have been well documented (Lader *et al.* 2000; Kroll *et al.* 2002; Harrington and Bailey 2005). Research on this topic is growing, although many of the studies conducted hitherto have had relatively small sample sizes with few studies of young women or young people from black and minority ethnic (BME) populations (Lader *et al.* 2000; Kroll *et al.* 2002). Prevalence rates of mental health problems vary from study to study, with the range being as wide as 50 to 100 per cent (Teplin *et al.* 2002; Ruchkin *et al.* 2003). Bailey and Kerslake (2008) argue that the variability across prevalence rates can be explained by differences in the method and timing of assessment: the psychiatric interviews employed vary; and some studies assess young people shortly after detention while others do so post sentencing. It is important to keep this timing in mind because coming into custody may affect pre-existing mental health difficulties or trigger new concerns (Harvey 2007). Bailey and Kerslake (2008) also point to differences across a number of variables from one study to the next in the age, gender, ethnicity, family structure, socio-economic status and criminal behaviour of respondents. They also draw attention to the important fact that some studies assess those adolescents already referred for psychiatric assessment, and therefore the information collected cannot be generalised to the whole offender population.

Kroll *et al.* (2002) conducted a study of 97 boys aged 12–17 in secure care. They identified depression and anxiety as the most frequent disorders and psychological assessment and CBT as the most frequently required intervention. They also discovered that 27 per cent of the sample had an intelligence quotient (IQ) of less than 70, which – depending on the pattern and nature of the learning difficulties – has significant implications for the delivery of interventions.

Harrington and Bailey (2005), in one of the most recent studies that included both young offenders in custody and in the community, found that 31 per cent of their sample of 301 adolescents had an identifiable mental health problem. They also found that almost one fifth were depressed and that a tenth had engaged in self-harm in the preceding month. Similarly about one in 10 exhibited symptoms of anxiety or post-traumatic stress. Seven per cent of the sample suffered from hyperactivity while five per cent showed psychotic-like symptoms. Co-morbidity is more common in adolescent offenders than in the general population (Harrington and Bailey 2004), and some disorders such as conduct disorder, depression and substance misuse frequently co-occur (Harrington and Bailey 2005).

Developmental issues in adolescence

When assessing young people with mental health problems it is important to consider the developmental context in which these difficulties have arisen. Certain behaviours might seem within normal limits for a younger child but could be viewed as indicative of mental health difficulties in an older adolescent (Reinecke et al. 2006; Kazdin and Weisz 2010). Adolescence is a period of change and this can make the process of assessment more difficult. The pattern of symptoms in some young people may be only just emerging and therefore not well established. The expression of symptoms may change over time and so careful, repeated assessment is necessary. Accurate assessment may also be hampered by the custodial setting; young people may remain guarded due to their mistrust of those in authority, their understandable worry about the stigma of reporting mental health difficulties, and their concern about whether the information they give may influence sentencing. The developmental context is equally important when planning and delivering therapeutic interventions (Reinecke et al. 2006). Indeed, Holmbeck et al. (2010) argue that therapists working with children and adolescents should have a knowledge of developmental norms, milestones and developmental psychopathology.

It is also necessary to consider the developmental tasks of adolescence, which include the developing identity, establishing a peer group and developing autonomy from parents/carers. Adolescence is a period of adjustment and, as Coleman and Hagell (2007) state, 'one of the most helpful ways of understanding adolescence is to think about it as one of life's major transitions' (p. 3). Entering custody is an additional major life transition for some young people and it may be expected to interfere with and influence the adolescent's ability to achieve normal developmental tasks. For example, the transition into prison may force some young people to develop independence from family members before they are ready or equipped to do so, and at the same time to mix with an anti-social peer group. Other young people may be at risk of becoming institutionalised and reliant on the structure and support provided by prison systems, impeding the development of independence. Seeing themselves as part of the prison system could be expected to impact on adolescents' views of themselves, thus influencing their developing identity: for example, they may see themselves as bad or dangerous and/or set apart from the rest of society. On a more positive note, some of the cognitive developments which occur during adolescence may provide opportunities for young people in custody to benefit from interventions that require skills such as taking the perspective of others and thinking about one's own thinking.

Later in this chapter, a case study will illustrate the use of CBT for psychosis with a young man in custody. Harrop and Trower (2001) propose that the psychosis which emerges in late adolescence is a disorder of adolescent development. They point out that there are many similarities between the common adolescent phenomena experienced by most people at that time (including difficult family relationships, grandiosity, magical thinking and egocentricity) and many of the experiences of psychosis. Harrop and Trower (2001) suggest that the problems of psychosis may arise because individuals have difficulties in defining a self that is autonomous from parents. Alternatively, the difficulties may primarily arise from an inability to make relationships with other young people. In either case, psychosis would be thought to result directly from adolescents becoming blocked in their psychological development.

An overview of cognitive behaviour therapy

This section of the chapter provides an overview of CBT in general; however, there is only room for this overview to be brief and fuller accounts can be found in, for example, Wells (1997) and Dobson (2010). Cognitive therapy was first clearly described as a manualised approach by Aaron Beck (Beck *et al.* 1979) for the treatment of depression. Since then the cognitive model has been applied to a number of psychological difficulties, including anxiety disorders, marital problems, anger, substance misuse and psychosis (Dobson 2010). Beck built on the foundations of behavioural principles but also stressed the relationship between cognition, physiology and emotion. In his theory, Beck outlined how early life experiences could influence the development of mental health problems in adulthood. He emphasised that early life experiences are highly relevant to the beliefs that a person forms about themselves, other people and the world (the 'cognitive triad'). Young people who have had disrupted early life experiences, which may include maltreatment and trauma, are more likely to see the world as a dangerous place and other people as frightening than are young people with a stable childhood. Their beliefs about themselves, the world, and other people are a reflection of their early experiences. Many young people import these negative life experiences into the prison (see Harvey and Smedley in Chapter 1 of this book).

Another important concept by Beck is that of 'assumptions', which are conditional because they 'represent contingencies between events and self-appraisals (e.g. "If I show signs of anxiety then people will think I am inferior")' (Wells 1997: 3). When working with young people it may be more appropriate to call these assumptions 'rules for living'. Examples may include: 'If I show my emotion, then people will use it against me' or 'If I'm not perfect, my family won't love me'. It is important to take these assumptions into account in the formulation of a young person's difficulties.

When underlying beliefs and assumptions are activated, then information processing becomes biased (Wells 1997) and events are interpreted in a distorted manner, but in a manner which is consistent with the underlying core beliefs and assumptions. Wells (1997) summarises the main cognitive distortions, or 'thinking errors'; they include: arbitrary inference, selective abstraction, overgeneralisation, magnification or minimisation, personalising, catastrophising and mind-reading. Helping young people in custody to recognise and challenge the biases in their thinking is an essential component of CBT intervention and one which can provide them with a valuable tool to use between sessions. A young man may be facing adjudication (a meeting with the governor of the prison to determine the consequences of breaking the prison's rules) following a fight with another prisoner on the wing. He may exhibit catastrophic thinking about the outcome of the meeting, expecting the worst and telling himself that he is sure to lose all his privileges for a long period of time. This way of thinking might result in a lowering of his mood. Another example of a cognitive distortion might be a young person who attends education in the prison and has poor levels of literacy. He may be asked by the teacher, 'Do you need any help with that?' and then think, 'She thinks I'm stupid.' This would be an example of mind-reading, that is, a cognitive bias whereby the individual jumps to a conclusion that they know what someone else is thinking. The prison is a low-trust and high-threat environment and therefore it is easy for such cognitive biases to flourish. On the other hand, the therapist must also be mindful of the possibility that the young person may be accurate in their appraisal of a situation; for this work, what is essential is some knowledge of the prison's environment and culture. For example, a young person may report feeling terrified because they believe they will be physically assaulted when they leave their cell; the therapist might discover that the young person owes money to another prisoner who has threatened him with violence and has a history of attacking other prisoners. If the young person's appraisal is factually accurate, then it would be inappropriate to attempt to modify or alter it.

It is argued that the activation of beliefs and assumptions (and the associated cognitive distortions) results in negative automatic thoughts. All the time that we are awake, our brains are generating thoughts, flowing through our minds in a steady stream. This is necessary for our survival and this constant flow of thoughts often acts as a trigger for more purposeful thinking. Automatic thoughts are constantly monitored and our brain then selects the most relevant ones for further attention. It is only then that we become aware of them as conscious thoughts. Automatic thoughts occur spontaneously and they cannot be consciously controlled by the individual. They may be in the form of words but automatic thoughts can also manifest as images, or as part of a thought flashing through the brain. The role of automatic thoughts in producing a feeling or a mood state is a key feature of the CBT model. A depressed feeling or mood may be triggered by a thought flashing through a person's mind, even when they are not consciously aware of this thought. The way we feel about a situation depends on what we think about it. For example, one person waking up in bed at night and hearing a noise downstairs may think, 'That'll be the cat making a mess', and feel a sense of mild irritation; another person may think, 'Someone is breaking into my house', and feel afraid; a third person might think, 'My partner has come home late again and woken me up', and feel angry: so the same situation can lead to different thoughts and so different feelings. The same thought can also lead to different emotional, physiological and behavioural responses. It is argued that these negative automatic thoughts result from the activation of core beliefs and assumptions that have been formed from earlier life experiences.

The cognitive model thus focuses on 'the way distorted thinking and unrealistic cognitive appraisal of events can negatively affect one's feelings and behaviour' (Dobson 2010: 14). Through a here-and-now approach to therapy, the focus can be on the vicious cycle of thoughts, feelings, physical responses and behaviour (Greenberger and Padeskey 1995). Many young people have little experience of attempting to distinguish their thoughts from their feelings and may need considerable help in doing so. Beck stated that the most important elements of CBT are engaging the patient, working collaboratively to develop a problem list, and setting a clear goal for each therapy session. A number of different cognitive and behavioural techniques in CBT (e.g. verbal reattribution, behavioural experiments) help people to evaluate and change their thoughts and behaviour, reducing their distress. Some of these techniques will be explored more fully in the case vignette later in the chapter.

It is important to highlight that at the core of CBT practice is the use of case conceptualisations or case formulations (Persons 1989; Tarrier 2006; Persons and Davidson 2010). Case formulation is the process in which a client's unique experience is blended with a psychological theory or model in order to understand the origins, development and maintenance of a presenting problem (Tarrier and Calam 2002). Persons and Davidson (2010) note that 'the formulation is a hypothesis about the factors that cause and maintain the patient's problems, and it guides assessment and intervention' (p. 173). Persons and Davidson state that once a formulation has been developed it should be revised through new assessment information and through a monitoring process in treatment. Friedberg and McClure (2002) argue that case conceptualisations are central to CBT with young people and have defined formulations as 'personalized psychological portraits' (p. 13). Through formulation in clinical work, the therapist moves away from a diagnostic model and provides an explanatory account of the presenting difficulties. This individual approach has particular value when working with young people with psychotic symptoms, whose symptoms may at first appear difficult to understand.

The evidence base for CBT

CBT is one of the most researched forms of psychotherapy; there were over 120 controlled clinical trials added to the literature between 1986 and 1993 (Butler *et al*. 2006). Butler *et al*. (2006) conducted a review of meta-analyses in order to establish the empirical status of CBT. They point out that the growing adaptation of CBT for a wider range of disorders and difficulties has led researchers to ask questions about the differential effectiveness by disorder and the extent to which positive outcomes are sustained. Butler *et al*. (2006) summarised findings across high-quality meta-analyses for 16 different disorders and concluded that CBT is highly effective for adult unipolar depression, adolescent unipolar depression, generalised anxiety disorder, panic disorder, social phobia, post-traumatic stress disorder (PTSD), and childhood depressive and anxiety disorders. In the case of adolescent depression, CBT was found to be superior to supportive/nondirective therapy.

There is a growing evidence base for the effective use of CBT with children and adolescents (Reinecke *et al*. 2006). Carr (2009) concludes that 'the results of these meta-analyses, reviews of meta-analyses and narrative reviews offer strong support for the effectiveness of therapies that fall broadly within the cognitive behavioural therapy tradition for a wide range of common psychological problems in children, adolescents and adults' (p. 38).

Using CBT with adolescents in secure settings

A CBT approach is well suited to young people in secure settings: it can be tailored to the individual's needs; it can be practical and problem-focused in the here and now, or very in-depth, drawing on the young person's childhood experiences. Its psychological formulations can be developmental in nature, taking in the young person's early childhood history and development of core beliefs and leading to an explanation of how their difficulties developed. A formulation can also explain how difficulties are being maintained, without alluding to historical information, or a formulation may explain a single symptom or problem area. This degree of flexibility is important when one considers the needs of different young people in the secure estate; some are not able or willing to talk about their past experiences, which often include traumatic events. A CBT approach to psychological intervention allows a young person to acquire the skills necessary to manage anxiety and/or low mood, which may even pave the way for trauma work (as noted by Rogers and Law in Chapter 7 of this book) if the young person wishes. Flexibility is also crucial to maintain engagement: a young person may initially agree to engage in an intervention in order to manage anxiety, or to understand certain difficulties better; but, once he or she has better established trust with the therapist, may progress to other types of intervention or may agree to think about more sensitive issues, perhaps related to offending behaviour or to early trauma.

There is also evidence that CBT can be adapted to meet the needs of those with learning disabilities (Kroese *et al.* 1997) and such adaptation has also been considered in relation to people in secure settings (Black *et al.* 1997), which is valuable as a high number of young offenders with mental health difficulties also present with learning needs (Kroll *et al.* 2002).

Having argued that CBT is applicable to adolescents in secure settings, the chapter will go on to consider a detailed case example of CBT with a young man who is experiencing psychotic symptoms in custody. Before examining this vignette it is important to review what is meant by the term 'psychosis' and to examine the evidence base for psychological intervention in relation to it and, in particular, for CBT in relation to it.

Defining and understanding psychosis

Psychosis is characterised by a loss of contact with reality and symptoms that alter a person's perception, thoughts, emotions and behaviour. Each person experiencing psychosis will have a unique combination of symptoms and experiences. Often there is a prodromal period during which the person's functioning deteriorates; this deterioration may include problems with memory and concentration, unusual behaviour and ideas, disturbed communication and affect, social withdrawal, a lack of motivation or a reduced interest in daily activities; these are sometimes called 'negative symptoms'. The prodromal period is usually followed by an acute episode marked by hallucinations, delusions and behavioural disturbances; these are sometimes called 'positive symptoms' and are usually experienced by the person as distressing. The term 'psychosis' is favoured in the current literature (Hirshfield *et al.* 2005), and will be used in this chapter, because the concept of schizophrenia, along with its validity and reliability, has been challenged (Bentall 2003), and the diagnosis can be unclear in an adolescent.

The stress-vulnerability model (Zubin and Spring 1977) is commonly used when developing a psychological formulation for a person with psychotic symptoms. This model stresses that anybody could experience psychotic symptoms if placed under sufficient stress; yet the model also describes how people vary in their vulnerability to a psychotic breakdown, due to individual differences which may be genetic, social, physiological or psychological: whether a person develops psychotic symptoms is dependent on the interaction between their pre-existing vulnerability and stressful events. For somebody with a high level of vulnerability, it may only take minor stressors to precipitate psychotic symptoms; somebody with a low level of vulnerability may nevertheless experience psychotic symptoms if subjected to immensely stressful events. This model promotes engagement because it is comforting for an individual to consider that anybody may experience psychotic symptoms under certain conditions. The stress-vulnerability model also provides a rationale for a range of psychosocial interventions to modify stress and/or to enhance coping.

Although the stress-vulnerability model can explain why a particular person has developed psychosis, it does not explain why he or she has developed a particular hallucination or delusion. Cognitive models of psychosis are attempts to make sense of the psychological factors linked to the onset of an episode of psychosis, but also to provide clarity about the psychological factors maintaining hallucinations and delusions and about the content and meaning of these experiences. Cognitive models outline how hallucinations and delusions can occur when anomalous experiences, which could affect other people, are misattributed to have extreme and threatening personal meaning (Morrison 2001).

Normalising is another important feature of CBT for psychosis. The therapist normalises psychotic experiences by giving information about the prevalence of unusual experiences in 'normal' people, which helps the person in therapy to desist from catastrophic thinking about what these experiences might mean. Research findings indicate that psychotic symptoms can be conceptualised with reference to normal psychological processes, and that this makes the content of symptoms understandable and suitable for CBT interventions (e.g. Chadwick *et al.* 1996).

There are many variants of the cognitive model that are proposed to explain the onset, development and maintenance of psychotic symptoms (Bentall 2003; Chadwick *et al.* 1996; Morrison 1998). However, Wykes *et al.* (2008) concluded that no specific cognitive model has been shown to be more effective than a generic cognitive model in the treatment of delusions. Dudley *et al.* (2010) point out that all these models 'share in common the notion that appraisals of events affect feelings and behaviour and therefore are all compatible with more generic cognitive models' (p. 189).

Psychosis and evidence-based practice

Pharmacological treatments are often regarded as the frontline intervention for first episode psychosis, but medication may not be sufficiently effective, and non-compliance is often a problem. These problems have prompted the development of psychological treatments. There have been promising results for the use of CBT as an adjunct to medication in the treatment of schizophrenia: there have been studies of the effectiveness of psychological interventions in psychosis in controlled trials with adults which have led to the conclusion that they are an important adjunct to medication in the treatment of the disorder (Haddock and Lewis 2005). However, the participants in this research have often been individuals with chronic, treatment-resistant psychosis rather than people experiencing a first episode. Drury *et al.* (1996) conducted a small controlled trial using CBT as an intervention with people suffering from acute psychosis. Although they reported good results for the use of CBT, not all the trial participants were experiencing their first episode of psychosis and there were methodological problems with the study.

The SoCRATES study – the study of cognitive realignment therapy in early schizophrenia (Lewis *et al.* 2002; Tarrier *et al.* 2004) – used a randomised sample of 309 patients to examine the impact of CBT on first-episode psychosis. This study evaluated the effectiveness of groups undergoing two psychological therapies – CBT and Supportive Counselling (SC) – and were compared to routine care alone. The overall findings of this study are that a brief package of CBT in acute early psychosis accelerated improvements in target symptoms. However, this difference between the CBT group and the routine care group was no longer apparent at six weeks. Haddock and Lewis (2005) suggest that this may well be due to the powerful main effect of drug treatment which is a part of routine care. The CBT intervention led to improved outcomes in symptoms at 18 months compared to routine care alone, although the effect was small. Both psychological therapies, CBT and SC, were evaluated as superior to routine treatment but individuals experiencing hallucinations appeared to have poorer outcomes over an 18-month period if they had received SC, compared to CBT or routine care alone. Haddock *et al.* (2005) stress the importance of tailoring treatment to meet the needs of the individual with early psychosis.

It should be noted that the studies described relate to adult populations. Some participants were inpatients while others received psychological intervention as part of intensive day care treatment. It is not unreasonable to assume that the evidence from the research with adults may be extremely useful when planning interventions with adolescents, but it is important to consider developmental issues and to adapt the therapy accordingly, and this will of course reduce treatment fidelity. Working in a secure setting presents particular challenges (to be discussed in more detail later in this chapter) and typically the process of engagement with young people detained or incarcerated against their will is more difficult than in community settings.

The psychosocial treatment recommendations of the schizophrenia Patient Outcomes Research Team (PORT) provide a comprehensive summary of current evidenced-based interventions for people with this diagnosis. The 2009 set of PORT recommendations also summarises the evidence relating to the different psychosocial treatments. In their paper describing this evidence, Dixon *et al.* (2010) recommend that individuals who experience persistent psychotic symptoms while receiving adequate medication should be offered CBT as an adjunct, to help to reduce the severity of their symptoms. They also state that 'the key elements of this intervention include the collaborative identification of target problems and symptoms and the development of specific cognitive and behavioural strategies to cope with these problems or symptoms' (Dixon *et al.* 2010: 52). The PORT recommendations also state that the benefits of CBT for individuals with recent onset of psychosis have not yet been clearly established; more research is needed into first-episode psychosis and psychological interventions. But there are promising indications that CBT can be a useful approach when working with individuals experiencing psychotic symptoms.

The NICE guideline for schizophrenia covers the 'treatment and management of schizophrenia and related disorders in adults (18 years and older) with an established diagnosis of schizophrenia with onset before age 60'. The guideline does not address the specific treatment of young people under the age of 18, 'except those who are receiving treatment and support from early intervention services' (NICE 2009). The NICE guideline recommends that CBT should be delivered on a one-to-one basis over at least 16 planned sessions and that it should include helping the individual to recognise the links between thoughts, feelings and actions and the links to current or past symptoms. NICE also recommends that the intervention

83

includes re-evaluating the person's perceptions, beliefs or reasoning as related to the target symptoms, as well as helping them to develop new ways of coping with their symptoms, reducing their distress and improving their functioning.

Case vignette

The following case study is a composite one, which does not reflect work with any one individual; rather, it combines clinical work with several clients over several years. This case study uses a generic cognitive model, based on the identification of predisposing factors to psychological difficulties which are described in relation to childhood experiences. The model then illustrates how these experiences shape the development of beliefs about the self, the world and other people, which are managed by rules for living. This model states that distress is caused by a triggering event that conflicts with, or breaches, these rules. The model also describes how an individual's psychological difficulties are maintained.

Background to the case vignette

Michael is a 16-year-old young man. He is the second eldest child born to his parents, Carol (38 years old) and John (40 years old). Michael has an older sister, Gemma (19 years old) and a younger brother, Tom (eight years old). There has been a long history of domestic violence since Gemma was a toddler. Carol and her children have been moved to safe houses and refuges on a number of occasions. Michael witnessed his father being extremely violent to his mother on a number of occasions, including occasions on which he used weapons; his mother required hospital treatment on several occasions. Michael was subjected to physical and emotional abuse by John, who returned to live with the family several times before he and Carol separated for good when Michael was 12 years old. John is alcohol dependent. Michael had no contact with his father for three years but contact between them had started again approximately a year before Michael entered custody. However, although Carol was aware of this contact, she asked Michael to keep it a secret from other family members to avoid upsetting them. Michael reported that he had retained a close relationship with his mother.

Michael entered custody for the first time just a week before the referral was made. He had received a 10-month detention and training order (DTO) for actual bodily harm after an assault on a young woman, Zoe. Michael and Zoe had been in a relationship for two months by the time of the offence; the relationship ended after the assault. Michael had a conviction for the robbery of a mobile phone when he was 15 years old and had received an intensive supervision order for a period of one year.

Carol, Michael's mother, had been very worried about Michael's mental health for some months prior to his entering custody. When Carol broached the subject with him, Michael had refused to see any mental health professionals. She subsequently went to her GP alone. In the absence of a clinical assessment, the GP believed that Michael was suffering from severe anxiety and referred him to a clinical psychologist in the local CAMHS. When the letter about the appointment arrived eight weeks later, Michael became very angry with his mother, perceiving she had gone behind his back, and refused to attend.

Later, when he was in custody, Michael's personal officer referred him to the mental health in-reach team (MHIRT) because his behaviour had recently changed on the wing, as several members of staff had noted. He had become increasingly withdrawn, spending all his time in his cell and refusing to attend education; it was noted that he had been tearful and anxious. He was assessed on the wing by a registered mental health nurse who reported that he seemed highly anxious and appeared to hold some paranoid ideas about other prisoners; however, Michael was very quiet and did not give much information during the interview. He was referred for both a clinical psychology and psychiatry assessment.

Initial assessment

Michael refused to leave his cell to attend an appointment in the health care centre, so it was necessary to go to the wing to see him. He presented as a tearful, frightened young man who was physically shaking but able to respond to questions. It became evident during the assessment that Michael was having psychotic experiences. It had been previously assumed by the wing staff that he was very anxious and probably depressed. Michael displayed paranoid delusions, stating that he feared for his life, that he had been followed by men in a silver car prior to coming into custody and that somebody was going to kill his family. He also reported that other prisoners on the wing were able to read his thoughts – which was one of the reasons why he was reluctant to leave his cell – and that other prisoners were in communication with Zoe and were observing him in order to report back to her. Understandably, he presented as highly distressed.

After this assessment, and liaison with the psychiatrist in the team, Michael was moved to the health care wing. From this point on, Michael attended twice-weekly psychology sessions. Initially, they were kept very short and frequent. He engaged well from the first session, despite the acute nature of his presentation, and showed himself capable of thinking psychologically and working with psychological concepts. It was during the second session, which took place on the health care wing, that Michael disclosed that he had been hearing voices for six months. He said that he had not told anyone, even his mother about these experiences; he feared that these voices meant that he was going mad.

After the initial assessments, by both the author and the consultant psychiatrist, a referral was made to adolescent medium-secure psychiatric services, with a view to a hospital transfer. However, there was no bed available immediately; there was an expected wait of three weeks. Therefore, further assessment and treatment (both medical and psychological) took place in the prison.

Michael responded well to antipsychotic medication, but the improvement in many of his psychotic symptoms revealed an underlying anxiety, which he said had been present for as long as he could remember. At times, Michael demonstrated a tendency to minimise or deny his symptoms in order to appear well and to avoid any increases in his medication. He stated that he did not suffer from any particular side effects but that he was cautious about increases in medication all the same. Michael could usually be coaxed to be more open and would often disclose symptoms when provided with reassurance about doing so.

Further assessment

A life path approach was used in order to help Michael to identify potentially stressful life events and to understand the development of his personality. Beck used the construction of a narrative to hypothesise how different problems arose, how they were linked to one another, and how they were maintained. There is evidence that this process of developing a coherent life story is therapeutic in itself (Roe and Davidson 2005). Key life events were drawn out on a large sheet of flip chart paper (kept by the author between sessions) in order to provide a chronology and to help Michael to consider possible triggers to his psychotic episode. This was used in conjunction with a stress-vulnerability model of psychosis, which Michael was able to grasp.

Formulation

The therapist developed a psychological formulation in collaboration with Michael (see Figure 4.1). Michael was able to recognise and understand how his childhood environment predisposed him to developing severe anxiety. He said that he had always been a worrier. Within his psychological formulation, his hyper-vigilance and intense worries about the safety of other family members were an understandable response to his prolonged exposure to witnessing domestic violence, the frequent family moves to escape from violence and the very real fear of the family being followed and attacked. Clearly, at some point, Michael's worries grew to the point where they were no longer rational and he came to fear attack from a number of sources – not just from his father. When his father finally left the family for good and stopped pursuing them, this was a relief. However, Michael also identified that he had begun to feel as though, being the oldest male member left in the family, he was more responsible for other members; this showed itself in controlling behaviours, such as wanting to know where other family members were going, who with, and when they would return. Michael was able to see how his controlling behaviours led other family members to keep their distance from him and in some cases begin to resent him.

Michael identified the death of his maternal grandmother from a heart attack as a potential antecedent to his psychotic episode. Michael had been close to his grandmother and her death was a shock. This loss would appear to have further activated Michael's worries about the safety of his family and worries about his own health too. Around this time, Michael recalled attending A&E with chest pains which were in fact due to a panic attack, but which Michael had at the time been convinced were a heart attack. He said that he stopped going out after that and became more isolated and withdrawn. One of the only friends he continued to see outside of school was Zoe, a school friend. Their relationship developed into a romantic one, although Michael stated that he felt uneasy about it and had little confidence in Zoe's wish to be with him. This would appear to be a reflection of Michael's low self-esteem and long-standing lack of confidence with his peers. Fowler (2000) suggests that it is possible that persecutory beliefs may reflect pre-existing negative beliefs about the self and others. Michael reported that he became convinced that Zoe was in communication with his father. Later in therapy, Michael suggested that he had developed this belief because he thought that Zoe must have had an ulterior motive for wanting to spend time with him, as he was unable to believe that she truly enjoyed his company. He also believed that she was having him followed, although he did not know why. These beliefs led Michael to challenge Zoe, and during this conversation he became angry when she would not admit that she had been speaking to his father; he pushed her and she fell, breaking a finger in the process; a few weeks later Michael confronted Zoe again, and during this argument he punched her. These offences were committed while Michael was on an intensive order.

Given the long-standing nature and the content of his anxious thoughts, it is not altogether surprising that Michael's psychotic symptoms have a similar flavour. The loss of his maternal grandmother and the stressful, and secret, nature of contact with his father appear to have been two events which increased Michael's stress levels in the lead-up to his psychotic episode. The impact of adolescence and the social challenges it brings may also have contributed to the deterioration in Michael's mental health. Harrop and Trower's (2001) theory of blocked psychological maturation is highly relevant to Michael. His beliefs about his responsibility to protect his family made it more difficult for him to establish autonomy and to develop peer relationships – both important psychological tasks of adolescence.

Michael was able to separate some of the long-standing behaviours which related to his developing personality from the symptoms of his psychosis; he was also able to reflect on how the former influenced the latter. In relation to maintenance cycles, Michael began to recognise how some of the ways he used to cope with his difficulties were in fact maintaining them. For example, Michael's feelings of anxiety and his fears about his family's safety led him to question family members repeatedly about their movements, in order to reassure himself that they were going to be safe if they left the house. This made them want to avoid him, and his sister in particular spent less time at home as a result. This in turn made Michael feel more worried about her safety. Michael's increasing isolation gave him more opportunities to ruminate about going mad and he reported that the voices increased in frequency when he was alone.

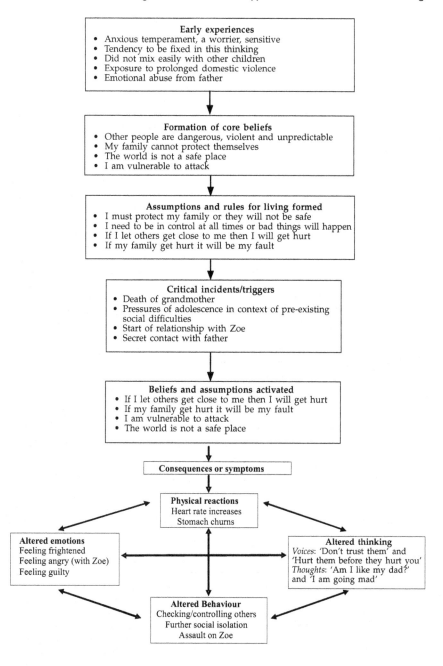

Figure 4.1   Psychological formulation

Intervention

Developing the formulation
The collaborative development of the psychological formulation was a therapeutic experience for Michael in itself. He expressed relief at understanding how his problems had developed and he felt reassured that his symptoms were in many ways an explicable response to his childhood environment and a series of challenging and stressful events. From the beginning of therapy, Michael demonstrated an ability and willingness to consider alternative explanations, suggesting that his level of conviction in some of his delusional beliefs was not high. A lower level of conviction in a delusional belief has been found to predict a good response to brief CBT for psychosis (Brabban *et al.* 2009).

Challenging negative automatic thoughts
Michael was socialised to the cognitive model using Greenberger and Padesky's (1995) five-factor model. He did not feel able to complete dysfunctional thought records in between sessions because he worried that an officer or another prisoner might find such records in his cell. It was agreed that thought records would be completed in sessions instead. During sessions Michael was asked to recall in detail the times during the previous few days when he had felt extremely distressed. A daily thought record was then filled in, initially by the therapist writing down what Michael said. The therapist explained and discussed different ways of challenging his negative automatic thoughts, for example, by examining the evidence for and against the thought and identifying cognitive distortions. Initially, Michael needed a lot of support to complete the thought record, but after a time he would pre-empt the therapist's response, and later still he was able to generate his own challenges to his thinking. One example of this occurred when (as Michael reported) he left his cell at lunchtime and thought, 'Everyone is staring at me, they can read my thoughts, they know I'm frightened'; but he was able to identify that he was jumping to the conclusion that other people staring at him meant that they could read his thoughts and to examine whether or not he had any evidence for this belief. Michael considered other reasons why people might be looking at him and came up with the statement, 'I have hardly left my cell since I arrived on health care so other prisoners might be curious about me and that's why they're looking over.' Michael's awareness of the link between his thoughts and his feelings was cemented by this approach.

The thought records were also used to show Michael the link between his own thinking and the content of the voices he heard. The records provided a visual way of showing Michael the significant similarities between his own thoughts and what the voices said to him. This paved the way for putting forward the idea that the voices might in fact be Michael's own thoughts.

Managing anxiety

Michael responded well to psycho-educational material about the cognitive model of anxiety and its relationship to physical symptoms. He was already familiar with challenging his thoughts and he was able to see how it was possible to reduce his anxious feelings by this method. Michael also began to recognise safety behaviours (reassurance seeking), for example, repeated phone calls home to check on the well-being of his family. Michael was able to recognise that these phone calls were maintaining his difficulties, because he believed that if he did not check on his family then they would be harmed. When he checked on them and they were unharmed, this reinforced his belief that his checking was productive and necessary and did not provide him with any opportunities to discover that his family would have remained unharmed had he not called them. In addition, he was able to see how this behaviour was placing a strain on family relationships. On his own initiative, he began to reduce these behaviours. When he became anxious he was able to challenge his unhelpful and catastrophic thoughts to good effect.

The therapy also addressed Michael's anxieties about his medication. It became clear that Michael viewed any increase in his medication as a sign that he was not making progress and that he would never get better. Through Socratic questioning he was able to turn this idea on its head and reach the conclusion that in fact an increase in his medication might be pivotal in helping him to remain free of some of his symptoms. He was also able to identify that minimising or denying symptoms in order to avoid an increase in his medication was counter-productive because he did not then get the support he needed to manage his symptoms – both psychologically and with medication.

Working with staff

In addition to the therapy described, it was felt to be important to work with other staff both to aid their understanding of Michael's presentation and to provide Michael with further support between sessions when the author was not on site. Part of the way through the intervention, after five sessions, Michael agreed that it would be helpful if his key nurse on the health care wing attended a psychology session; this was facilitated, and a less detailed formulation was shared with her. She developed a greater understanding of Michael's behaviour, for example, of his repeated requests to make phone calls to his family, and she also agreed to prompt Michael to use strategies he had learned between sessions.

Risk issues

Michael worked collaboratively to develop further the psychological formulation of his psychosis so that it included aspects of his risk to others. Michael remained clear in his view that he had never considered hurting himself, even when very psychotic. However, this work was difficult because there remained some events Michael could not recall with accuracy and he was unsure whether they had actually occurred or were a part of his psychotic thinking. For example, Michael was uncertain whether Zoe had been conspiring against him in some way or whether that was all in his mind. He recalled feeling hostile towards her, but he could not understand the strength of this feeling now and no longer felt that way. Initially, Michael was extremely uncomfortable with the idea that he might be a risk to others in the future, if he had another psychotic episode. At first he stated categorically that he would never hurt anyone again and became very defensive. He brought his concerns to a later session, stating that he had some worrying thoughts about his potential risk that he wanted to discuss further. The vertical arrow technique (Burns 1980) was used to elicit the 'bottom line', that is, to identify what lay at the heart of Michael's concerns. The dialogue is shown below:

> *Therapist*: If you were to acknowledge that you might be a risk to others what would that mean to you?
> *Michael*: That I can't control myself.
> *Therapist*: If that was the case, what would be so bad about that?
> *Michael*: I might lose control and hit out at any time.
> *Therapist*: If that were true, what would be the worst thing about that?
> *Michael*: That other people would be scared of me, people I care about.
> *Therapist*: If that were true, what would it mean to you?
> *Michael*: That I am like my dad.

Michael became very tearful at this point; he said that worries about becoming like his father had been bothering him ever since he assaulted Zoe. It was important for Michael to recognise his potential risk to others and yet also to challenge the thoughts that he would inevitably turn out like his father: this was a delicate balance. In one session, the therapist encouraged Michael to list the differences between himself and his father and he generated many such differences. One of the most important was that Michael's one and only incident of aggression occurred in the context of a psychotic episode. Michael's desire to avoid hurting anyone again was a motivating factor, in that it increased his commitment to continue taking medication and to engage in relapse prevention work.

Michael's transfer to hospital

Michael was transferred to a hospital setting after 10 psychology sessions in the prison. The author worked across both settings and so was able to continue with the intervention. Initially, in the first few days after transfer, Michael deteriorated: once again, he became worried about others being able to read his thoughts and he refused to leave his bedroom. However, with support and frequent reminders about the skills he had learned, he was able to challenge his thoughts again and he gradually became integrated into the life of the unit.

In the medium-secure unit for adolescents, Michael, his mother and his siblings engaged well with family therapy and Michael reported that he felt better understood by his family; the feelings of guilt about what he had put them through began to reduce. In turn, family members reported that Michael had a better awareness of the impact of his controlling behaviour on them. Both Michael and his mother reported a new atmosphere of increased communication and they acknowledged the negative impact of keeping secrets. Michael decided to put decisions about contact with his father on hold until he left hospital, because he recognised that this contact was too much for him to cope with at the current time. He also engaged with the occupational therapist and began a programme of gradually increasing his community leave, which served to reduce his level of anxiety in social settings.

The psychological intervention came to an end by mutual agreement after a further eight sessions in the hospital setting (thus after 18 sessions in total). This included work on preventing relapse and on early warning signs, undertaken jointly by the author and Michael's key nurse. Michael left hospital six months later, having served his sentence.

The challenges of providing therapy in prisons

This case study illustrates some of the many and varied challenges of delivering therapeutic interventions in a custodial setting. It is pertinent now to consider challenges to the delivery of therapy in prisons in more detail.

Some of the problems are practical ones. For example, the practice in the Prison Service of moving a disruptive prisoner to a different prison may well be effective in reducing disruption in the prison but it may also result in the abrupt termination of therapy and, from the therapist's perspective, it may well exacerbate the client's difficulties. On average there were more than 6,000 inter-prison transfers between April 2007 and February 2008; such transfers present a major challenge for therapy providers, given that they often occur without warning (PRT 2009). There are also problems with the movements of prisoners within any one prison. The prisoners may be kept in their cells or 'locked down' when there are security concerns in the prison. This may, at times, prevent people from attending therapy sessions. Even mere attendance at therapy sessions can be difficult to achieve in a prison. Typically, prison officers move the prisoners together to a variety of destinations within the prison at the start of the morning and the afternoon shifts. It is the author's experience that there are rarely other opportunities for prison staff to facilitate a prisoner's attendance at a session. If an error is made and a prisoner is not put 'on the list' for the health care or mental health unit, it is often not possible to rectify this oversight to ensure the prisoner's attendance. There are other reasons why a young person may not be able to attend regularly. A young person in custody must see a range of professionals – some of whom play a role in preparing them for court or parole hearings. A therapist may discover that the young person did not attend a session because they were meeting their solicitor, barrister or parole officer.

Problems are also caused by the fact that demand for mental health assessment and interventions in the prison far outstrips supply; therefore, there are frequent dilemmas about who should be seen. This can lead to mental health nurses and other professionals in the prison having constantly to re-prioritise those prisoners who are viewed as most in need of psychological assessment or therapeutic work. In the author's experience, it is not uncommon for young people deemed to be at high risk of suicide or serious self-harm to be prioritised for assessment by visiting mental health professionals. While this is understandable and often necessary, it can mean that prisoners engaged in therapy inevitably become a lower priority as their sessions are cancelled to allow for the emergency assessment of high-risk individuals. Clearly this impacts on the pace of progress and the level of trust and engagement between the young person and the therapist.

Other, broader challenges stem not just from such practicalities but directly from the differing and, at times, competing aims of the mental health professional and the Prison Service. The priorities of the Prison Service are security and containment for the prison as a whole, whereas mental health professionals focus on the psychological needs of the individual. There are often times when it does not seem possible for these two sets of priorities to co-exist easily. It is important for a psychologist to develop an understanding of these differing priorities which can easily lead to misunderstanding and even to conflict between the two groups. If disagreements about the management of a particular individual, or about prison practice or procedure, go unaddressed, then it is easy for misperceptions to flourish on both sides.

Another important issue affected by the differing aims and objectives of health care and prison staff is that of measuring the outcomes of psychological interventions. What is obvious is the need to establish an evidence of what works, and with whom, in prison; what is less obvious is who defines improvement and how. In a traditional health care setting, the psychologist and the patient set goals at the start of therapy and measure their progress against them throughout the intervention. In prisons and other secure settings, the situation is more complicated as the psychologist seeks to balance engagement of the patient in addressing psychological difficulties with the task of public protection. Prison staff may view progress in therapy as best measured by indicators such as a decrease in assaults on staff, adjudications and damage to property. While these indicators would be viewed positively by psychologists, they may not be the targets of intervention as such. In prisons and other secure settings, there is a need for a balance in evaluating therapeutic interventions in ways that serve both the individual and the institution.

Many mental health professionals are used to working in the NHS or other health care settings in which mental health professionals typically work as part of a wider, usually multidisciplinary, team, especially when working with complex cases. In prisons, however, a psychologist may well be working alone or, even if alongside other professionals, rarely with the opportunities for team discussion and care planning meetings that exist in secure hospitals. In most

MHIRTs, demand far outstrips the resources and the focus is on providing psychological assessments and interventions with the people who are most in need. This pressure can mean that there are fewer opportunities to reflect with colleagues on one's work, say, on a client's formulation or on the direction of therapy. Clearly, supervision is vital under these circumstances. The case described in this chapter illustrates the difference between offering interventions in a hospital and a prison, especially in relation to the multidisciplinary input available to a young person. While a range of psychological approaches is used in prisons to address the mental health needs of offenders, rarely are all of them offered to one person at the same time or in the same prison. Yet it is more common for a range of therapies and interventions – for example, occupational therapy, family therapy, psychology, and psychotherapy – to be offered in secure hospitals. Young people in prison are no less complex in their presentation than those in secure hospital settings, yet the range and type of interventions available is much narrower. As a result, it is likely that at least some young people in prison are receiving a particular treatment simply because that is what is available. The clinician may well be aware of more suitable and more effective therapies which he or she is not able to offer.

Practical characteristics of the prison can make aspects of therapy difficult. Historically, CBT has involved the patient completing diaries of their thoughts, feelings and behaviours in private, outside therapy. But in prison, there is little privacy for prisoners: the prison staff may search their cell at any time and some prisoners share cells. It is the author's experience that this lack of privacy means that prisoners are understandably reluctant to record their private thoughts and feelings in written form. Therefore, in order to undertake the diary-keeping which is an important feature of CBT the therapist and the patient can, instead, complete diaries within sessions. This may not capture the 'in the moment' thoughts and feelings of a young person in the same way but may nonetheless provide valuable information.

One of the challenges for all psychologists is how to help the individual to use what was learned in therapy in everyday situations and settings. This is much more difficult in prisons and other secure settings. CBT involves the person learning new skills and coping strategies and if he or she cannot apply these to life outside the therapy space then the intervention has not been successful. Some skills can be tried out in the prison but others cannot. Some behavioural experiments cannot be set up and for some young people the focus of their difficulties, for example, interactions with the opposite sex, form no part of life in prison. For many young people in prison, being cut off from the outside world limits the generalisability of any interventions or therapeutic encounters experienced in prison.

Finally, there are frequent challenges with risk and confidentiality. Psychologists and mental health professionals working in prisons and secure settings must address both the needs of the individual and the protection of the public. Risk assessment will always form part of the work even when the main focus is therapeutic. There is a need to strike a delicate balance between effectively managing risk, trying to maintain trust between the young person and the therapist, and helping the young person to address their mental health needs in therapy. The young person engaging in therapy must be fully aware at the start that the psychologist has a duty to pass on certain kinds of information to other agencies, for example, to children and family services, MAPPA or prison security. At times this duty may affect engagement, when information that the young person would prefer to keep confidential must be shared. While this may be true in ordinary health settings as well, the possible level of risk and the frequency of disclosures may occur more often in work in prison. On a positive note, it is the author's experience that, if the conditions of confidentiality are set out at the start of therapy, most young people understand them and engage with the therapist all the same.

Conclusion

There is no doubt that adolescents in the secure estate present with high levels of need in relation to their mental health. There is a window of opportunity in secure settings to address these needs, especially as socially excluded individuals are often not good attendees in the community. CBT is a useful approach to both engagement and therapy in secure settings and it is appropriate for use with a wide variety of different problems and diagnoses. This is important in the prison, where many of those in contact with mental health professionals have complex needs and several different problems. Young offenders in particular show high rates of co-morbidity (Harrington and Bailey 2004). They require a treatment intervention that can be used flexibly to address different problem areas in turn and to provide either a 'here and now' approach to understanding their needs, or a developmental formulation, or both. CBT fits the bill for all these reasons. Despite this, there remains a paucity of research in this area. There is a need to develop an evidence base for what works with young people (as well as other client groups) who have mental difficulties in secure settings. Research provides evidence which can then be used to argue for more resources to provide psychological interventions.

References

Bailey, S. and Kerslake, B. (2008) 'The process and systems for juveniles and young persons', in K. Soothill, P. Rogers and M. Dolan (eds), *Handbook of Forensic Mental Health*. Cullompton: Willan Publishing.

Beck, A.T., Rush, A.J., Shaw, B.F., Emery, G. (1979) *Cognitive Therapy of Depression*. New York: The Guilford Press.

Bennett-Levy, J., Butler, G., Fennell, M., Hackmann, A., Mueller, M., Westbrook, D. and Rouf, K. (eds) (2004) *Oxford Guide to Behavioural Experiments in Cognitive Therapy*. Oxford: Oxford University Press.

Bentall, R. (2003) *Madness Explained*. London: Penguin Books Ltd.

Black, L., Cullen, C. and Novaco, R.W. (1997) 'Anger assessment for people with mild learning disabilities in secure settings', in B.S. Kroese, D. Dagman and K. Loumidis (eds), *Cognitive-Behavioural Therapy for People with Learning Disabilities*. London: Routledge, pp. 33–52.

Brabban, A., Tai, S. and Turkington, D. (2009) 'Predictors of outcome in brief cognitive behaviour therapy for schizophrenia', *Schizophrenia Bulletin*, 35(5): 859–64.

Burns, D. (1980) *The Feeling Good Handbook*. New York: New American Library.

Butler, A., Chapman, J., Forman, E. and Beck, A. (2006) 'The empirical status of cognitive-behavioural therapy: A review of meta-analyses', *Clinical Psychology Review*, 26: 17–31.

Carr, A. (2009) *What Works with Children, Adolescents and Adults? A Review of Research on the Effectiveness of Psychotherapy*. Abingdon: Routledge.

Chadwick, P., Birchwood, M. and Trower, P. (1996) *Cognitive Therapy for Delusions, Voices and Paranoia*. Chichester: John Wiley & Sons.

Close, H. and Shuller, S. (2004) 'Psychotic symptoms', in J. Bennett-Levy, G. Butler, M. Fennell, A. Hackmann, M. Mueller, D. Westbrook and K. Rouf (eds), *Oxford Guide to Behavioural Experiments in Cognitive Therapy*. Oxford: Oxford University Press.

Coleman, J. and Hagell, A. (2007) 'The nature and risk of resilience in adolescence', in J. Coleman and A. Hagell (eds), *Adolescence, Risk and Resilience: Against All Odds*. Chichester: Wiley, pp. 1–16.

Department of Health (2004) *National Service Framework for Children, Young People and Maternity Services*. London: Department of Health.

Department of Health and HMPS (2001) *Changing the Outlook: A Strategy for Developing and Modernising Mental Health Services in Prisons*. London: Department of Health.

DH, DCSF and Ministry of Justice and Home Office (2009) *Healthy Children, Safer Communities: A Strategy to Promote the Health and Well-being of Children and Young People in Contact with the Youth Justice System.* London: Department of Health, Department for Children, Schools and Families, Ministry of Justice and Home Office.

Dixon, L., Dickerson, F., Bellack, A., Bennett, M., Dickenson, D., Goldberg, W., Lenman, A., Calmes, C., Pasillas, R.M., Peer, J. and Kreyenbuhl, J. (2010) 'The 2009 Schizophrenia PORT psychosocial treatment recommendations and summary statements', *Schizophrenia Bulletin,* 36(1): 48–70.

Dobson, K.S. (2010) *Handbook of Cognitive-Behavioural Therapies,* 3rd edition. New York: The Guilford Press.

Drury, V., Birchwood, M., Cochrane, R. and McMillan, F. (1996) 'Cognitive therapy and recovery from acute psychosis: a controlled trial. I. impact on symptoms', *British Journal of Psychiatry,* 169: 593–601.

Dudley, R. and Kuyken, W. (2006) 'Formulation in cognitive-behavioural therapy: There is nothing either good or bad, but thinking makes it so', in Johnstone and Dallos (eds), *Formulation in Psychology and Psychotherapy.* Abingdon: Routledge, pp. 17–46.

Dudley, R., Park, I., James, I. and Hodgson, G. (2010) 'Rate of agreement between clinicians on the content of a cognitive formulation of delusional beliefs: The effect of qualifications and experience', *Behavioural and Cognitive Psychotherapy,* 38: 185–200.

Fowler, D. (2000) 'Psychological formulation of early episodes of psychosis: A cognitive model', in. M. Birchwood, D. Fowler and C. Jackson (eds), *Early Intervention in Psychosis.* Chichester: John Wiley & Sons.

Friedberg, R.D. and McClure, J.M. (2002) *Clinical Practice in Cognitive Therapy with Children and Adolescents: The Nuts and Bolts.* New York: The Guilford Press.

Goldson, B. (2006) 'Penal custody: Intolerance, irrationality and indifference', in B. Goldson and J. Muncie (eds), *Youth Crime and Justice.* London: Sage, pp. 139–56.

Goldson, B. and Muncie, J. (eds) (2006) *Youth Crime and Justice.* London: Sage.

Greenberger, D. and Padeskey, C. (1995) *Mind over Mood: Change The Way You Feel By Changing The Way You Think.* New York: The Guilford Press.

Haddock, G. and Lewis, S. (2005) 'Psychological Interventions in Early Psychosis', *Schizophrenia Bulletin,* 31(3): 697–704.

Harrington, D. and Bailey, S. (2005) *Mental Health Needs and Effectiveness of Provision for Young Offenders in Custody and in the Community.* London: Youth Justice Board.

Harrington, R.C. and Bailey, S. (2004) *The Scope for Preventing Antisocial Personality Disorder by Intervening in Adolescence. NHS National Programme on Forensic Mental Health Research and Development, Expert Paper.*

Harrop, C. and Trower, P. (2001) 'Why does schizophrenia develop at late adolescence?', *Clinical Psychology Review,* 21(2): 241–66.

Harvey, J. (2007) *Young Men in Prison: Surviving and Adapting to Life Inside.* Cullompton: Willan Publishing.

Hirshfield, R., Smith, J., Trower, P. and Griffin, C. (2005) 'What do psychotic experiences mean for young men? A qualitative investigation', *Psychology and Psychotherapy: Theory, Research and Practice*, 78: 249–70.

Holmbeck, G.N., Devine, K.A. and Bruno, E.F. (2010) 'Developmental issues and considerations in research and practice', in J.R. Weisz and A.E. Kazdin (eds), *Evidence Based Psychotherapies for Children and Adolescents*. New York: The Guilford Press.

Kazdin, A.E. and Weisz, J.R. (2010) 'Introduction: Context, background and goals', in J. R. Weisz and A.E. Kazdin (eds), *Evidence Based Psychotherapies for Children and Adolescents*. New York: The Guilford Press.

Kroese, B.S., Dagman, D. and and Loumidis, K. (eds) (1997) *Cognitive-Behavioural Therapy for People with Learning Disabilities*. London: Routledge.

Kroll, L., Rothwell, J., Bradley, D., Shah, P., Bailey, S. and Harrington, R.C. (2002) 'Mental health needs of boys in secure care for serious or persistent offending: a prospective longitudinal study', *The Lancet*, 359: 1975–9.

Lader, D., Singleton, N. and Meltzer, H. (2000) *Psychiatric Morbidity among Young Offenders in England and Wales*. London: Office for National Statistics.

Lewis, S., Tarrier, N. and Haddock, G. (2002) 'Randomised controlled trial of cognitive-behavioural therapy in early schizophrenia: acute-phase outcomes', *British Journal of Psychiatry*, 181: 91–7.

Morgan, R. and Newburn, T. (2007) 'Youth justice', in M. Maguire, R. Morgan and R. Reiner (eds), *The Oxford Handbook of Criminology*. Oxford: Oxford University Press.

Morrison, A.P. (1998) 'A cognitive analysis of the maintenance of auditory hallucinations: are voices to schizophrenia what bodily sensations are to panic?', *Behavioural and Cognitive Psychotherapy*, 26: 289–302.

Morrison, A.P. (2001) 'The interpretation of intrusions in psychosis: an integrative cognitive approach to hallucinations and delusions', *Behavioural and Cognitive Psychotherapy*, 29: 257–76.

NICE (2009) *Core interventions in the treatment and management of schizophrenia in primary and secondary care (update).* London: National Institute for Health and Clinical Excellence.

Persons, J.B. (1989) *Cognitive Therapy in Practice. A Case Formulation Approach.* New York: W.W. Norton.

Persons, J.B. and Davidson, J. (2010) 'Cognitive-behavioral case formulation', in K.S. Dobson (ed.), *Handbook of Cognitive-Behavioural Therapies*, 3rd edition. New York: The Guilford Press.

PRT (2009) *Bromley Briefings Prison Factfile*. London: Prison Reform Trust.

Reinecke, M.A., Dattilio, F.M. and Freeman, A. (eds) (2006) *Cognitive Therapy with Children and Adolescents*. New York: The Guilford Press.

Roe, D. and Davidson, L. (2005) 'Self and narrative in schizophrenia: time to author a new story', *Med Humanities*, 31: 89–94.

Ruchkin, V., Koposov, R., Vermerien, R. and Schwab-Stone, M. (2003) 'Psychopathology and age at onset of conduct problems in juvenile delinquents', *Journal of Clinical Psychology*, 64: 913–20.

Solomon, E. and Garside, R. (2008) *Ten Years of New Labour's Youth Justice Reforms: An Independent Audit*. London: Centre for Crime and Justice Studies.

Tarrier, N. (ed.) (2006) *Case Formulation in Cognitive Behaviour Therapy: The Treatment of Challenging and Complex Cases*. Abingdon: Routledge.

Tarrier, N. and Calam, R. (2002) 'New developments in cognitive behavioural therapy case formulation: epidemiological systemic and social context: an integrative approach', *Behavioural and Cognitive Psychotherapy*, 30: 311–28.

Tarrier, N., Lewis, S., Haddock, G., Bentall, R., Drake, R., Kinderman, P., Kingdon, D., Siddle, R., Everitt, J., Leadley, K., Benn, A., Grazebrook, K., Haley, C., Akhtar, S., Davies, L., Palmer, S. and Dunn, G. (2004) 'Cognitive-behavioural therapy in first-episode and early schizophrenia – 18-month follow-up of a randomised controlled trial', *British Journal of Psychiatry*, 184: 231–9.

Tarrier, N. and Wykes, T. (2004) 'Is there evidence that cognitive behaviour therapy is an effective treatment for schizophrenia? A cautious or cautionary tale?', *Behaviour Research and Therapy*, 42: 1377–401.

Teplin, L.A., Abram, K.M., McClelland, G.M., Dulcan, M.K. and Mericle, A.A. (2002). 'Psychiatric disorders in youth in juvenile detention', *Archives of General Psychiatry*, 59(12): 1133–43.

Wells, A. (1997) *Cognitive Therapy of Anxiety Disorders: A Practice Manual and Conceptual Guide*. Chichester: John Wiley & Sons.

Wykes, T., Steel, C., Everitt, B. and Tarrier, N. (2008) 'Cognitive behaviour therapy for schizophrenia: effect sizes, clinical models and methodological rigour', *Schizophrenia Bulletin*, 34: 523–37.

Youth Justice Board (2010) *Youth Justice System Custody Figures*. Available at: www.yjb.gov.uk/en-gb/yjs/Custody/CustodyFigures/

Zubin, J. and Spring, B. (1977) 'Vulnerability – A new view on schizophrenia', *Journal of Abnormal Psychology*, 86: 103–26.

Chapter 5

Cognitive analytic therapy with young adult offenders

Abigail Willis

Introduction

In March 2009 over nine thousand young adults (aged 18–20 years) were in custody in England and Wales (Ministry of Justice 2009).[1] This sizeable group presents very high levels of mental health concerns: an evaluation of 1,254 young male offenders aged 16–20 years under sentence found that 41 per cent exhibited significant neurotic concerns; that 4 per cent exhibited psychosis; and that 88 per cent met the criteria for a personality disorder (Lader *et al.* 2000). Their mental health concerns are compounded by the difficulties that they have experienced in the community, including alcohol and substance misuse, low levels of social support, low levels of employment, reduced engagement in training and education, accommodation concerns and financial difficulties (HMCIP 1997; Lader *et al.* 2000; Howard League for Penal Reform 2003, 2005a, 2005c). Many have experienced loss and abuse and have entered the 'looked after' system (HMCIP 1997; Lader *et al.* 2000; Howard League for Penal Reform 2005c). The group presents high rates of reoffending; nearly two thirds were reconvicted within two years (Howard League for Penal Reform 2005c; HMCIP 2006). Clearly young adult offenders present very high levels of social and psychological needs.

The transition into custody is identified as a particularly stressful time across prison populations, characterised by higher levels of self-injury and attempted suicide (HMPS 2004). The transition may be especially difficult for young adults. On entering custody approximately half strongly agreed that they experienced major feelings of distress and often felt depressed; nearly one third were concerned about their mental health (Harvey 2007). Reasons for a difficult transition include the prison environment, but also the developmental context; young adults are attempting to meet the demands of early adulthood including increasing independence, responsibilities and establishing identity (Cole and Cole 1989).

The young offender custodial environment has been recognised as deprived; Her Majesty's Chief Inspectorate of Prisons (1997) has suggested that overcrowding can lead to a breach of operating standards and to resource cuts which affect regime activities. Bullying has been recognised as highly prevalent in young adult offender establishments (HMCIP 1997; Ireland 2002). Moreover, many young people have reported feeling unsafe (Howard League for Penal Reform 2005b). There have been records of a high level of assaults both between young people, and by young people towards staff (Howard League for Penal Reform 2007).

People of this age group are in the process of moving to adulthood, and they can experience incarceration as an untimely separation from community support structures such as family and friends on which they usually rely. For other young people who are experiencing a poorly supported transition to independence in the community, custody can represent an opportunity for containment, for example in the routine, or in clear consequences for behaviour, and can represent an opportunity for their basic practical needs such as housing and food to be met. However, for these young people, there is also the risk of becoming reliant on institutional structures.

Identity development is a key aspect of adolescence and young adulthood (Cole and Cole 1989). During therapy, young people have reported that they perceive the experience of entering custody impacting on their identity as it develops. Custody isolates young people from wider relationships through which they might have the opportunity to engage in varied roles and status positions. Goffman (1961) refers to this isolation as 'role dispossession' (p. 124). During therapy young people have said that being in prison can be stigmatising: they can internalise people's identification of them as 'scum' or they perceive themselves as being 'the lowest of the low'. Others have emphasised that imprisonment reinforces identities that they have been developing in the community. Custody increases their exposure to a custodial peer group and culture and increases their allegiance with gangs and peer offenders from their local community. Furthermore, custody marks that their behaviour has reached a threshold and that they can withstand the severest sanctions that authorities have to offer. During therapy, young people have stated that custody will thus be recognised by an anti-social peer group as a maturational trophy, as a 'badge of honour'. Werthman (1967) interviewed boys in America and noted that for some of them incarceration marked to their peers 'evidence that they have paid and were willing to pay a more significant price for maintaining an identity' (p. 38). Their identity could become defined exclusively in relation to the authorities. Goffman (1961) writes that inmates may engage, or be under pressure to engage, in activities with symbolic implications which are in conflict with their identity; for example, in compliance with a regime they might find conflict with a belief that they should not allow themselves to be controlled by others, while being bullied might conflict with their identity as an aggressor. These identity conflicts can be of increased salience to young adults who are in the process of establishing their identity, exacerbating the impact of the transition into custody.

Understanding these various needs of young adult offenders within their custodial context and understanding how those needs can be addressed is clearly important to people charged with their care. Yet despite the overt importance of these needs within the criminal justice system there has been a failure to develop a comprehensive understanding of them. Indeed, 'young adult offenders have languished in a prison system which has no clear idea what to do with them, how best to meet their needs nor how to tackle re-offending' (Howard League for Penal Reform 2005b).

A thematic review by HMCIP in 1997 highlighted that 'institutions for young prisoners must recognise them as adolescents' (section 2.09). The 2001 Labour manifesto aimed to 'improve the standard of custodial accommodation and offending behaviour programmes for 18–20 year old offenders'. However, there is more recent evidence to suggest attention has been deflected from young offenders aged 18–21 years, and to suggest that they have received poorer services at all joint establishments (local prisons, split sites with adults and children; HMCIP 2006).

Failure to offer a positive experience of mental health services is likely to be a costly oversight, potentially resulting in a failure to affect the trajectory of psychological difficulties. Psychological difficulties may impair people's ability to undertake the transition into adult roles (DH 2004); it may be through undertaking some of these developmental tasks that young people disengage from offending (based on evidence from HMCIP 1997).

Engaging young adult offenders in mental health services

Young adult offenders are reluctant to seek support for mental health needs from statutory services. Anecdotal evidence would suggest a number of young people are offered contact with mental health services prior to their incarceration but do not engage with mental health services (Durcan 2008). Few young adult offenders voice their mental health needs at interview (HMCIP 2007) and only 29 per cent of young adult offenders are willing to seek emotional support from in-reach services (Harvey 2007). Traditional mental health services may not be seen as an accessible or acceptable means of support for young adult offenders.

These findings may reflect a pattern in the community, by which young adults are referred in proportionate numbers yet demonstrate higher levels of non-compliance at every point in the service, whether opt-in, assessment, therapy or planned discharge (Willis 2005). A community population of young men aged 13–30 years identified reasons for not engaging, including: difficulties in naming upsetting emotions, or the use of names which did not equate with mental health concerns; self-reliance associated with a concept of masculinity; the expectation that disclosure would be perceived as a weakness and attract criticism; a distrust of services and doubt in the efficacy of talking therapies (Halperin *et al.* 2008). An exploration of the culture of a young offender institution suggests additional barriers to engagement, including the need to maintain a strong veneer and to hide vulnerabilities (Harvey 2007). Harvey (2007) found that for young adult offenders, who had learned self-reliance, seeking support was not a usual means of coping; they did not anticipate that support would result in sustained benefits. Moreover, young people perceived costs in seeking support; costs which included stigmatisation, a lowered sense of worth, potential empowerment of others, a perceived affiliation with the institution and a burdening of others. Factors salient to young adult offenders when establishing supportive relationships included trust and the manner in which support was offered (Harvey 2007).

This chapter aims to consider what cognitive analytic therapy (CAT) offers when addressing the psychological difficulties of young people sentenced to custody, and the adaptations that are required to apply the approach. CAT is of likely benefit having been applied both to forensic populations (Pollock and Belshaw 1998; Pollock *et al.* 2006) and to young adult populations (Chanen *et al.* 2006; Jenaway and Mortlock 2008), to teams working with psychological difficulties

(Carradice 2004) and to psychologically damaging environments (Walsh 1996). CAT has begun to be recognised as a therapy model in prison establishments (see Mason 2008a and b).

Cognitive analytic therapy

Anthony Ryle developed CAT as an integrative psychotherapy meeting the needs of clients presenting within the National Health Service, a system which has limited resources (Ryle 1998). Its evolution has incorporated ideas from personal construct theory, object-relations theory, cognitive theory, activity theory and sign mediation. CAT provides a social model of the construction and experience of self. The key concepts utilised are described below (and the reader is referred to more detailed texts for the points at which the ideas rest on the listed models: Ryle 1990; Ryle and Kerr 2002).

Reciprocal role procedure

Through mutual engagement with a caregiver (or significant other) an infant develops templates for understanding and predicting the self and others; these templates are called reciprocal role procedures. The reciprocal role procedures include aspects derived from both the child and the parent, for example, ideas of both how to care and how to be cared for; ideas both of feeling bullied and of bullying. A repertoire of reciprocal patterns is usually internalised and it is these relationship experiences, in interaction with the biological temperament of the child, that influence what is internalised. However, for some individuals the range can be restricted due to overwhelming or depriving interpersonal experiences.

The reciprocal nature means that the self is always in dialogue with an aspect of the self or with another person. The enactment of a reciprocal role procedure can be internal (intra-personal) enabling self-management, for example, utilising an internal dialogue to soothe oneself or achieve comfort; or alternatively an enactment can be interpersonal, with another person, for example, seeking to care for another, or seeking to elicit care.

Psychological problems might reflect the enactment of reciprocal roles derived from care in early development which was harsh or neglectful. Difficulties might be long-standing and repetitive, as the person with such difficulties will not tend to graduate to a wider repertoire, due to the self-reinforcing reciprocations from others. As an individual adopts one pole of the pairing, the other person in the interaction will feel pressured to adopt the reciprocal pole. For example, when somebody becomes needy and overwhelmed, others may be pressured to adopt a rescuing position.

Procedural patterns trace the sequence of steps, which begins with an aim, an appraisal in terms of values, plans and predicted consequences, enactment, and the consequences of acting, followed by the confirmation or revision of the aim depending on the consequences. The enactment of a procedure moves an individual between different reciprocal role positions. Procedures frequently self-confirm the limited reciprocal role repertoire. For example, if it feels intolerable to think that I have been rejected, I aim to escape this position, and I assume that the only means to achieve this is to withdraw from others; but others then perceive me as rejecting them and so, ultimately, I feel more alone.

Self-repeating patterns

Ryle identified three particular self-repeating patterns from therapies: traps, snags and dilemmas.

Traps are negative beliefs that generate actions with consequences that confirm the original beliefs. For example, assuming that others are probably untrustworthy, I keep a watchful distance from others; I do not develop mutually trusting relationships; but others do not know my wishes and so are more likely to behave in a way I do not want; therefore, I continue to assume they are likely to be untrustworthy.

Snags are characterised by the abandonment of appropriate aims because of the prediction that their achievement will result in negative consequences. For example, I would like to engage in employment but assume that I am unlikely to be successful and so do not seek to find work, but return to offending.

Finally, dilemmas occur when the options for roles, choices or acts are restricted to false dichotomies where both alternatives are unsatisfactory and self-confirming. For example, either I am passive and mistreated by others, or I aggressively assert my wishes, bullying others in the process.

Self-reflection

Self-reflection is an important skill: the capacity to review one's engagement of reciprocal role procedures, to consider the consequences and to revise accordingly. Self-reflection is learnt through the experience of caregivers reflecting on oneself as a child. An individual develops signs (including language) which are symbols that convey meanings between people through their creation in social interaction. For example, a child may spontaneously pout while pushing away his food, and his mother may interpret the pout as conveying dissatisfaction and seek to placate him or her by removing the food. Over time the pout may become a sign between the two of them meaning 'Placate me now'. It is through these processes that an individual develops the capacity for language, internal thought and self-reflection.

Self states

Self states are reciprocal roles associated with a specific narrative, that is, specific cognitive and affective processes, disassociated from other roles and self states. The existence of dissociated self states can lead to a disintegrated sense of self, in which an individual is not fully aware of all the self states comprising the overall self. He or she will accordingly have a reduced capacity to reflect on different reciprocal role procedures in order to decide that which is most appropriate for implementation. Furthermore, he or she is less likely to revise them according to consequences. This can be associated with reduced reflection and a sense of discontinuity and unpredictability in the movement between different reciprocal role procedures.

In summary the cognitive analytic model uses a variety of psychological ideas to provide a description of a social development of personality, associated interpersonal and coping styles, and the means by which these are maintained.

What does cognitive analytic therapy involve?

CAT reflects the child's early learning relationship procedures: joint, collaborative activity and the creation, use and internalisation of tools enable initially supported activity to be internalised for eventual independent skill acquisition. Reference is made to Vygotsky's activity theory and zone of proximal development: 'what the child does with an adult today she will do on her own tomorrow' (Ryle and Kerr 2002).

The duration of therapy is brief but typically constitutes eight, 16 or 24 sessions, with additional follow-up sessions scheduled. The contract is agreed at the beginning of the therapy. Therapy can be understood as comprising three phases: reformulation, recognition and revision.

Reformulation

Reformulation is the focus of the first four to six sessions. During these sessions the therapist enquires widely about an individual's presenting concerns, early experiences and later relationship experiences (Moorey *et al.* 2006). The aim is to build a therapeutic relationship – including a working relationship but also likely to convey aspects of the reciprocal role procedures – to raise morale and to begin to develop an understanding of the difficulties within the relational history. The aim of the process is to identify an individual's target problems (the difficulties he or she wishes to address) and the self-reinforcing procedures within which the target problem is embedded and which contribute to those target problems (the target problem procedures) and the implicated reciprocal role procedures.

For example, a young person might raise concerns about their binge misuse of substances (target problem). Their substance misuse might be identified as part of a procedure comprising an aim (say, to escape from unmanageable feelings), an appraisal (the assumption that the only way of managing is to distract from, and to override, feelings), enactment (substance misuse and other functionally equivalent enactment behaviours, such as risk-taking behaviours), and the consequences of that behaviour (sanctions, withdrawal by other people, and an increased risk of harm to self). The reciprocal role in this example might include enactment of a reciprocal role of feeling wary and cautious in response to internal unsafe and unpredictable feelings.

A psychotherapy file can be used which enquires about different procedures, with provided examples of snags, traps, dilemmas, and about different states. The file encourages the client to adapt the wording, in order to collaborate in developing the individualised formulation. Versions of the psychotherapy file are available in both narrative and diagrammatic formats. Mood monitoring or other tools may be used to gain information. Client and therapist reflect on the information and then collaboratively develop the target problem procedures and reciprocal roles.

Tools generated within the therapy include a descriptive reformulation presented as a letter. This is usually drafted in sessions four to six. The descriptive reformulation identifies the individual's target problems (the difficulties they wish to address), the self reinforcing procedures which contribute to the target problems (that is, the target problem procedures), and the implicated reciprocal role procedures. The narrative outlines how early experiences have shaped current reciprocal role procedures and how they are currently maintained. The letter is written with an empathic style, aiming to provide a containing summary of the collaborative work undertaken. A sequential diagrammatic reformulation is also developed collaboratively in order to provide a diagrammatic representation of reciprocal roles and procedures, including the self-reinforcing patterns and their contribution to target problems. The diagram can provide a succinct summary of the understandings generated in the therapy and a reminder of triggers and of the consequences of familiar ways of responding.

Recognition

These tools, the reformulation letter and the diagram, together provide the support for accurate self-observation required for the recognition phase of therapy. The CAT therapist reflects on the therapeutic relationship and seeks to explore when the enactment of reciprocal role procedures is likely or is in fact occurring, in order to strive for a non-collusive and so new relationship experience. Recognition focuses on the reflective process of identifying enactments of reciprocal role and target problem procedures within and outside the therapy.

Revision

Revision occurs from the internalisation of a new reciprocal role procedure developed through the experience of therapy. This internalisation enables a new inner dialogue and an integration of what may be a fragmented procedural system. In addition the client is encouraged to identify exits from the self-reinforcing procedures, exits which might support the development of new reciprocal role procedures. The range of techniques which might be used to facilitate an exit is not model dependent, and so can be derived from a range of psychological approaches.

The end of therapy is addressed by the exchange of goodbye letters; these letters seek to address what has been achieved, what remains to be worked at and the feelings around the ending. The letter can be used as a reminder of areas agreed for continued work after the end of weekly contracted sessions. Reviews are usually offered after the therapy to evaluate and support maintenance of the work.

CAT has only limited exclusion criteria. Exclusion has been defined by significant impairment in the verbal and sequential logic skills required to undertake the therapy, usually due to very significant brain injury, psychosis or cognitive deficits, or current alcohol/substance misuse (Pollock and Belshaw 1998). Recent practice examples indicate that engagement in the process can still be facilitated by attentiveness and foundation work addressing areas of deficits required to undertake the therapy (see Ryle and Kerr 2002; Yeates *et al.* 2008). The therapy aims to increase the scope of individuals able to benefit by taking account of the zone of proximal development and initiating the skills of working in therapy in the initial phases. Determining suitability among the young offender custodial population also involves consideration of the available time frame within which a young person can engage in therapy – a number are serving short sentences or likely to undergo transfer to other establishments. Other considerations include the motivation of the young person to engage in a regular focused therapy and whether he is in a sufficiently secure position to engage in reflective work (e.g. not experiencing significant bullying, further court appearances).

The following sections aim to illustrate the utility of the approach, and adaptations required, in providing CAT to young adult offenders in custody.

Cognitive analytic therapy reformulation with young adult offenders

Using reciprocal role procedures to predict therapy engagement

CAT allows for an early reflection on the reciprocal roles and procedures that young people enact in custody and which may impact on their engagement with mental health services and in therapy. Frequently encountered reciprocal roles are battling, rebellious and undefeated in response to unrelenting constraints and control, with a feared position of being defeated and crushed, and being abandoned, forgotten and alone with others distant or absent. The reciprocal roles may reflect roles emphasised in the wider custodial environment, such as the roles controlling–controlled and inattentive–devalued. Reflection on these roles can be used to make predictions about the therapeutic relationship, and likely threats to it, and can highlight some of the client's fears about engaging in therapy, for example that the work will lead to increased vulnerability and weakness.

The therapist and young person collaboratively consider fears about engaging and this allows for a flexible and responsive containment in how the therapy proceeds.

Using reformulation to assess factors impacting on motivation

Early reformulation work can also increase motivation as young people develop an awareness of the impact of their behaviour on both themselves and others, and its self-reinforcing nature. Reframing challenging behaviours by focusing on aims, restricted repertoires and self-limiting patterns can increase motivation by enabling collaboration rather than a direct challenge. Some young men exploring the development of reciprocal role procedures voice their disappointment with, and resentment towards, their own caregivers, and highlight their motivation to ensure that they do not have a negative impact on their real or future children (20 per cent of young men in custody are fathers; Howard League for Penal Reform 2005b). The costs of change may also become more evident as they note the hidden reinforcements provided by some reciprocal role positions, for example, when bullying enables them to feel powerful and to avoid the bullied position.

Forming a scaffold through tools to increase self-reflection

Attentiveness to the language and metaphors used during reformulation allows the mirroring of language and signs which are acceptable to both parties, and this mirroring can be a means of joint understanding. Commonly young people will initially deny feelings of anxiety, due to the tendency in custody to equate such feelings negatively with vulnerability and weakness. However, young people may accept the use of the terms 'edgy' or 'on guard' as phrases which allude to feelings that they do not wish to be more precisely named during the initial discourse. Terms such as 'aggressive' or 'angry' may be tolerated early in the therapy, where later more descriptive terms such as 'bullying' or 'sadistic' may be more appropriate and accepted.

The process of appraising the zone of proximal development means that, during reformulation, it is possible to attend to difficulties without accessing dreaded or overwhelming feelings too early on. The establishment in therapy of the joint tools of the sequential diagrammatic reformulation and the reformulation letter forms scaffolding within which a young person can develop increased confidence and curiosity in self reflection, extending the zone of proximal development.

Negotiating with young people about where they wish to keep the tools is necessary. Many young people do not feel able to keep these tools on the wing due to concerns about confidentiality, or they require specific assistance in keeping them protected. The therapist works with young people to consider their safety while engaging in therapy, actively helping them to manage concerns such as returning to the wing after accessing upsetting feelings.

Reformulation in practice

To consider reformulation more closely, it helps to examine a case study of a composite, fictitious sort. The case example of 'Sam' comprises elements from real clinical examples, but is a composite from many of them, so it does not identify any one client.

Sam, aged 19 years, was referred for assessment of his suitability for therapy by his care coordinator. The care coordinator identified a history of aggressive and self-injurious behaviour, low mood, negative self-identity and the experience of an internal voice directing him to harm others. His functioning in custody was marked by high levels of social withdrawal and limited engagement with activities.

Sam was the elder of two children born to his mother and father. His father was domestically violent. His parents separated when Sam was five years old, due to his father forming a new relationship; his father resided in the local community but did not maintain contact. His mother experienced depression, engaged in alcohol misuse and twice attempted to kill herself. She referred to him as the 'little man' in lieu of his father. Sam saw his mother mistreated by partners, some of whom were also physically abusive to him. The family experienced significant financial and housing difficulties. Sam spent a brief period in residential care after he assaulted a partner of his mother during a family argument.

At school Sam was bullied; his academic performance was marred by difficulties in concentrating and by low attendance. Within the school environment he presented sporadic aggressive behaviour towards peers; over the course of his development the severity of the risk behaviour increased. He received a warning when he was found in possession of a weapon, and received exclusion after an assault on a teacher. He subsequently engaged in increasing cannabis use.

At 17 years of age, after an increase in disputes with his sister, his mother asked him to move out. Sam lived in a supported hostel for young people. He attended college but at 18 years of age he was convicted for severely assaulting a man aged 27 who regularly visited the hostel. The staff had been concerned the man was forming exploitative relationships with women at the hostel.

Sam expressed anger towards his father and a desire to punish him for harming his mother. He highlighted a wish to protect and provide for his mother and sister, and to hide his needs in order to ensure others did not worry about him. He raised concern that his aggressive behaviour was escalating and he saw that his behaviour was not fully under his control. He stated that he was unsure what he could expect to gain from attending therapy.

An initial six-session contract was agreed with Sam in order to complete reformulation work. The aim of this reformulation work was to develop a joint understanding, to enable Sam to try out therapeutic work and, from this position, to enable him to consider whether he wished to complete further individual therapy. Acknowledgement was made of the potential risks of reformulation through reflection on hard-to-manage states and feelings. Sam's use of emotional distance as a means of self-management was acknowledged as a means of flexibly managing reformulation work.

Sam engaged in providing the information to aid the process of developing the sequential diagrammatic reformulation but he maintained an emotional distance from the content and passivity in developing ideas. He expressed anxiety about the vulnerability that might result from openly exploring the difficulties in a relationship. Four predominant reciprocal roles were recorded (detailed in Table 5.1). It was acknowledged that the roles might not be fully conveyed in the words used but that these words were the signs currently acceptable at this stage of therapy.

Identification of the reciprocal roles enabled conversation about what roles were reinforced in the different settings of community, custody and therapy. He experienced less opportunity to adopt the 'hero' position in custody and more often was positioned in 'alone' and 'rejected'. A risk of aggression was noted whereby he might seek to enact the 'terminator' position if he perceived himself as 'bullied' or under threat. A risk of self-injury might be most probable if he felt that he was failing in his coping or in his support of others that depended on him in the community. The reciprocal roles identified were developed into reciprocal role procedures. These are detailed in Figures 5.1, 5.2 and 5.3.

Identification of reciprocal role procedures contextualised the difficulties outlined at referral. Sam's presenting concerns became psychologically congruent responses to his learning experiences. His

Table 5.1 Predominant reciprocal roles

	'Terminator' Powerful Ruthless —— Respectful Defeated	'Hero' Protective Provider —— Loyal Cared for Appreciative	Abandoning Unreliable Caught up in own problems —— Alone Unsafe 'In the shadows'	Rejecting Bullying —— Bullied Rejected Humiliated 'Lowest of the low'
Reciprocal role				
Historical example	Aggressive behaviour directed towards adults and peers perceived as a threat	Protection to younger sister and mother Fantasy of what a father figure might have offered The 'little man'	Lack of appropriate parental support Social avoidance and isolation	Observation of domestic violence Rejection by father Experience of bullying Aggressive behaviour
Current example	Internal voice at times of perceived threat Belief that he can ultimately protect himself due to ruthless actions		Social withdrawal on wing Wing staff distracted by other concerns	Self-injury associated with denigrating self-talk and self-punishment
Transference example		Protect therapist from extent of undisclosed feelings	Assumption that the limits of therapy will be insufficient or insecure	Instances when enquiry experienced as criticising

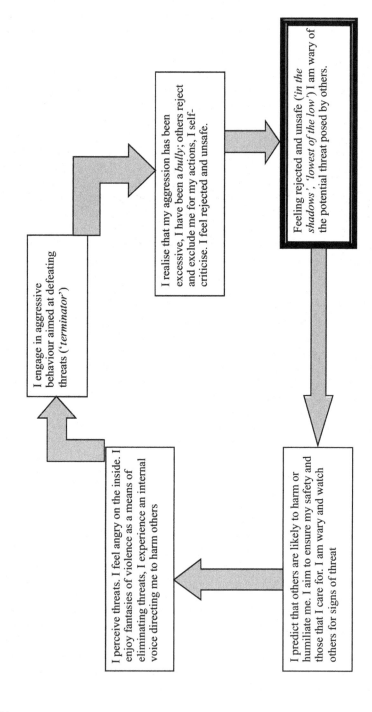

Figure 5.1 Aggression trap

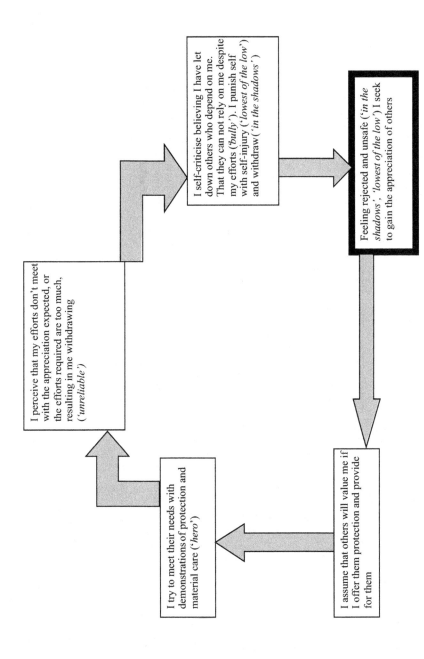

Figure 5.2 Caring for others trap

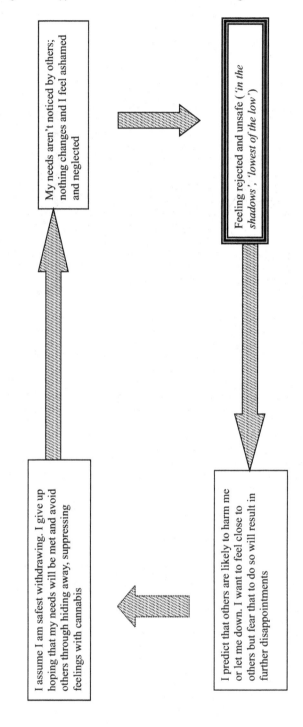

Figure 5.3 Avoidance snag

ambivalence about engaging in mental health services and therapy could be understood both as his usual means of coping and as a reluctance to use interpersonal support. The reformulation process provided the opportunity to evaluate what an integrative therapy might offer, and the means of developing ideas for increasing understanding and change.

Cognitive analytic therapy recognition with young adult offenders

The recognition phase of CAT requires the client to apply the jointly developed model of their difficulties, and of their identified reciprocal roles and their procedures, to their experiences both within and outside the therapy. Through conversations mapping the understandings, the young person undertakes a reflective process and develops reflective skills.

A collaborative investigation of the working model developed and factors associated

The process of reviewing the working model which the client and therapist have developed allows them to collaborate in investigating the influential factors which the research literature has identified as relevant to young adult offenders. In the case of Sam, substance misuse might be part of an intrapersonal procedure around affect regulation; the use of violence might be part of the behavioural enactment of an interpersonal reciprocal role procedure. More generally, identity and role models are mirrored in the restricted roles enacted. Peer groups take on particular reciprocal role positions. By addressing recognition of the model the young person considers how factors are intertwined with the working model.

Addressing therapy ruptures

Therapeutic ruptures occur as the reciprocal role procedures are enacted within the therapeutic relationship. Recognising and attending to enactments have been associated with more positive therapy outcomes (Bennett *et al.* 2006). When ruptures in the therapeutic relationship occur, the understandings and tools are a means of actively addressing them and learning from them. Bennett *et al.* (2006) identify a number of the stages in the process including acknowledgement, exploration, linking and explanation, negotiation, consensus, new ways of relating and closure. In custody, ruptures sometimes occur due to barriers in the custodial environment; for example an escort is not available to bring a young person to an appointment. Clients and therapists can discuss the therapeutic barriers which the environment raises and, where possible, can solve these problems and reflect upon the reality of the young person's situation.

Recognition as increasing self-reflection and addressing cognitive functioning linked with offending

Many young offenders' early experiences did not provide a relationship which facilitated their ability to reflect on their experiences and responses (see Day *et al.* 2008 research reviewing literature pertaining to children in custody). Young offenders' cognitive functioning has been observed to include impulsivity and low levels of social perspective taking and reflection (Ross and Fabiano 1985). Impulsivity can be an obstacle for achieving desired change and can result in early termination of therapy. Recognition in CAT can begin to develop the individual's capacity to reflect on the consequences of one's actions; recognition, and the associated development of a capacity for self-reflection, represent the beginning of exits from reciprocal role procedures.

Self-reflection is usually retrospective at first, but over time it can be used to generate the capacity to reflect on oneself *in situ* and in anticipation of how one might react to a given state or aim. For example, the diagram (see Figure 5.1, p. 116) was used by Sam to consider, 'I am feeling alone and unsafe; how do I often respond to entering this reciprocal role?' The tools provide an indication of where the enactment of a procedure might lead; this indication can help the young person to begin to consider the consequences of usual patterns of responding for them and others. (Notably some clinicians have highlighted how these initial skills can facilitate risk management, see Shannon 2008.)

Cognitive analytic therapy revision (developing exits) with young adult offenders

Identification of exits from self-reinforcing procedures

Exits are usually developed by reflecting on, and recognising, procedural patterns both within and outside therapy. The means by which exits are generated and learnt is not therapy specific; rather the exits are developed in negotiation between the therapist and the client. For example, exits might comprise a different means of:

1 achieving an aim, for example achieving the respect of others through alternative behaviour;
2 appraisal, for example the reappraisal of assumptions (such as 'expecting me to wait is to disrespect me');
3 forming plans and predicted consequences, for example developing new skills;
4 recognising the consequences of acting, for example developing an awareness of the impact of one's behaviour on oneself and others.

Returning to Sam, exits from the patterns might include acknowledging and developing wider ways to gain respect and value. He might reappraise his hypervigilance and assumption that other people pose a threat, discriminating more carefully between cues in order to establish when this is likely. He might learn new behavioural skills in handling interpersonal situations and conflicts, and these skills would offer alternative means of managing threatening situations and of managing his own needs and his internal world, with less avoidance and suppression. The process of bonding, rupture and repair during therapy could be a relational experience through which to learn how to recover from conflict and mis-attunement, for example, to learn to tolerate, to integrate and to regulate feelings (see Bristow 2006).

Having received advice and intervention prior to therapy, young people commonly have an awareness of potential exits. Without sufficient recognition skills to implement these exits appropriately, or at a point when they have enough reflective capacity, this knowledge of exits remains redundant. CAT focuses on recognition and on increasing the zone of proximal development and can increase the implementation of previously rehearsed but unimplemented skills.

Identification, experience and internalisation of a new reciprocal role procedure

Within the therapeutic relationship, stepping outside the self-reinforcing patterns can offer *in vivo* learning of a different relationship style. Reflecting on the experience of therapy, many young people identify the therapy relationship as an experience offering them solidarity, respect and value, sometimes in contrast to other relationship patterns in custody. Reflection on their engagement in this new reciprocal role *within* therapy – on how they experience it and how it impacts on them – is a means of developing a template for a different means of relating both to themselves and others *outside* therapy.

This process of considering which new reciprocal roles could be worked towards often parallels young adults' other developmental tasks, as it offers an explicit consideration of their identity, and of the identities that they might wish to develop. For example, Sam might suggest that he would like to develop a sense of value and integrity. Conversations offer a chance to consider which experiences would facilitate this development, and which are the factors in his life which inhibit it. The therapeutic relationship itself would aim to model for him the processes of both offering and receiving value and integrity.

Contextual challenges for achieving change: the role for consultation and systemic approach

Does CAT bring about change for young people in custody? The present author completed a small audit of the outcomes for eight young people who had undertaken CAT while in custody. The results showed that almost all young people felt that they had an improved understanding of their difficulties: half of them rated their understanding of their difficulties as 'a lot better' and three as a 'bit better'. The majority felt that they had an improved understanding of what might assist in achieving change: two indicated this as 'a lot better' and five 'a bit better'. Their ratings for implementing such changes were slightly lower: only one considered his ability to implement change 'a lot better' and five 'a bit better'. As Smail (2001) noted, 'one should not ... underestimate the value psychotherapy might have as a means of clarifying [the client's] situation ... but nor should one overestimate its ability to change them' (p. 351).

The results of this small audit suggest that the strongest benefits were in understanding concerns. Importantly, none of the young people indicated a negative outcome from the therapeutic input. The findings bear the caveat that all the therapies were undertaken by a single therapist, and that adherence to the CAT model was not measured. Also, the measurements only incorporated subjective ratings, only observed small differences and were not statistically assessed. However, other studies have also suggested that CAT may need to improve more in the revision process (Marriott *et al.* 2007). The finding is also likely to reflect some of the difficulties undertaking revision in a custodial environment.

The introduction to this chapter referred to some of the social and environmental characteristics of young adult offender custodial settings, including bullying and deprivation and a culture in which vulnerability is hidden. Goffman (1961) highlights features of relationships between staff and inmates in total institutions and notes the prevalence of social distance and stereotyping and the implications of 'batch living' (p. 22). Nieland *et al.* (2001) explored coping styles in custody and found that the expression of aggressive impulses and insincere engagement in social relationships were protective: 'the culture within which incarcerated young offenders live is one in which factors that protect an individual from psychological distress might ordinarily (in a non-incarcerated population) be considered antisocial' (p. 42). It is a challenge for CAT to encourage clients to risk new ways of relating to people and to internalise a healthy reciprocal role outside therapy in what is often an unhealthy environment; that wider environment often does not offer naturalistic reinforcement for change.

Revision work includes consideration whether and how young people intend to implement exits in custody and upon release, for example, by considering with the young person the systemic contexts that inhibit or reinforce change, such as the prison staff, family, peers, other mental health professionals and wider agencies. These conversations may establish whether it would be beneficial to consult with people in the wider system who work with the client and their family, in order to help them to plan how they will continue work upon release. For example, Sam may require the wider custodial staff to be aware that he is attempting to develop different communication skills so that those skills are appropriately reinforced.

Kerr *et al.* (2007) highlight the need for 'psychologically informed management' (p. 64) by mental health teams which work with clients who show severe and complex difficulties. Mental health team members can experience stress, splitting and burnout when attempting to support these clients, and prison staff may experience similar difficulties. Prison officers receive only minimal training in the mental health needs of people in custody, and they often have numerous competing demands in managing a regime for a large number of young adults. CAT is increasingly applied to teams to develop an understanding of, and psychologically informed means of working with, clients who present complex concerns (Carradice 2004). The reformulation derived from individual work can be shared with the team, or the reciprocal roles and enactments can be mapped with people working in the wider system. This process may reduce the likelihood that the wider system reinforces or colludes with reciprocal role procedures associated with the concerns being addressed by therapy.

Although these avenues can be rewarding, there are challenges to working in this manner, including physical distance, lack of familiarity with local service providers and complex family networks. Moreover, only 12 per cent of mental health in-reach teams report genuine cooperative working with residential staff in the management of prisoners (HMCIP 2007; see also Mills and Kendall, Chapter 2, this book).

The need for a flexible application of the cognitive analytic therapy model and tools

Moving between reformulation, recognition and revision

Therapy would usually proceed from sufficient reformulation to sufficient recognition to revision. However, maintaining engagement with some young adults requires amendment of the model. An exploration of therapy with young adults who were leaving care observed that some young people found the initial reformulation process too shaming and likely to provoke unmanageable states and reciprocal roles (Jenaway 2006). In these situations, a possible means of maintaining engagement is to use only a limited reformulation derived earlier and based on current experiences. Jenaway (2006) highlights that focusing on aims and potential exits can facilitate a client's sense of control of disclosure and engagement in the therapeutic relationship, and the enactment of more positive reciprocal roles, as resilience and other strengths are emphasised. However, revision work without sufficient reformulation and recognition is less likely to be sufficient for achieving the desired change, as young people may not have established the recognition skills to implement the exits effectively. Nevertheless, it is possible to return to these areas over the course of the therapy, as the therapeutic alliance strengthens and as the potential risks of the relationship fragmenting reduce.

Creative methods

Creative ways of communicating and engaging young adults in the tasks of therapy can be beneficial. Many young adults lack confidence in literacy-based tools. It is possible to develop their understanding and recognition of the working model through pictures, colours, facial expressions and body language, creative writing, the voicing of reciprocal roles, and mask work in order to explore different reciprocal roles and states. One way to reduce the demands of literacy during the process is to use captions, such as 'terminator', 'in the shadows' or 'happy bubble' (personal communication with young people during therapy), to refer to positions on the sequential diagrammatic formulation. A different way of completing a goodbye letter might be writing a rap or drawing a picture. The strategies used should be considered in collaboration with the individual young adult, in order to reflect their strengths and interests.

Consultation to the young offender institution

CAT has been used to understand psychologically harmful working environments: it has been used to explore the relating styles of individuals and groups; to explore the procedures enacted in the working environment; and to consider useful approaches to ameliorating these procedures (Walsh 1996). The theoretical analysis has been applied to the forensic environment of a special hospital (Stowell-Smith 2006). It may, then, be of interest to apply the model to understanding the young offender institution – to understanding what might contribute to a psychologically harmful environment, and how such an environment might be ameliorated.

Ethical considerations

The strengths of the approach include its broadly based understanding of difficulties, its flexibility and the adaptability of its structure. These strengths also raise ethical considerations. Many young adults who attend are ambivalent and uncertain about what they want to gain from therapy. It is necessary to strike a balance between adapting the process so that it facilitates further therapeutic work, and ensuring that a young person wishes to progress the therapy accordingly. An ongoing enquiry is required in order to establish that individuals are consenting to the directional moves of the therapy.

There is also a conflict between increasing adaptability and a reduced adherence to practice that is empirically based. The research base for CAT is still being developed, and the current research is dominated by scientific methods that are acknowledged to be less rigorous than randomised control trials. Moreover, when adaptations are made to the structure of CAT, the relationship with this evidence becomes further fragmented. Therefore, more work is required to evaluate the effectiveness of CAT, its applicability with specific populations and the acceptability of adapting its methods.

Conclusion

Young adult offenders present with a wide range of psychological needs. CAT offers a means of responding to the individual needs and resources of young people, and does so within a structured framework that helps them understand the multiple difficulties they have experienced. CAT also acknowledges the importance of the current and historical social context of these difficulties. The approach can be used to develop change and also to support systemic intervention and consultation. Importantly, aspects of the approach can be used to enhance the client's engagement and motivation which, if not attended to, might have impeded the therapeutic endeavour.

Note

1 Figure includes those 21-year-olds who were aged 20 or under at conviction who have not been reclassified as part of the adult population.

References

Bennett, D., Parry, G. and Ryle, A. (2006) 'Resolving threats to the therapeutic alliance in cognitive analytic therapy of borderline personality disorder: A task analysis', *Psychology and Psychotherapy*, 79(3): 395–418.

Bristow, J. (2006) 'Change of state: Learning how to manage unmanageable feelings and states', *Reformulation*. Available at www.acat.me.uk/catclientview.php

Carradice, A. (2004) 'A case study describing group staff consultation to help care planning for a client in the inpatient service', *Reformulation*. Available at www.acat.me.uk/catclientview.php

Chanen A., Jackson, H.J. and McCutcheon, L. (2006) 'A randomised controlled trial of psychotherapy for early intervention in borderline personality disorder', *Acta Neuropsychiatrica*, 18(6): 319.

Cole, M. and Cole, S. (1989) *The Development of Children*. New York: Scientific American Books.

Day, C., Hibbert, P. and Cadman, S. (2008) *A Literature Review into Children Abused and/or Neglected Prior to Custody*. London: Youth Justice Board.

Department of Health (2004) *National Service Framework for Children, Young People and Maternity Services*. London: Department of Health.

Durcan, G. (2008) *From the Inside: Experiences of Prison Mental Health Care*. London: Sainsbury Centre for Mental Health Care.

Goffman, E. (1961) *Asylums: Essays on the Social Situation of Mental Patients and Other Inmates*. London: Penguin.

Halperin, J., Leibowitz, J., Crocker, L., Gsödl, M., Campbell, J., Parrett, N. and Underhill, J. (2008) 'So who is avoiding whom? Bridging the gap between young men and mental health professionals', *Clinical Psychology Forum*, 191: 25–9.

Harvey, J. (2007) *Young Men in Prison: Surviving and Adapting to Life Inside*. Cullompton: Willan Publishing.

HMCIP (1997) *Young Prisoners: A Thematic Review by HM Chief Inspector of Prisons for England and Wales*. London: Home Office.

HMCIP (2006) *Young Adult Male Prisoners: A Short Thematic Report*. London: HM Inspectorate of Prisons.

HMCIP (2007) *The Mental Health of Prisoners: A Thematic Review of the Care and Support of Prisoners with Mental Health Needs*. London: HM Inspectorate of Prisons.

HMPS (2004) *Recorded Self-Harm in the Prison Service. Safer Custody Group Research Briefing 2*. London: Safer Custody Group.

Howard League (2003) *Busy Doing Nothing: Young Men on Remand*. London: Howard League Trust for Penal Reform.

Howard League (2005a) *The Key to the Future? The Housing Needs of Young Adults in Prison*. London: Howard League Trust for Penal Reform.

Howard League (2005b) *A Sobering Thought: Young Men in Prison. Research briefing 1*. London: Howard League Trust for Penal Reform.

Howard League (2005c) *Young Neglected and Back: Young Men in Prison. Research briefing 2*. London: Howard League Trust for Penal Reform.

Howard League (2007) *News Release: Imprisoned Children Trapped in 'Hotbeds of Violence'*. London: Howard League Trust for Penal Reform.

Ireland, J. (2002) *Bullying Among Prisoners: Evidence, Research and Intervention Strategies*. Hove: Brunner-Routledge.

Jenaway, A. (2006) 'CAT with teenagers and teenagers leaving care'. *Reformulation*. Available at www.acat.me.uk/catclientview.php

Jenaway, A. and Mortlock, D. (2008) 'Service innovation: Offering cognitive analytic therapy in a child and adolescent mental health service', *Reformulation*. Available at www.acat.me.uk/catclientview.php

Kerr, I.B., Dent-Brown, K. and Parry, G.D. (2007) 'Psychotherapy and mental health teams', *International Review of Psychiatry*, 19(1): 63–80.

Labour Party (2001) Labour Party General Election Manifesto. *Ambitions for Britain*. London: Labour Party.

Lader, D., Singleton, N. and Meltzer, H. (2000) *Psychiatric Morbidity among Young Offenders in England and Wales*. London: Office for National Statistics.

Marriott, M., Kellett, S. with a comment by Ryle, T. (2007) 'Generating practice-based evidence for CAT', *Reformulation*. Available at www.acat. me.uk/catclientview.php

Mason, K. (2008a) 'Providing primary care psychological services in prison using a stepped care model. Improving Access to Psychological Therapies (IAPT) in Prison. Conference by Department of Health, National Offender Management Service, Ministry of Justice and HM Prison Service. Manchester, UK.

Mason, K. (2008b) 'Implementing CAT as part of the stepped care model in HMP Liverpool'. Celebrating 10+ years of CAT Training: Innovations in the Application of Cognitive Analytic Therapy. Manchester, UK.

Ministry of Justice (2009) *Population in Custody Monthly Tables March 2009 England and Wales. Ministry of Justice Statistical Bulletin.* London: Ministry of Justice.

Moorey, J., Davidson, K., Evans, M. and Feigenbaum, J. (2006) *'Psychological therapies for personality disorder'*, in M.J. Sampson, R.A. McCubbin and P. Tyrer (eds), *Personality Disorder and Community Mental Health Teams.* Chichester: John Wiley & Sons.

Nieland, M.N.S., McCluskie, C. and Tait, E. (2001) 'Prediction of psychological distress in young offenders', *Legal and Criminological Psychology*, 6: 29–47.

Pollock, P. and Belshaw, T. (1998) 'Cognitive analytic therapy for offenders', *The Journal of Forensic Psychiatry*, 9(3): 629–42.

Pollock, P.H., Stowell-Smith, M. and Göpfert, M. (eds) (2006) *Cognitive Analytic Therapy for Offenders: A New Approach to Forensic Psychotherapy.* Abingdon: Routledge.

Ross, R.R. and Fabiano, E.A. (1985) *Time to Think: A Cognitive Model of Delinquency Prevention and Offender Rehabilitation.* Johnson City, TN: Institute of Social Sciences and Arts.

Ryle, A. (1990) *Cognitive Analytic Therapy: Active Participation in Change.* Chichester: John Wiley & Sons.

Ryle, A. (1998) 'The whirligig of time', *Psychiatric Bulletin*, 22: 263–7.

Ryle, A. and Kerr, I.B. (2002) *Introducing Cognitive Analytic Therapy: Principles and Practice.* Chichester: John Wiley & Sons.

Shannon, K. (2008) 'Using what we know: Cognitive analytic therapy's contribution to risk assessment and collaborative risk management'. Celebrating 10+ years of CAT Training: Innovations in the Application of Cognitive Analytic Therapy. Manchester, UK.

Smail, D. (2001) *Why Therapy Doesn't Work and What We Should Do About It.* London: Robinson.

Stowell-Smith, M. (2006) 'States and reciprocal roles in the wider understanding of forensic mental health', in P.H. Pollock, M. Stowell-Smith and M. Göpfert (eds) *Cognitive Analytic Therapy for Offenders: A New Approach to Forensic Psychotherapy.* Abingdon: Routledge.

Walsh, S. (1996) 'Adapting cognitive analytic therapy to make sense of psychologically harmful work environments', *British Journal of Medical Psychology*, 69: 3–20.

Werthman, C. (1967) 'The function of social definitions in the development of delinquent careers', cited in P.G. Garabedian and D.C. Gibbons (eds) (2006), *Becoming delinquent: Young Offenders and the Correctional Process.* New Brunswick: Transaction Publishers.

Willis, A. (2005) 'Comparing the compliance rate of young adults (aged 16–25 years) with the general adult population', *Clinical Psychology*, 47: 29–33.

Yeates, G., Hamill, M., Sutton, L., Psaila, K., Gracey, F., Mohamed, S. and O'Del, J. (2008) 'Dysexecutive problems and interpersonal relating following frontal brain injury: Reformulation and compensation in cognitive analytic therapy (CAT)', *Neuro-Psychoanalysis*, 10(1): 43–58.

Chapter 6

Systemic psychotherapy in prison

David Shelton

This chapter examines the use of systemic psychotherapy in prison. The chapter begins by outlining the development of the practice of systemic and family psychotherapy from the 1950s to the present day. It provides a brief overview of the literature on systemic practice in prisons and forensic mental health settings. The chapter describes a number of key systemic concepts underpinning the author's practice with young people in prison and ends by presenting a case vignette demonstrating the application of these concepts.

A brief history and context

Systemic and family therapy has developed since the 1950s and consists of a number of approaches and concepts (see Dallos and Draper 2005). Hitherto, its practice has largely been confined to community outpatient settings, as opposed to the type of challenging secure settings described in this book.

Cybernetics, and the study of robotics, was at the heart of western society's development during the 1950s. Two World Wars and an economic depression had led to a demand for luxury household items that required mass production, and the automisation of labour was key to this process. Underpinning this process was the reliance on automated, semi-independent mini-systems that could work more or less independently of each other but could combine in order to produce cars, television sets or washing machines. The 'systems' part, then, of 'systemic psychotherapy' has its roots in this period and refers directly to this idea that human behaviour, and that of families in particular, could be understood in terms of a number of mini- or sub-systems such as parents or siblings, combining to create a whole system (the family). Much of the language and terminology of early systemic schools of thought was linked directly to this notion of engineering systems, and proponents wrote about behaviour in terms of 'feedback mechanisms', while the interventions were clearly thought about in terms of engineering. Indeed, the therapist would 'restructure' the family in order to change the nature of the interactions that were thought to be sustaining the unwanted behaviour; or the therapist would devise certain 'strategies' for the family members to follow in order to upset the 'equilibrium' or 'homoeostasis' that was maintaining the problem. Gregory Bateson, who was a pioneer in the field of systemic psychotherapy, took many of the concepts from the field of engineering and transplanted them into the field of psychology and human behaviour. His early work was concerned with the idea that an individual's mental illness could be understood in terms of the wider family system, and this work, published in the 1950s, laid the foundation for future schools of systemic practice (Bateson et al. 1956).

The structural therapy movement of the 1960s and early 1970s, largely credited to the pioneering work of Salvador Minuchin (Minuchin et al. 1967), advocated looking for organisational patterns within families in order to create change within the therapy session. The strategic therapists of the 1970s, led by Jay Hayley, were more interested in the patterns of interaction around problematic behaviours and intervened with tasks and directives to help change these patterns. For strategic family therapists, change was expected to happen outside of the session.

The Milan and post-Milan schools of thought of the late 1970s and early 1980s (Selvini-Palazzoli et al. 1978) saw a shift in emphasis to eliciting patterns of beliefs within families, between families and agencies, and so on. The Milan therapists intervened by challenging beliefs and enabling family members to see different patterns emerging. Change was expected to be unpredictable.

By the 1990s, the main systemic school of thought was underpinned by the ideas of constructivism, typified by the co-construction with the therapist of an individual's story about his or her experience of the world; the emergence of the reflecting team, working typically with what the client may bring to the session. Leading authors and practitioners of this period were Karl Tomm (USA), Tom Andersen (Norway) and David Campbell (UK). From the late 1990s to the present day, the main systemic school of thought has been underpinned by the philosophy of social constructionism (the idea that all information is socially constructed) in which the therapist works to return the power for change to the client, with less emphasis on technique and more on thinking about the position of the therapist and how he or she can usefully connect to the client and client's system.

Thus, over the six decades or so in which systemic psychotherapy has developed, there has been a radical shift from the early practices, in which the therapist was clearly the expert and would be seen as being responsible for bringing about change, to current practice in which the therapist 'joins' with the family, individual, or couple in order to empower them to realise change. This may involve the therapist taking the 'expert' position, but that position is the only one of a number open to the therapist.

The author's work context

This chapter is based on the work of the author in a large young offender institution (YOI) in England. The prison detains approximately 600 males aged 15 to 21 years. These young people have either been remanded into custody, are awaiting sentencing, or are serving a relatively short-term sentence (up to two years). In common with the majority of remand centres in the UK, this institution has an unsettled feel to it: each day up to 100 young prisoners are transported from prison to court for various legal procedures (sentencing, plea and directions). The uncertainty of the young person's future makes for an uneasy alliance between the young prisoners and the staff, and there is a temporary feel about much of the prison (see Harvey 2007). The prison has an inpatient mental health care wing which also experiences this uncertainty. There is a total of 15 inpatient beds on this unit, and there is a dedicated multi-disciplinary team (MDT) of nurses, psychiatrists, psychologists, occupational therapists, arts therapists who provide treatment and care to this group. If the young person is discharged back into the prison (on 'ordinary location') he is followed up by a member of the in-house community mental health team (CMHT). If there are mental health concerns or the young person cannot be managed on 'ordinary location' by his unit's officers or the CMHT, then he is referred to the inpatient mental health unit for an initial assessment. Thus the service functions in much the same way as does a child and adolescent mental health (CAMH) service.

One of the biggest challenges to providing therapy in prison is to respect the context in which the therapist is operating and yet simultaneously to bring a difference to the lives of the young people who are being looked after. This tension between the role of 'custodian' and 'carer' has been well documented (Shapiro 1988; Greenberg and Shuman 1997) and can often lead to polarised and frozen positions by both prison officers (custodians) and mental health workers (carers). Systemic practitioners are in an excellent position to move between these positions while being mindful of the needs of the patient.

In a prison setting, health care staff, including therapists, are not operating in an institution whose highest contextual marker is care. My personal experience of working in this environment is that it is like being a guest in someone else's house, and I am acutely aware that the therapeutic work I undertake is not always seen by the prison as one of its key tasks. Working therapeutically within a prison requires constant reflection and revision in order to take into account the demands of the clinical context. For example, a typical referral of a young man to health care is often accompanied by a view from prison staff that 'there is nothing wrong with the lad' and that he is 'acting out' or 'misbehaving' and requires a firm hand to 'bring him back into line'. To be an effective clinician one has to be able to speak both to the world of prison and the world of mental health without alienating one from the other while also keeping in mind the young person's perspective.

Research and systemic practice in prisons and forensic mental health settings

Researchers and practitioners have studied and written about systemic psychotherapy in prisons and hospital secure settings only to a limited extent (see Richards et al. 2009 for a review), whereas considerably more has been written about systemic approaches with offenders in the community (Henggeler et al. 1998; Schoenwald et al. 2000; Littell et al. 2004). This discrepancy may reflect the difficulties of practising health care in a custodial environment, as well as the emphasis on keeping people out of the prison by skilling them up with preventative strategies via community-based services.

Two studies of family therapy with young people in custody concern the USA (Perkins-Dock 2001) and Israel (Elizur 1994). Perkins-Dock (2001) reviewed the literature in the USA and found that, although the treatment focusing on the family unit may be more effective than individual treatment with delinquent youth, it is often difficult to involve families in the treatment process while juvenile offenders are incarcerated. Perkins-Dock (2001) concludes with the observation that 'family therapists should become an integral part of the treatment process for incarcerated juvenile offenders as well as part of the preventive process prior to and after adjudication and during incarceration' (p. 621). The work of Elizur (1994) also looked at working with families in institutions for juvenile offenders in Israel. Elizur describes the necessity of introducing modifications into the correctional system in order to create a therapeutic space that supports closer relationships between the offender and his family and between the family and the institution, in an attempt to prevent the further marginalisation of the families. Both studies acknowledge the need for therapy somehow to transcend the barriers and hurdles of the prison setting, in order to connect the prisoners with key outside individuals and systems.

Literature on work with the families of mentally disordered offenders in UK forensic mental health settings is sparse (Lam 1991; Cordess et al. 1991; Kuipers 1998) and a review of family work undertaken 10 years ago in restricted clinical settings, such as medium- or high-level secure units in the UK (Geelan and Nickford 1999), suggested that there was little evidence of its use in these settings, despite the high incidence of people diagnosed with schizophrenia. This is particularly problematic given that the NICE national guidance is that individuals with the diagnosis receive at least six months of family therapy (NICE 2009).

Vivien-Byrne (2001) has explored the use of systemic ideas in a forensic mental health unit and the challenges that such work poses. In particular, she outlines the limits of applying ideas popular in systemic practice, acknowledging the forensic context as one in which extremes of clinical practice and theoretical positions are apparent. She suggests the need for an approach that balances the often conflicting demands of clinical and forensic perspectives, particularly with regard to responsibility, reality, illness and risk (Vivien-Byrne 2001).

Recent developments

Work on the wider systems involved in a forensic patient's life is described by Bownas (2007), and specifically looks at the work of a family work team (FWT) in an adult inpatient forensic setting. In this setting, the role of the FWT extends beyond that of working with the presenting patient and his family; it also liaises with 'significant other' systems involved in the patient's care, such as the patient's MDT. In practice, this means that the process by which the FWT becomes engaged in the work with the patient and his family and other services is negotiated after a referral by the MDT. This negotiation involves the FWT inviting the MDT to an initial consultation, often without the patient, in order to negotiate aims and specific outcomes the MDT have in mind for any future work between the FWT and the referred patient. Following this initial consultation, the patient and/or family member is then invited to a consultation with the FWT where these aims and ambitions are shared. Thus the FWT joins with the patient and MDT and attempts to optimise transparency and engagement in negotiating treatment aims and goals, constantly attempting to hand responsibility for change back to the client and the people in his support systems. Those instances where there is some distance between the aims and ambitions of the MDT and those of the referred patient often require a series of consultations, in which the FWT shuttles between the two parties in an effort to commission a piece of work which can be mutually agreed by the patient and the MDT. Working with the FWT has been most influential to the present author's thinking and his application of systemic ideas to a YOI context.

Key systemic concepts in the author's practice

Context and multiple perspective taking

Consideration of an individual's context is fundamental to systemic practice. This notion has its roots in the work of Gregory Bateson (Bateson 1973), and his simple assertion that context is the key to understanding. He developed this idea from the study of cybernetics and the various 'systems' involved in industrial engineering and applied it to the study of the mind and eventually to mental illness (Bateson *et al.* 1956). A young man in prison may be seen as a 'prisoner', but in other contexts he is also a 'brother', a 'student', a 'patient', and so on. Context, be it prison, college, home or hospital, determines identity and gives meaning to a person's behaviour and thoughts, and each context is important to an all-round understanding and appreciation of that person.

Just as a person's identity will change according to context, so will the accompanying story or narrative about that particular identity. Humberto Maturana, the Colombian biologist, used the term 'multiverse' to express the idea that a person can have multiple stories about himself, compared to a 'universe' where the emphasis is on one dominant story about a person, often held as the 'truth' (Mendez *et al.* 1988). The challenge for therapists working in prison is to balance the unhelpful, dominant view (often 'mad' in hospital, 'bad' in prison or both for someone in a mental health care unit in a prison) with other more hopeful and positive views that may become marginalised, ignored or forgotten during the person's detention or admission. A discourse based solely on the medico-legal view of the person, in which ward round discussion is focused exclusively on practicalities of 'leave' and 'medication', will limit the range of therapeutic conversations, thus reducing, rather than increasing, the opportunity for the therapist and patient to 'connect' in a way that is helpful to the patient. The role of the systemic therapist in developing an alternative narrative to the dominant pathological view is vital to the individual's recovery, as well as connecting the patient to other systems that share an alternative (non-pathological) view of the individual, such as family and friends.

Communication

Transparent and open communication has not always been the practice in family therapy. In the 1980s and 1990s, a typical experience of family therapy for the family was to find itself with a member of the team, usually the lead clinician, sitting in a room in front of a one-way mirror, behind which sat the rest of the team. At key moments throughout the session, the telephone in the room would ring and the team would send a message to the family, which the therapist then had to manage as best he could. Or in some practices communication came through an earpiece through which the therapist would receive a running commentary from the team while attempting to work with the family. This traditional approach, in which the family could be seen by, but not see, the team, had its origins in the work of Gregory Bateson and his colleagues who advocated this arrangement in order to keep the 'team-behind-the-screen' comparatively free from the emotional temperature of the encounter and therefore able to generate different ideas about and solutions for the family's difficulties in a relatively calm atmosphere. Over the past 10 years or so, this practice has changed, thanks largely to the work of Tom Andersen, a Norwegian psychiatrist who introduced the practice of reflecting teams (Andersen 1987; 1991). Andersen advocated that as part of the therapeutic process, the mystery of the one-way screen should be removed, and the team be situated in the same room as the family and lead therapist, but at a distance, making no eye contact with the therapist or family during the conversations between the therapist and family. At an agreed interval, the roles are reversed, and the reflecting team will talk among themselves, reflecting on what they have heard, while it is the turn of the family and lead therapist to listen. A number of guiding principles to conducting this reflection ensure that it is marked by tentative and speculative suggestions, as opposed to authoritative assertions, which are connected to the words and phrases uttered by the family in their conversation with the therapist. Following the team reflection, the roles are again reversed and the therapist invites the family to comment on what the reflecting team has said, paying attention to ideas or questions that were of particular interest to the family.

The strength of this particular model of communication lies in the respect it affords the family's ideas and words. This validation and witnessing of the family's (and patient's or prisoner's) voices can be a very different experience for families in a forensic institution that can often have difficulty hearing such views, or that hears anything too different from the medico-legal position as problematic or difficult.

Neutrality/curiosity

The notions of neutrality and curiosity were first written about by Selvini-Palazzoli *et al.* (1980) and later by Cecchin (1987). Systemic practice sets much value in giving equal weight to the different stories and perspectives concerning the client. This process is invaluable in setting the perspective of the prison or secure hospital that this person is a 'prisoner' or 'mentally ill patient', alongside the perspective of the client that he is, for example, a 'hard worker' or a 'social mixer', or alongside the perspectives of significant others that he is a 'husband' or 'son' or such like. Once these stories are identified, an important task for the therapist is to keep these alive, as a healthy counterbalance to the stories that emphasise pathology and deviance. By remaining curious about 'other' aspects of the client, it is hoped that the therapist is seen by the other family members as being neutral, unbiased in the weight or preference given to different identities or preferred areas of work. Because the balance between being a 'carer' versus 'custodian' which is prevalent in forensic settings tends to polarise and freeze staff in extreme positions, the systemic therapist needs to be able to hold these positions as well as 'other' stories in mind, while remaining connected to the prison staff and also the mental health workers. It is important that the therapist is disciplined enough to remain neutral to any particular position as well as curious about how that position will impact on other staff members. Jones argues that 'the therapist maintains neutrality towards points of views, towards persons, towards outcomes and towards the overall system itself in order to demonstrate impartiality as well as ensuring equal attention and weight is given to the very different stories about an individual' (Jones 1993: 145).

Connectivity

Leading on from neutrality is the notion of connectivity, and the importance of 'connecting up' the disparate stories about an individual's identity. This avoids simply focusing on the prison or mental health issues, such as risk, or relapse, or illness, to the exclusion of all other aspects of the person's life, and instead talks to the collective individual rather than to an isolated fragment of that person. A major challenge to this work is the impact of the social and physical environment of the prison not only on the behaviour of the prisoner but also on that of the therapist; remaining mindful of contexts and systems other than the immediate one is a skill essential to effective systemic practice in such a challenging environment. Connectivity also refers to the ways in which the very many different aspects of a person's life are mutually affected by his and others' behaviour, including conversations.

Circularity

In the systemic literature, a stimulus-and-response model of communication is preferred over the more traditional cause-and-effect deterministic model, recognising that human interaction is relational and subject to feedback and recursivity or circularity. Human systems are regarded as showing circular interaction: Person A might say or do something that will affect what Person B does or says, whose response in turn affects Person A and whose response then influences or shapes the behaviour or verbal responses of Person B, and so on. This is in contrast to the so-called 'first order' or prescriptive view of communication typical of forensic settings. Emotions, too, are subject to this circularity; Bertrando talks about the process thus: 'I like to say that every emotion comes from somewhere and goes somewhere, meaning that any emotion one of us feels and displays [...] is a consequence of and a response to an emotion displayed by someone else' (Bertrando 2010). This idea of circular feedback loops was one of a number of concepts that were extrapolated from the fields of cybernetics and applied to human systems (Bateson 1973) and is key in understanding the process of human communication. For example, the therapist (Person A) talks to the client (Person B) and asks a number of questions; the response that the patient gives the therapist will affect the next question that the therapist asks: thus the interaction of therapist and client is seen as subject to change and flux, depending on what is said in the exchange between the two people. This is significantly different from the older model that saw communication as something more akin to a cause-and-effect (that the therapist gave expert advice to the client, and the client improved or not). Ways in which the therapist could work with this more realistic notion of communication was further developed both by the Milan therapists (Selvini-Palazzoli *et al.* 1978) and Karl Tomm in his work on 'interventive interviewing' (Tomm 1987a, 1987b, 1988). This period in the development of systemic practice saw a movement away from the therapist giving advice to the family from an objective, non-involved expert position (known as the 'first-order' position), to the therapist acknowledging that he is part of the system and not 'outside' it and has a great influence on the family system ('second order'). For a therapist to interact with young prisoners from a second-order position, where collaboration about aims and goals is key to the development of a therapeutic relationship, requires careful judgement on the part of the therapist; the therapist will typically find himself moving between both first- and second-order positions, depending on the demands of the situation.

Collaboration

In systemic work, as in other related fields, a strong therapeutic alliance is vital to engagement and progress. This is particularly so in a prison setting with a mandated client group whose motivation to attend and participate is often, at best, ambivalent. An essential point in the initial meeting is an understanding of what the client wishes the work to address, in addition to the areas identified by third parties. Obvious as this sounds, the client's understanding and ownership of at least some of the issues is a major and often underestimated part of the engagement process. Inherent in this negotiation is the understanding that the aims and ambitions of the work may also change over time in response to the feedback and position of the client. Such a position reflects the openness of the systemic treatment approach, and the therapist's task is to retain a reflexive and responsive stance, weaving into the work issues proposed by the client and by third parties so that they remain relevant and pertinent to the work as a whole.

Case example

This section describes an example of a systemic-based approach carried out by the author and the trainee clinical psychologist with a young man who had completed a cognitive-behavioural therapy (CBT)-based anger management group. After completing that six-week group, the young men were invited to think about anger in the context of key relationships outside prison.

Background to the referral

The clinical psychology service comprises a full-time qualified clinical psychologist and a part-time assistant psychologist. The service offers a training placement to the local clinical psychology doctoral training courses. There is no 'prison' or 'forensic' psychology service within the prison – it was disbanded several years ago following a change in status of the prison to a 'remand' prison – and so, as a way of regulating the number of referrals it receives, the department receives its referrals via the weekly referral health care meeting for both in- and outpatients.

The referral was of a young man aged 19 years, 'Danny', who was serving an 18-month sentence for robbery. Danny had been referred to the CMHT by his personal officer (Mr Smith) who had noticed that Danny had difficulties controlling feelings of anger. He noticed that Danny would lose his temper very quickly, often acting impulsively on his anger, resulting in a high rate of incidents of confrontation with both peers and officers. This behaviour therefore had an impact on the system around him and on the response of the system to manage his difficulties. According to Danny's prison file, he typically lost his temper following telephone conversations with his girlfriend and his mother. The referral noted that there were 'anger issues' and 'relationship problems' and that this referral might lend itself to a systemic approach. The referral form provides space for elaboration, but the invitation is rarely taken up by referrers and so the first step is usually either a telephone call or meeting with the referrer to develop the picture further.

Danny had grown up with his mother and his two older sisters. At a young age he had witnessed his father being violent to his mother; his father left when he was aged seven. Social care had been involved with the family and reports indicate that Danny's mother had difficulty monitoring and supervising Danny. The task of supervising him and his younger sister often fell to Danny's older sister, and Danny remembered having the run of the house from an early age. Danny had been referred to CAMHS in the past and it was thought that he possibly had conduct disorder, but he did not engage with this service.

At the prison a professionals meeting was arranged with the clinical psychologist, trainee clinical psychologist, Danny's personal officer and a community psychiatric nurse (CPN) from the CMHT. Such meetings are good practice when working with young people in prison as they allow information to be drawn together from different sources and enable different perspectives of the problem to be heard. Danny's personal officer explained that Danny had been having problems on the unit following telephone calls to his girlfriend and/or mother and this would lead to him doing something that the other young men would find confrontational. Danny was invited to attend the anger management group run on the health care wing, which he attended with four other young men. Danny's progress through the group was good: he engaged with the therapeutic process and was very constructive and helpful with ideas for the other group members; he appeared to understand the cognitive-behavioural model of anger management. After the standard six sessions, the group reviewed its progress and Danny was keen to think about how he could apply what he had learned to the outside world. In particular, he wanted to think about how this could be applied to his relationship with his girlfriend, as he felt that he risked losing her if he continued to behave as he had, losing his temper and becoming verbally and physically threatening towards her. Danny agreed to have sessions which included his girlfriend, Sharon. The clinical psychologist and trainee clinical psychologist thought about whether Danny's mother should also attend, but neither Danny nor Sharon were keen on this happening too quickly, and his mother was also unable to find time off work.

Taking a 'reflective team' approach

A 'reflecting team' approach was used, but rather than the reflection taking place behind a one-way screen, it took place in front of Danny and his girlfriend. Using a one-way screen in a prison setting, where prisoners are closely observed by staff 24 hours a day, and whereby some young people may experience symptoms of anxiety and feel paranoid, was not thought to be ethical or helpful; but reflecting in front of the client avoided these difficulties. Thus, while retaining the benefits of having a number of different eyes, ears and minds in the room during the therapeutic session, it also had the added benefits of transparency and accountability (Andersen 1987). Therefore, there were no mysterious telephone calls mid-session to perplex the client or surprise the therapist.

The therapy

A total of six sessions were agreed initially. Each session was divided roughly into thirds: the pre-session, in which the therapists meet to think about how to approach the session; the session itself, in which the clients talk with the lead therapist and then hear a reflection from the two therapists (reflecting team); and finally the post-session, in which any developments or outcomes are acknowledged and reflected on by the team. The clients are not present for the pre- or post-session.

Session I

Pre-session
The therapists thought briefly about the engagement of the couple in the work, the sorts of questions that might be helpful in understanding what Danny and Sharon wanted from these sessions, and how any future work might be used to thicken the connections between what Danny had learnt in the anger management group work programme and his application of that in real-life situations, particularly in his relationship with Sharon.

Session

In the first part of the session Danny and Sharon explained what they wanted from the work and what impact they expected it to have on their relationship. In discussion with the couple about the real-life situations in which Danny's temper becomes a problem, it was helpful to hear to what extent Sharon's attempted solutions to the problem of Danny's anger might in fact have been maintaining his difficulties. A neutral stance by the therapist coupled with a curiosity about 'what happened when' allowed the build-up of a detailed picture of incidents in which Danny and Sharon experienced difficulties in their relationship. This meant that the reflection between the two therapists, with Danny and Sharon listening, was able to highlight the attempted solutions of the couple and how these helped or exacerbated the situation, and to be curious about what would need to happen between the two people in order to arrive at a different and more positive conclusion.

Outcome

In the final part of the session, Danny and Sharon agreed to meet again the following week, and to think about what would need to happen differently during a difficult telephone conversation in order for both of them to experience a better outcome.

Session 2

Pre-session

The pre-session was used to check what Danny and Sharon thought had been more or less helpful in the previous session and to explore more the idea of understanding each other's different contexts, and how this might influence behaviour.

Session

The couple spoke about the intervening week and Danny remarked that having someone work with them on their relationship felt like there was an 'arm round my shoulder' rather than 'fingers pointing at me'. Much of the session was spent thinking with the couple about what the consequences might be for Sharon and Danny's relationship when Danny feels supported or accused.

Outcome

The eliciting of multiple perspectives or positions and exploring the different outcomes that arose from these supported the idea that Danny's behaviour was not solely something that was 'wrong' with him, but could be influenced by Sharon. Equally, the reflecting team suggested that Sharon would need to feel an arm around her shoulder as well. The notion that an emotional response is a consequence of, and a response to, an emotion displayed by someone else, is central to systemic thinking and practice (as is described earlier in the section on circularity).

Session 3

Pre-Session
During this pre-session the therapists briefly spoke about keeping in mind the purpose of the work: to help Danny to generalise his learning about anger control from group work to a real-life situation, namely his telephone calls with his girlfriend, Sharon.

Session
The couple were keen to talk about an example in the intervening week of a telephone conversation that got off to a bad start but ended up OK. The reflection enabled both therapists to wonder aloud about what had been different about this interaction from other, less successful ones. They did not ask the couple directly; asking Danny and Sharon directly would have run the risk of them feeling pressured to give an answer that they thought the therapist wanted to hear, when they might not have known at this time what made the difference. A popular systemic question following a change in outcome refers to who, besides the couple, noticed this change, often asked in an attempt to broaden out the relational aspect of the difficulty. In response to this sort of argument, Danny spoke about his personal officer, Mr Smith, talking to him later that day, mentioning he had been impressed with how Danny had not 'lost it' on the telephone to Sharon.

Outcome
Success was acknowledged and plans were made to include Danny's personal officer in the following session.

Session 4

Pre-session
In the pre-session it was confirmed that Danny's personal officer would attend session four. One idea was to 'interview' the personal officer and position Danny and Sharon with the other therapist as the reflecting team. The personal officer had reported that Danny had managed well further telephone conversations with Sharon in the preceding week.

Session
Danny's personal officer was very positive about the way Danny had managed his phone calls. In their reflection with the therapist, Danny again said that feeling that he had an 'arm round his shoulder', had

made him less 'cross' with Sharon when she did not give him the response he immediately wanted. Sharon said that she was more mindful how she spoke to Danny, and tried not to make her words sound as though she was 'pointing the finger'. Danny was pleased that his behaviour had been noticed by his personal officer. Sharon also thought that her work colleagues had noticed a difference in her mood after she had spoken with Danny. The notion of recursivity and circularity was key to this session.

Outcome
The reflection included an appreciation by Danny's personal officer and Sharon's work colleagues of the small but important changes in Danny and Sharon's telephone interactions. These responses had helped to 'thicken' the link between what Danny had learnt in his group work and its application to a real-life situation.

Session 5

Pre-session
In the two weeks since the previous session, there had been about 12 phone calls, the majority of which had been positive. The plan for the session was to hear about them from Danny and Sharon, with a reflection to acknowledge the progress that both partners had made, and to think about how this experience might be remembered and used in the future.

Session
Danny's progress on the unit had meant that he had increased his privilege status to enhanced level[1] which had resulted in increased access to telephone calls, which Sharon was particularly pleased with. She had needed to talk to Danny about a family matter and his increased amount of telephone time had made her feel more supported by him. Danny also felt that he was able to be supportive even though he was locked up in prison. When asked how this experience might be useful in the future, Danny mentioned his relationship with his mother: although he was not especially concerned with the relationship at the moment, he felt he would be more confident in addressing it at some point in the future, after his release.

Outcome
A final follow-up session was agreed for four weeks' time.

Session 6
The majority of the sixth and final session involved the therapists reviewing the work that had been carried out. This could be considered as a 'live' therapeutic letter discussed in front of Danny and Sharon.

Conclusion

Creating a suitable clinical context (in this case systemic) in order to work with young men in a YOI requires enormous effort, focus, persistence and support from like-minded colleagues. There are many hurdles to therapy, and despite the move over the past decade to commission NHS-based services for the treatment and care of the mentally ill in prison, the context in which these services operate is nevertheless still a prison, in which the assessment and treatment of young people with mental health problems is not a priority. (For example, the assessment and management of young prisoners with mental health problems was not part of any of the key performance indicators for the remand prison in 2007 to 2008: Ministry of Justice 2008). The emphasis on 'security', the transient nature of the young person's experience in a remand YOI, and the closedness of the prison system all appear to work against the notion of providing a stable base from which the young person can reconnect with the outside world. Indeed, the author's clinical impression is that the remand process often exaggerates and exacerbates the young person's experience of disconnection, which, for those vulnerable individuals, can ultimately manifest itself in problematic mental health symptomatology. The clinical example of Danny and Sharon, however, was chosen because it illustrates the systemic process by which skills learned in a prison context can then be applied to a 'real-life' situation that has some merit and meaning for the young person. Being mindful of the very many different 'positions' that a young person can occupy allows the therapist to think with the young person about life beyond the prison walls and helps the young person to connect with those significant systems outside of prison, providing different contexts for putting into practice those skills learned from various prison programmes. Systemic practitioners are in a fairly unique position to work across systems in this way.

Note

1 The prison runs an Incentives and Earned Privileges scheme (IEP) which has three levels: 'basic', through to 'standard' and 'enhanced' level; each level attracts certain privileges, such as being able to spend more on canteen, more telephone credit, and so on.

References

Andersen, T. (1987) 'The reflecting team: Dialogue and meta-dialogue in clinical work', *Family Process*, 2(4): 415–28.

Andersen, T. (1991) *The Reflecting Team: Dialogue and Dialogues about the Dialogues*. New York: W.W. Norton.

Bateson, G. (1973) *Steps to an Ecology of Mind: Collected Essays in Anthropology, Psychiatry, Evolution and Epistemology*. London: Paladin/Granada Publishing.

Bateson, G., Jackson, D., Hayley, J. and Weakland, J. (1956) 'Towards a theory of Schizophrenia', *Behavioural Science*, 1(4): 173–98.

Bertrando, P. (2010) 'Emotional positioning and the therapeutic process', *Context*, 107: 17–19. Available at: www.aft.org.uk/publications/publications. asp.

Bownas, J. (2007) 'Using a systemic family perspective in a secure in-patient setting for adults with psychoses', *Context*, 93: 30–3.

Cecchin, G. (1987) 'Hypothesising, circularity and neutrality revisited: An invitation to curiosity', *Family Process*, 26(4): 405–13.

Cordess, C., Driscoll, R., Robinson, S. and Vivian-Byrne, S. (1991) 'Family work with victims and offenders in a secure unit', *Journal of Family Therapy*, 13(1): 105–16.

Dallos, R. and Draper, R. (eds) (2005) *An Introduction to Family Therapy: Systemic Theory and Practice, 2nd edition*. Maidenhead: Open University Press.

Elizur, Y. (1994) 'Working with families in institutions for juvenile offenders: an ecosystemic model for the development of family involvement', *Human Systems*, 5: 253–66.

Geelan, S. and Nickford, C. (1999) 'A survey of the use of family therapy in medium-secure units in England and Wales', *Journal of Forensic Psychiatry and Psychology*, 10(2): 317–24.

Greenberg, S.A. and Shuman, D.A. (1997) 'Irreconcilable conflict between therapeutic and forensic roles', *Professional Psychology, Research and Practice*, 28: 50–7.

Harvey, J. (2007) *Young Men in Prison: Surviving and Adapting to Life Inside*. Cullompton: Willan Publishing.

Henggeler, S., Schoenwald, S., Borduin, C., Rowland, M. and Cunningham, P. (1998) *Multisystemic Treatment of Antisocial Behaviour in Children and Adolescents.* New York: The Guilford Press.

Jones, E. (1993) Family Systems Theory: Developments in the Milan-Systemic Therapies. Chichester: John Wiley & Sons.

Kuipers, E. (1998) 'Working with carers: Interventions for relatives and staff carers for those who have psychosis', in T. Wykes, N. Tarrier and S. Lewis (eds), *Outcome and Innovation in Psychological Treatment for Schizophrenia.* Chichester: John Wiley & Sons.

Lam, D. (1991) 'Psychosocial family interventions in schizophrenia: a review of empirical Studies', *Psychological Medicine,* 21(2): 423–41.

Littell, J.H., Popa, M. and Forsythe, B. (2004) 'Multisystemic treatment for social, emotional, and behavioral problems in children and adolescents aged 10–17'. *Protocol for a Campbell Collaboration Review.* Available at: www.campbellcollaboration.org/doc-pdf/mstprot.pdf

Mendez, C.L., Coddou, F. and Maturana, H. (1988) 'The bringing forth of pathology', *The Irish Journal of Psychology,* 9(1): 144–72.

Ministry of Justice (2008) *Re-offending of Juveniles: New Measures of Re-Offending 2000–2005, England and Wales.* Ministry of Justice Statistics Bulletin. London: Ministry of Justice. Available at: www.justice.gov.uk/publications/docs/re-offending-juveniles-2000-2005.pdf

Minuchin, S., Montalvo, B., Guerney, B.G., Rosman, B.L. and Shumer, F. (1967) *Families of the Slums: An Exploration of Their Structure and Treatment.* New York: Basic Books.

NICE (2009) *Core Interventions in the Treatment and Management of Schizophrenia in Primary and Secondary Care.* London: National Institute for Health and Clinical Excellence.

Perkins-Dock, R. (2001) 'Family interventions with incarcerated youth: A review of the Literature', *International Journal of Offender Therapy and Comparative Criminology,* 45(5): 606–25.

Richards, M., Doyle, M. and Cook, P. (2009) 'A literature review of family interventions for dual diagnosis: implications for forensic mental health services', *British Journal of Forensic Practice,* 11(4): 39–49.

Schoenwald, S., Henggeler, S., Brondino, M. and Rowland, M., (2000) 'Multisystemic therapy: Monitoring treatment fidelity', *Family Process* 31(1): 83–103.

Selvini-Palazzoli, M., Boscolo, L., Cecchin, G. and Prata, G. (1978) *Paradox and Counterparadox.* New York: Aronson.

Selvini-Palazzoli, M., Boscolo, L., Cecchin, G. and Prata, G. (1980) 'Hypothesizing–circularity–neutrality: three guidelines for the conductor of the session', *Family Process,* 19: 3–12.

Shapiro, D.L. (1988) 'Ethical constraints in forensic settings: Understanding the limits of our expertise', *Psychotherapy in Private Practice,* 6(1): 71–86.

Tomm, K. (1987a) 'Interventive Interviewing: Part I. Strategizing as a fourth guideline for the therapist', *Family Process,* 26: 3–13.

Tomm, K. (1987b) 'Interventive Interviewing: Part II. Reflexive questioning as a means to enable self-healing', *Family Process*, 26: 167–83.

Tomm, K. (1988) 'Interventive interviewing: Part III. Intending to ask lineal, circular, strategic and reflexive questions', *Family Process*, 27: 1–15.

Vivien-Byrne, S. (2001) 'What am I doing here? Safety, certainty and expertise in a secure unit', *Journal of Family Therapy*, 23(1): 102–16.

Chapter 7

Working with trauma in a prison setting

Andrew Rogers and Heather Law

When you feel you know the future, you can be sure that you are reliving the past ... because nobody knows the future.

(Annie Rogers 1996: 235)

Introduction

The following chapter draws on the authors' experience of working with young people (children and adolescents) with offending histories within community youth offending teams, secure children's homes and a young offenders institution (YOI). While the chapter focuses particularly on the adolescent population in prison, it is the authors' view that the developmental perspectives and systemic approaches described within the chapter have meaning and value for understanding clients' behaviour and our approaches to it within the wider mental health and criminal justice systems.

The first part of the chapter explores trauma theory in simple terms and relates it to our evolutionary responses, and experience of attachment and brain development through childhood. It examines the concept of post-traumatic stress disorder (PTSD) including definitions of trauma, the symptoms required for diagnosis and the recommendations from the National Institute for Health and Clinical Excellence (NICE) for interventions. It discusses interventions including trauma-focused cognitive behaviour therapy (CBT) or eye-movement desensitisation reprocessing (EMDR) and reviews them in the context of working in the prison system. A case study then illustrates a systemic approach to addressing the needs of young people with complex trauma histories within prisons. The final part of the chapter describes some of the particular opportunities, challenges and ethical dilemmas that can be encountered when working with this client group and highlights the need to incorporate an understanding of trauma and its effects on the treatment rationale of many young people in prison.

Brief trauma theory and the 'fight or flight' response

All animals, including humans, are biologically pre-programmed to protect themselves from harm. The term 'fight or flight' was first coined by the Harvard physiologist Walter Cannon in 1929, who used it to describe the response of animals to threat, involving the autonomous reaction of the central nervous system. The flight or fight reaction (also known as the 'fight, flight, freeze reaction') is an innate mechanism used to protect ourselves whenever we perceive that we are in danger. When we experience it the whole body reacts to prepare us to 'fight' or to 'flee' from the perceived threat or danger, and we undergo a physiological response that affects all of our bodily systems and functioning (see Bloom 1999 for an overview).

With each fight or flight response, the brain forms a new network of connections that are triggered with each new experience of threat or danger. Consequently, the more threatening or dangerous experiences we are exposed to, the more sensitive we become to possible threats and danger. Developmentally, children who are repeatedly exposed to dangerous and/or threatening situations become hypersensitive to threat, and consequently even mild threats can activate the fight or flight response. This can result in long-term physical and psychological changes, which can only be countered by the creation of a safe, protective environment (Bloom 1999).

When individuals are successful in fleeing danger or fighting it, the physical and psychological impact is reduced. However, when the victim of a traumatic event cannot escape or fight, they begin to feel helpless. If this helplessness occurs repeatedly, and the brain becomes accustomed to trauma, the individual will fail to try and escape from danger or threat, which is known as 'learned helplessness' (Maier and Seligman 1976). Interventions must overcome this obstacle by focusing on empowerment and mastery before addressing the traumatic experience directly.

Similarly, when an individual experiences a traumatic event, 'dissociation' acts as a kind of protective device. Dissociation is defined in DSM-IV-TR as 'a disruption in the usually integrated functions of consciousness, memory, identity, or perception of the environment' (APA 2000: 519). Under normal circumstances, it is this ability that allows us to do more than one thing at once, a phenomenon we often refer to as going on 'autopilot'. It is likely that human beings have evolved this ability in order to be more efficient.

However, in people who have experienced traumatic events, this ability is adapted as a protective mechanism and is used as a built in 'safety valve'. In its most extreme form, fainting allows a complete stop of consciousness. More commonly, we split off an experience from the feelings that accompany that experience, a process known as 'emotional numbing'. In this situation, it may appear to others that an individual is 'coping well' or 'is not fazed' by a traumatic event. Whilst dissociation is an adaptive and protective process, this form of emotional numbing may also mean that an individual's ability for normal emotional interactions may be reduced (Bloom 1999).

Traumatic re-enactment

It has long been noted that fragmented memories of traumatic events seem to dominate the lives of traumatised individuals. These memories may return as physical sensations, flashbacks, nightmares and even behavioural re-enactments. Freud (1914, 1920) called this process 'repetition compulsion', stating that the patient 'reproduces it not as a memory but as an action; he repeats it, without, of course, knowing that he is repeating [...] he cannot escape from this compulsion to repeat; and in the end we understand that this is his way of remembering' (Freud 1914: 150). It would seem that individuals are programmed to repeat what they cannot remember and individuals seem compelled to expose themselves to situations reminiscent of the original trauma. Children are particularly vulnerable to behavioural repetition (Horowitz and Becker 1971) and, as adults, those who have been traumatised are more likely to behave in an anti-social or self-destructive manner (Bloom 1999). A major cause of violence is believed to be due to the re-enactment of victimisation; the majority of violent offenders have been physically or sexually abused as children (van der Kolk 1989). Similarly, abused children are likely to display self-destructive behaviours, including self-harm, self-starving or self-mutilation (van der Kolk 1989).

Thus, it is relatively easy to understand how victims of traumatic experiences, such as physical abuse, can in turn become the abuser. It results in part from the phenomenon of behavioural re-enactment, but it can also be seen as a reaction to the feelings of helplessness and a loss of power experienced during their time as a victim. Commonly, the victim will take on the role of the abuser and will victimise others in turn (Bloom 1999), which prevents them from feeling helpless and enables them to regain feelings of power and control.

Attachment, trauma and brain development

When a person experiences a traumatic event, their initial appraisal of the situation is governed by their sensitivity to threat. Once the situation is viewed as threatening, the thinking brain, the part that regulates emotion, is bypassed to some degree in favour of survival responses (fight/flight/freeze) which are governed by the 'emotional brain' and the limbic system. When a young person experiences something traumatic, they rely on their developing brain to help them to recognise the danger, to respond, and ultimately to regulate the emotional impact of the trauma.

In very simple terms, the brain may be viewed as three distinct areas: the 'old' brain (the reptilian complex), which basically maintains autonomic bodily functions such as homoeostatic functions, heart and breathing rates; the 'emotional' brain (the limbic system), which produces automatic responses such as fight, flight or freeze, and the 'thinking' brain (the cortex), which in this context is involved in higher mental processes involving problem-solving, consequential thinking and emotional regulation (Sunderland 2006). In effect, the thinking brain develops to regulate the impulsive and emotional nature of the emotional brain. At birth, the connections between the thinking brain and the emotional brain are highly underdeveloped and therefore babies and young children can become quite easily emotionally overwhelmed. The process of attachment, involving sensitive, timely and emotionally 'tuned-in' caregiving helps to develop and strengthen the connections between the two parts of the brain, literally sculpting the very nature of the child's developing brain (Teicher 2000).

Children are predisposed to seek comfort and care from their primary caregiver, particularly when they are distressed. Indeed, 'people in general and children in particular seek increased attachment in the face of external danger' (van der Kolk 1989). This interaction between caregiver and child, particularly in the first two years of life, is the basis for developing the child's emotional regulation system and develops the child's model for interacting with the world. When the primary caregiver can provide 'good enough' comfort and care to meet the child's physical and emotional needs in an accurate and timely way (co-regulation), the child begins to develop for themselves a model of the world and relationships built on this 'primary' relationship. They then use this 'internal working model' (IWM) as a blueprint for future experiences and relationships (Bowlby 1988; and see Haley in Chapter 3, this book).

Children brought up in relatively safe, consistent and caring environments develop an IWM of the world as safe, of others as caring and consistent and of themselves as worthy of care. The children then organise themselves and their behaviour according to these developing assumptions. These processes impact at a biological level and affect the nature and course of brain development. These processes are important in the child's development of self-esteem, empathy (Golding *et al.* 2006) and emotional regulation (Perry 2000).

Disruption to this early attachment process through parental inconsistency, neglect and abuse has a direct impact on the development of a child's brain, attachment style and emotional regulation systems. When children grow up in a neglectful, inconsistent or abusive environment, they will develop alternative attachment strategies that maximise their chances of receiving care from their caregiver or in the most extreme cases maximise their chances of survival. The developing brain wires itself, in an adaptive way, to manage these experiences. People who have had less than ideal early experiences of care, including a lack of exposure to the process of co-regulation by a caregiver, are less likely to have developed the structures and connections in the brain which keep the thinking brain regulating the emotional brain. They are more likely to have developed structures and connections between the two parts of the brain based on recognising and interpreting threat (Sunderland 2006). In any given situation, therefore, not only will they be more likely to view an event or situation as threatening, they are more likely to react in a survival way (fight or flight) and less able to regulate their behavioural and emotional response to that situation. This is highly relevant to the prison context where many people appear to have a history of early attachment disruption, neglect and trauma (Crighton and Towl 2008).

Post-traumatic stress disorder

One main focus in the field of traumatic stress over the past 30 years has been that of PTSD. The concept of PTSD grew out of the experiences of clinicians working with veterans following the Vietnam War. PTSD was a specific construct introduced in the third edition of the *Diagnostic and Statistical Manual of Mental Disorders* (DSM). For any significant traumatic event, approximately a third of people will develop PTSD (NICE 2005). However, most people are likely to experience some transient trauma symptoms in the few days or weeks after the traumatic event, but may be relatively unaffected in terms of psychological functioning in the long term.

The DSM-IV-TR defines trauma as: 'direct personal experience of an event that involves actual or threatened death or serious injury, or other threat to one's physical integrity; or witnessing an event that involves death, injury, or a threat to the physical integrity of another person; or learning about unexpected or violent death, serious harm, or threat of death or injury experienced by a family member or other close associate' (DSM-IV-TR; APA 2000: 463–4). Similarly, ICD-10 defines trauma as 'a stressful event or situation (either short- or long-lasting) of an exceptionally threatening or catastrophic nature, which is likely to cause pervasive distress in almost anyone (e.g. natural or man-made disaster, combat, serious accident, witnessing the violent death of others, or being the victim of torture, terrorism, rape, or other crime' (WHO 1992: 147).

There are three main elements to a diagnosis of PTSD: re-experiencing the event, for example, in the form of flashbacks, nightmares or recurring intrusive images and sensations; hyper arousal; and avoidance, for example trying not to remember, avoiding situations and people that may remind you of the event. Associated symptoms may include substance misuse, depression, emotional numbing and unexpected anger. For a diagnosis to be made, these symptoms need to have been present for at least one month after the event (APA 2000).

Estimates of the prevalence of PTSD in the general population are fraught with difficulties. Variations in definitions and diagnostic thresholds make comparable population estimates difficult. The most recent US National Comorbidity Survey used a threshold based on the criteria of DSM-IV and estimated a lifetime prevalence of just under 7 per cent, and a 12-month prevalence of just under 4 per cent. There is an increased risk within certain population groups, for example those working in professions such as the police, fire and rescue and ambulance services, as well as individuals in prison (Koren *et al.* 2005; Wright *et al.* 2006). Within the prison population, estimates of the prevalence of PTSD range from 4 to 21 per cent (Goff *et al.* 2007). PTSD is thought to be even more prevalent within the juvenile offender population, with estimates varying between 2.3 per cent and as high as 32.3 per cent (Abram *et al.* 2004).

Research into PTSD in children has identified both protective factors and risk factors. Protective factors include parental warmth, high intelligence, family support and low family conflict (Piquero *et al.* 2007). In adults, risk factors include lack of social support, poor physical health, poor quality of life and family or marital problems (Crighton and Towl 2008). Recently, Breslau (2002) identified three global factors associated with PTSD: pre-existing psychiatric disorders, a family history of psychiatric disorders and trauma during childhood. Similarly, two recent systematic reviews showed a variety of risk factors for both the development and chronicity of PTSD (Brewin *et al.* 2000; Ozer *et al.* 2003). Both reviews found a strong association between a lack of social support after a traumatic event and symptoms of PTSD. There was also a weak but significant association in both reviews between a family history of mental illness, prior psychiatric history and prior trauma with PTSD. Yet it remains unclear exactly how these risk factors and protective factors moderate and interact in the development and chronicity of symptoms of PTSD, and more generally in the development of mental health problems and delinquency (Piquero *et al.* 2007).

From clinical experience, however, the diagnosis of PTSD appears to capture only a limited aspect of post-traumatic psychopathology; it does not on its own provide a meaningful way of classifying people presenting with more pervasive and complex presentations. While it is undeniable that many of the young people in prison will meet the criteria for a diagnosis of PTSD, the reality of clinical experience is that the majority of clients referred to mental health services in the criminal justice system will have experienced repeated traumatic experiences in the context of disrupted early attachments, neglect, social and emotional deprivation and family breakdown. In addition, they may also be experiencing a traumatic response to their own index offences. Consequently, many of the young people in prison often arrive with multiple diagnoses (including early onset psychosis, conduct disorder, attention deficit hyperactivity disorder (ADHD), autistic spectrum disorder, depression, and attachment disorder to name but a few. While such multiple diagnoses are in part an attempt to classify and 'understand' the complexity of a young person's presentation, and can be useful in communicating the scale of the difficulties, it is our opinion that these multiple diagnoses often serve to confuse the intervention, the professionals and more importantly the client and their family system. In our experience, all too often young people with these complex difficulties have been offered individual 'trauma therapy' in response to a diagnosis of PTSD, or simply the fact that they have experienced a 'traumatic' event, without due consideration to the complexity of their presentation and their ability to tolerate the process of individual therapy. As a consequence, at best the results are that the young person disengages or actively avoids such interventions, and at worst the young person is overwhelmed and goes into crisis.

To address these more complex presentations, over the past 20 years there have been a number of attempts to describe more effectively the pervasive difficulties of people who have experienced long-term chronic trauma, often viewed under the auspices of 'complex trauma'. These include terms such as disorder of extreme stress not otherwise specified (DESNOS) (Pelcovitz *et al.* 1997), complex PTSD (Herman 1992; Briere and Scott 2006) and self-trauma disturbance (Briere 2002). More recently, van der Kolk (2005) and Cook *et al.* (2005) have proposed a new diagnosis of developmental trauma disorder. These 'complex trauma' descriptions, in contrast to the diagnosis of PTSD, generally highlight the long-term developmental impact of multiple, chronic traumatic experiences usually of an interpersonal nature which occur over time during childhood.

While it cannot be denied that there are people within prisons who present with 'simple' PTSD, the vast majority of clients referred will be experiencing complex trauma reactions, allied to a history of exposure to repeated trauma and disrupted attachment histories. Therefore, we would argue that we need to adapt the traditional evidence-based interventions for PTSD, such as trauma-focused CBT or EMDR, in order to take these developmental considerations into account; these interventions certainly should not be seen as 'stand-alone' or even primary interventions in this context. Before detailing a composite case example of clinical work, the following section will examine in more detail the evidence-based treatments for PTSD. This perspective is highlighted to some degree in the *Position Statement on Complex Post-Traumatic Stress Disorder* (UK Trauma Group, n.d.).

Intervention approaches

NICE (2005) guidelines for the treatment of PTSD are split into three stages of intervention: early intervention, interventions where symptoms are present within three months of a traumatic experience, and finally interventions where symptoms are present for more than three months after a traumatic experience.

In the early intervention stage, 'watchful waiting' is advised in cases where symptoms are mild and have been present for less than four weeks; a follow-up appointment should be offered within one month. Immediately after a traumatic event, a single-session psychological debriefing should not be routinely offered; however, post-incident, caregivers should have an awareness of the psychological impact of the trauma and offer practical and emotional support.

When symptoms are present within three months of the trauma, NICE recommends that interventions, including trauma-focused CBT, should be offered to those with severe symptoms of PTSD. This should ideally consist of eight to 12 sessions of up to 90 minutes. These sessions should be offered on a regular basis (for example, weekly) and should be delivered by the same person. Drug treatment may be considered for sleep disturbance, including short-term use of hypnotic medication. For the longer term a suitable antidepressant should be considered, preferably introduced at an early stage to reduce the chance of dependence. NICE guidelines suggest that routine, non-trauma-focused interventions, including relaxation and other non-directive therapy, should not be offered to individuals presenting with symptoms within three months of a traumatic event.

For interventions where symptoms have been present for more than three months after a trauma, NICE guidance recommends that *all* patients are offered individual trauma-focused psychological treatment such as trauma-focused CBT or EMDR, usually on an outpatient basis. For single-incident trauma, eight to 12 sessions of trauma-focused psychological treatment delivered regularly and by the same person should be considered. For individuals who have experienced multiple traumatic events, traumatic bereavement, or where there is a chronic disability as a result of a traumatic event or significant co-morbid disorders or social problems, psychological treatment may be extended to more than 12 sessions and should ideally be part of an integrated care plan.

NICE advises health care professionals to consider devoting sessions to building a trusting therapeutic relationship and to ensuring that the client is emotionally stable before they are able to disclose the details of the traumatic event. Where individuals show little or no improvement following specific trauma-focused psychological treatment, consideration should be given to the addition of pharmacological treatment or an alternative form of trauma-focused psychological treatment.

Although a range of treatments for sufferers of PTSD are offered on the NHS, ranging from generic psychological treatments to those specifically for PTSD, NICE (2005) guidelines recommend the use of those treatments for which there are randomised controlled trials (RCTs) demonstrating the efficacy of a particular approach. These evidence-based treatments use psychological models and techniques but can be delivered by a range of mental health care professionals, including psychologists, mental health nurses, psychiatrists and social workers to name but a few. The most commonly used of these evidence-based treatments are EMDR and trauma-focused CBT.

EMDR

This technique was developed by Shapiro in 1989 on the basis of a theoretical model suggesting that improper processing and storage of the memory of a traumatic event causes the physical and psychological symptoms associated with PTSD (Shapiro 1989). During a traumatic event, emotional arousal is so strong that it interferes with our ability to process the experience and form a cohesive, contextualised memory. Consequently, recalling the event can be extremely distressing and the individual may feel as though he is reliving the event. Similarly, because the memory had not been contextualised it can be triggered by experiences in the present and can therefore have a significant debilitating impact on daily life. Shapiro's (2001) Adaptive Information Processing Model states that stimulating the patient's information processing with eye movements, taps or tones while they are recalling a traumatic memory can help the reprocessing and reintegration of that memory and, as a result, reduce the distress associated with that memory. During EMDR therapy, the client will be asked to identify a target image of the traumatic event and the negative beliefs related to this memory. They will then be asked to recall this target image while the therapist leads them through a series of rapid eye movements. This dual processing task is hypothesised to allow reprocessing of the original trauma and the desensitisation of the negative emotions associated with it.

Recent research has called into question the value of the eye movements in the therapeutic effectiveness of EMDR, suggesting that success may be due to other procedures during the therapy which are common to other treatment programmes (Davidson and Parker 2001). These procedural elements include the recall of a target image, desensitisation and cognitive restructuring, all of which are common to other treatment programmes such as CBT. However, the author of the treatment model (Shapiro 1996) and others (Welch and Beere 2002) have maintained that bilateral stimulation is a core therapeutic element.

Trauma-focused CBT

The cognitive-behavioural model focuses on the relationship between thoughts, emotions and behaviours and therapy is based around techniques that aim to influence an individual's distressing emotions by adapting their thoughts, beliefs and/or behaviours. CBT programmes designed specifically for PTSD generally include psycho-education about the common reactions to a traumatic event in order to normalise the sufferer's symptoms, and generally use treatment techniques including exposure, cognitive therapy and stress management.

For the treatment of PTSD, the exposure technique usually consists of either imaginal exposure/narrative writing or *in vivo* exposure. Imaginal exposure and narrative writing involve a detailed and emotional recounting of the traumatic event either as a verbal commentary or in written form. This is repeated until the individual no longer experiences high levels of distress during the recollection. *In vivo* exposure involves identifying 'safe' situations which the individual now avoids due to the associations with their traumatic memory. The therapist will then guide repeated exposures to these situations until the client is no longer fearful and anxious of them (see Foa and Kozak 1986).

Cognitive therapy was initially developed in the 1970s for the treatment of depression (Beck 1976) and then for anxiety (Clark 1999). This kind of therapy is concerned with addressing a patient's excessively negative thoughts and beliefs to reduce distress and to improve daily functioning. Cognitive treatments of PTSD focus on the patient's hypersensitivity to threat and the way in which this stems from interpretations of the traumatic experience and its aftermath. The therapist helps the client to test out predictions about their interpretations of what is safe and gathers evidence for and against these predictions. In doing so, the client is encouraged not to use avoidance behaviours nor to ruminate excessively about what may or may not happen, and thus the client ultimately arrives at more adaptive conclusions.

Stress management is concerned with building up skills for coping and managing anxiety and is a central theme in CBT. Generally this management can include relaxation training, breathing retraining, positive thinking and distraction. For PTSD, stress management aims to increase the client's sense of mastery by improving their coping skills and creating opportunities to test out those skills in an 'inoculated' or gradual manner (see Meichenbaum 1985).

Integrated Interventions

Thinking more systemically about intervention and with particular relevance to clients with more complex presentations, Briere and Scott (2006) describe a number of central treatment principles when working with traumatised clients. These include:

- providing and ensuring safety;
- providing and ensuring stability;
- maintaining a positive and consistent therapeutic relationship;
- tailoring the therapy to the client;
- taking gender issues into account;
- being aware of and sensitive to socio-cultural issues;
- monitoring and controlling transference.

If therapists are to follow these principles it seems unhelpful to be working individually with the client on their trauma without first (or at least simultaneously) working with their environment and in particular with those people charged with providing safety and care for them. In our experience, individual intervention with the client, as well as intervention within the wider system, can be summarised into three very broad areas of intervention:

- psycho-education, for both the client and the caregiving system;
- regulating distress and building coping resources, for both the client and the caregiving system;
- reprocessing the trauma, for the client.

Working with the traumatised system

Research shows that prison officers are also at increased risk of PTSD (Wright *et al.* 2006) and the authors have been approached by prison officers who are seeking help for symptoms of PTSD as well as other emotional difficulties. In addition, the prison environment itself can be a source of negative experiences that could be deemed to be traumatic for both prisoners and staff, for example restraint situations, witnessing extreme self-harm behaviours, bullying, and so on. If the caregiving system itself is experiencing symptoms allied to a PTS response (for example, hyper-vigilance to threat or high anxiety) it is unlikely that it will be able to provide an attuned, emotionally sensitive caregiving approach and therefore unlikely to provide enough safety and consistency for trauma treatment to be effective. Therefore, it is suggested that one of the core tenets of working with trauma presentations in a prison should be to work firstly with the staff team, in order to develop an environment in which trauma resolution can be maximised. This approach of working with caregivers as the primary intervention is a growing method of effective intervention particularly with young people and carers in the 'looked after' system (Golding *et al.* 2006).

Case example

The composite case study described in this chapter is developed from the clinical experience of the authors. It illustrates work with young people who had early attachment disruption, showing an approach which integrates more traditional individual treatment for PTSD alongside working with caregivers within the environment. This case study is a composite and, for the sake of the narrative, it omits some details and employs artistic licence. It is recognised that this may present an 'ideal' and that the often limited resources and the systems in which we work make it difficult even to approach some of the interventions suggested here. In addition, it is important to note that any assessment and intervention process would only be undertaken within the context of a robust risk assessment and management plan.

Background to the case example

Luke is 15 years old and is the biological son of Julie (42 years old) and Dave (45 years old). He has two older brothers, 23 years old and 20 years old, both of whom have been involved in criminal behaviour in the past. Luke also has a half-sister, Charlie, who is eight years old. Julie's first husband, Dave, was violent towards her and left the family home before Luke was born. When Luke was three years old,

Julie met and married Pete. Julie and Pete's relationship was also violent and Luke witnessed much of this violence. Pete left the family home when Luke was eight years old, just prior to the birth of his younger half-sister, and after a particularly violent incident between Pete and Julie, in which Luke witnessed his mother being beaten and subsequently hospitalised. Luke is reported to have tried to intervene in the argument and Pete hit him too. Although Pete left the family home when Luke was eight years old, he continued to return home occasionally.

Julie has a long history of depression, alcohol and substance misuse. She had post-natal depression following Luke's birth and her alcohol and substance misuse worsened during this time. Julie remains committed to helping Luke, but their relationship has been quite volatile throughout Luke's childhood and more recently Julie's attempts at putting behavioural boundaries in place for Luke have resulted in violence between them.

Luke was involved in a serious road traffic accident when he was 12 years old, having been a passenger in a stolen vehicle. One of the passengers was killed in the accident. Luke's behaviour in primary school was described as 'challenging', but manageable, although there were a number of fixed-term exclusions in Year 6 (when he was 11 years old).

Luke first became known to the youth offending team (YOT) at the age of 12 due to several incidents of criminal damage and vehicle offences. His first conviction for taking a vehicle without the owner's consent (TWOC) was at the age of 13, for which he received a six-month referral order. Luke had a number of subsequent offences involving violence, including two assaults on his mother. He received various community orders and has served a previous prison sentence of six months on a detention and training order (DTO) at the age of 14. His current index offence involved a violent assault with a weapon and robbery for which he received a three-year custodial sentence.

Luke was referred by his caseworker within the prison as he was reporting recurring thoughts of violence and 'paranoia' about other young people trying to assault him. Luke was also reporting difficulties with sleep and recurring nightmares about his car accident and also 'seeing his own death in different violent ways'.

Since being in prison Luke has been particularly difficult for staff to manage. He has had a number of serious fights with other young people and with staff, resulting in the loss of privileges and some time spent on the care and separation unit. He is reported by staff to be particularly reactive during the early morning routine. Luke has been refusing to attend education. Given the difficulties in managing Luke's behaviour, he is under threat of being moved to another establishment under the disruptive prisoner protocol.

In the past, Luke was receiving a number of different interventions across the prison and has also received a number of similar interventions in the general community either through his YOT or local child and adolescent mental health service (CAMHS). These included, in no particular order, individual anger management, anger management group, family therapy, art therapy, victim empathy and awareness work, substance misuse awareness, offence-focused work and counselling. However, it appeared that Luke's presentation was deteriorating despite the level of intervention he was receiving. Luke also had a number of tentative diagnoses including conduct disorder, ADHD and a query regarding early-onset psychosis (in relation to his violent thoughts). He had had a trial of medication for his ADHD, but this had been discontinued due to non-compliance.

Assessment

Luke was seen in a quiet room on the wing, as he had initially refused to attend the mental health day unit within the prison. Luke said that he did not attend the unit as he 'did not want the other young people to think he was mental'. Luke initially presented as highly anxious and hostile. He found it difficult to sit still for more than about five minutes and was extremely distractible, particularly when there was any movement outside the window. He needed a lot of reassurance regarding the therapist's role and remit, the safety of the room and the limits of confidentiality. As the session progressed Luke became more settled and began to engage. Luke reported feeling constantly 'on edge' as if something bad was going to happen. He reported frequent nightmares, all with a theme of violence, both perpetrated by him and with him as the victim. Luke also spoke about experiencing 'flashbacks' to the car accident in which another young person was killed. He reported these occurring 'most days'. He also described constantly feeling 'paranoid' about other young people attacking him, although he denied being bullied or experiencing any particular problems with other young people on the wing. He spoke about having 'violent thoughts', but not wanting to act on the thoughts. He was clear that these thoughts were within his head and he did not report any auditory or visual hallucinations. He said that his main concern was that he loses his temper quickly, often 'for no reason', and that he is worried what violent things he might do when this happens.

Luke talked about using distraction and 'trying to forget' as his main way of managing his intrusive thoughts. He spoke about using drugs and alcohol as a way of helping to forget and 'feel better'. He said that he never actively thinks about the car accident and avoids going near the crash site. Luke also said that he does not like watching 'the soaps', because often these remind him of the arguments at home. He said that he carries a weapon 'for protection' and has always slept with a weapon under his pillow.

Luke spoke negatively about his previous experiences of accessing support. He acknowledged that he rarely talked about his difficulties, preferring to 'bottle them up'. He spoke about feeling anxious in groups of people, linking this to his sense of 'paranoia', and gave this as his reason for refusing to attend education, preferring to stay in his cell as he 'can stay out of trouble'.

Luke described losing his temper as 'being out of control'. He said that he becomes violent and is unsure why it happens and how he can stop it. Luke said these violent episodes are often accompanied by vivid thoughts and images of violence and a sense of release. Luke said that he has little memory of the episodes and it seems as though he is 'somewhere else'; he takes a long time to calm down; and once he is calm he regrets what he has done. However, this makes him feel very negative about himself, and as he feels worse he begins to have thoughts of violence again.

Brief formulation

In formulating Luke's presentation in relation to attachment theory and complex trauma, the following was hypothesised.

Luke's early history was characterised by a chaotic family environment with witnessing violence and an inconsistent availability of care. These very early experiences are likely to have impacted on Luke's emotional development, his ability to take for granted other people's care and emotional availability, and his ability to maintain secure and supportive relationships; they are also likely to have impacted on his feelings of self-worth and his ability to manage and regulate extremes of emotion.

In addition to these very early experiences, Luke's presentation is highly likely to have been compounded by his later experiences of trauma, including witnessing extreme violence and being involved in a road traffic accident. His presentation and his profile on the Trauma

Symptom Checklist for Children (TSCC; Briere and Runtz 1989) are consistent with a young person who is experiencing post-traumatic symptoms and associated anxiety and distress.

Luke's experience of others is that they are inconsistent or ineffective in helping him to regulate his emotions – and he is therefore unlikely to seek help from others when distressed, preferring to 'keep things in'. He has developed some ability to regulate his emotions, albeit in an avoidant and arguably maladaptive way. Consequently, feelings are masked, but build up over time and at some point become overwhelming. Once these feelings are released, the response is often likely to be out of proportion to the trigger or stimulus.

In addition to his arguably maladaptive emotional regulation system, Luke's sensitivity to threat is likely to be heightened. This is like a 'double-blow': Luke is more likely to feel threatened in any given situation and less likely (over time) to tolerate effectively the anxiety this produces. Thus, he has become highly reactive to threat, with violence (fight, rather than flight) being the preferred survival mechanism. In part, Luke's experience has taught him that it is too much of a risk for him to wait to find out whether a situation is actually threatening – 'fight first, survive and deal with the consequences afterwards; wait and you will get hurt'.

In addition, the experience of being violent, and the associated feelings of power, could be serving to help him maintain self-esteem and a sense of having some power and control over his world. In our experience, this 'powerless–powerful' dynamic is a particularly common theme for young people who have witnessed domestic violence. It seems that the feeling of powerlessness to intervene or protect as a child when a parent is being assaulted is avoided at all costs when the child grows up and is more physically able to have an impact. The young person or adolescent then presents themselves as 'powerful' and aggressive and also seems to respond in a heightened way to witnessing or experiencing the bully–victim dynamic. In simpler terms, it could also be argued that Luke has learned from watching others in his environment that violence is an effective way to behave.

Intervention

Working with the system

The initial intervention endeavoured to bring together all those working with Luke and to provide training and psycho-education about attachment theory, the fight and flight system, complex trauma and brain development. After that, the staff were involved in developing a shared formulation of Luke's presentation, both in terms of managing the potential risk he posed of violence to others, as well as understanding and addressing his post-trauma symptomatology. This formulation included identifying potential situations within the prison environment and therapeutic day that might trigger the oversensitive fight or flight system. For example, the staff identified that Luke's challenging behaviour often occurred first thing in the morning after the wing had been 'woken up' by a prison officer shouting loudly (albeit jovially) along the corridor. Having discussed this with Luke, we realised that as he woke to this loud shouting he experienced high levels of anxiety and flashbacks to his stepfather returning home drunk in the early hours and shouting at his mother. This insight enabled staff to develop a management strategy whereby they would knock on his cell door five minutes prior to the officer doing his morning call. This gave Luke a chance to reorientate himself to his environment and almost immediately reduced the violent incidents against staff in the mornings.

In further consultation with staff it was clear that Luke's behaviour evoked very strong emotions among them. These emotions were often polarised between, on the one hand, feeling desperately sorry for him and wanting to rescue him from his distress (particularly following the trauma training) and, on the other hand, feeling extremely hostile to him and rejecting of him. Staff reported that these emotions led to them taking very different approaches to the management of Luke's behaviour. When feeling the need to rescue him, some staff reported ignoring some of his high-risk behaviours, whereas when feeling hostile to him some staff acknowledged implementing harsh sanctions as a response to his behaviour.

Allowing staff to verbalise these feelings enabled them to recognise the inconsistent management of Luke's behaviour, even within the context of one shift, and their inadvertent reinforcement of some of the difficulties – and their recreation of the 'ambivalent parenting style' that Luke is reported to have experienced during his childhood. As a result, staff became more consistent in their management of Luke's behaviour.

Direct work with Luke

The individual work with Luke initially involved psycho-education about trauma and the fight or flight response. His thoughts, nightmares, perceived 'paranoia' and violent outbursts were discussed in relation to experiencing and witnessing violence and as ways of coping with these experiences that were initially adaptive, but were now proving maladaptive. The traumatic memories themselves were not discussed in this early part of treatment. It was agreed with Luke that the primary aims of the initial intervention were to reduce the potential risk of violence, to increase his confidence in managing his symptoms and to develop strategies to help him sleep more effectively.

As the sessions progressed, Luke began to make links between his violent thinking and behaviour and the times when he felt threatened. He also began to talk about his offence, his feelings of vulnerability at the time and his intrusive memories, specifically of his own offence, that he had not shared previously. He spoke of being shown photographs of the victim after he had been charged for the assault and of 'not being able to get them out of his head'. Luke also started to express his confusion about the fact that he had been violent even though he greatly disliked violence, and he related this to his own experiences as a child.

In collaboration with his personal officer, a safety plan was developed which identified the most likely times when Luke would experience intrusive thoughts and memories, along with Luke's ideas of what would be helpful and unhelpful responses from other people. Luke was encouraged to think about the triggers and situations when he felt most under threat (whether perceived or real threat) and these ideas were shared with staff. Staff were encouraged to notice changes in Luke's presentation and to reflect them back to him sensitively. Increased support was offered in attending education and he was placed in a smaller working group. A key focus was to work with Luke to start to let other people know what he was experiencing and how he was feeling. The idea was for Luke to begin to develop a sense that other people can be effective in helping him to regulate his emotions – in other words to recreate those early experiences of co-regulation that Luke had little experience of. Without staff being aware of this process and developing their skills in 'attunement', this aspect of the individual work would have been much less effective, as his attempts to test out the availability of others' care could have been thwarted.

Specific sessions were dedicated to helping Luke develop self-soothing strategies. He was encouraged to develop a 'safe place', using visualisation as well as learning soothing breathing techniques, along with ways to help him orientate himself to his environment when he was feeling particularly distressed and/or experiencing flashbacks. These strategies were shared with relevant staff and Luke was encouraged to seek support from others to implement them as 'real-time' experiments. For example, when Luke was involved in an adjudication (a meeting with the Governor to determine consequences for a serious infringement of prison rules), he recognised that it was a situation where he might feel threatened; but Luke was able to plan his coping strategies and requested support to manage this situation and the staff member present was able to help him to recognise the changes in his presentation and prompt him to use his coping strategies 'in the moment'.

As sessions progressed over a 12-month period, Luke's presentation improved, particularly in his reactivity to threat. He began to engage better in the prison regime and gained 'enhanced' status, allowing him more access to association with other young people and activities that required less supervision. Luke still experienced high levels of anxiety, although his sleep routine improved and his experience of intrusive thoughts decreased. He began to reappraise situations as neutral that previously he would have appraised as threatening. At times, Luke continued to have 'flashbacks' to his car accident, although he began to report them as less intense.

At this point and in agreement with Luke and the staff team, the therapist began to discuss Luke's traumatic memories and thoughts in more depth. In this sense the intervention took on a more traditional trauma-focused cognitive-behavioural approach in addressing traumatic memories directly (although consideration of using EMDR would not be discounted at this stage). Luke began to talk through individual memories of his car accident and his witnessing violence as a child. While Luke's intrusive memories of his offence remained, albeit reduced in intensity and frequency, he made the decision not to focus on these memories directly; he stated that he did not want to feel 'completely OK' about what he had done as he thought that not feeling so would act as a deterrent to future displays of violence. Throughout this period of the work, Luke would frequently return to his safety plan, and his ability to engage in the sessions fluctuated, often depending on the amount of perceived or actual 'threat' within the prison. Big shifts in the dynamics on the wing with new staff members or young people brought about a heightened sense of vulnerability, and the therapist would often have to return to working with the staff, in order to recreate the safety and stability that Luke required to access the therapeutic process, and return to reviewing Luke's coping skills. A significant additional change was that Luke began to talk more with his mother outside of the therapeutic sessions, about their shared experience. His mother commented on how much more 'open' Luke was in sharing his thoughts and feelings with her.

After approximately 18 months of intervention, Luke decided that while he was at times still experiencing some intrusive thoughts and heightened anxiety, they were manageable in terms of his daily life and were not impacting significantly on his ability to engage effectively within the prison. Luke's self-reports and scores on the TSCC showed significant improvements in terms of post-traumatic symptomatology. Staff reports indicated much less reactivity in Luke's presentation and an improvement in his overall mood and engagement. It was agreed to end the involvement at this point, albeit recognising that there was scope to continue the work, particularly in aiding the transition back into the community. However, it seemed important to recognise the progress Luke had made and the therapist was more confident that Luke would be able to access support independently in the future.

Challenges and ethical considerations

One of the most difficult decisions to make when working with clients in prison is whether it is ever safe enough in the prison environment to engage with the client in direct intervention which focuses on re-experiencing the trauma. If we ask our clients to work directly with their trauma memories before their emotional regulation systems are able to manage this, we potentially increase the risk to themselves of increased distress and retraumatisation. Within an offender population, with increased distress and emotional reactivity, we could also argue that we increase the risk to others. Therefore, ongoing liaison with prison staff and shared 'care plans' are vital. This is not work that should be carried out in isolation and certainly not without understanding the context of the young person's current environment.

Even if we are able to create a 'safe enough' environment to engage in direct trauma-focused intervention, the timescales in a prison often mean that the work is unfinished. There must be a clinical judgement about what, if any, direct work needs to be made; one which takes into account the potential risks of harm, as well as the potential benefits to the client. Being open, honest and realistic with clients about what is achievable, and involving them in the decision to proceed with intervention both seem important in keeping young people engaged. In our experience, young people are often more realistic about what can be achieved from intervention than the therapists and other professionals.

Once engaged in direct work, the practicalities of meeting young people in the prison can hinder the therapeutic process. The notion of a traditional therapy 'space' and of a '50-minute hour' is simply unrealistic, and these are all factors that need to be considered in the decision about safety to proceed. Protecting confidentiality while balancing issues of risk is also a constant challenge, as frequently, for example, when young people who are experiencing intrusive violent thoughts or images and/or pseudopsychotic features such as 'hearing voices', report their own fears about their potential for violence. An open, honest approach, incorporating clear statements about maintaining safety and the limits of confidentiality and revisiting the topic frequently, seems to aid engagement and the disclosure process. Furthermore, in our experience young people's anxieties about confidentiality often seem to be much lesser than those of the professionals working with them.

A further consideration when working with trauma in a prison is the possibility that the client may be traumatised by his or her own offence. Indeed, many young people are initially referred to our service for experiencing flashbacks or nightmares about their offence. More commonly, they report thoughts and nightmares with a theme of violence, but are unable to distinguish whether they are related to their offence or to their own experiences of witnessing or experiencing violence. Alternatively, a young person may present with trauma symptoms seemingly unrelated to their offence, only for the relationship to be disclosed later on in the process.

This raises a major ethical consideration about how comfortable individuals and society may be about young offenders being 'helped' to feel less distressed about their offence. Some might argue that the resulting distress is potentially a deterrent to further offending. But others might argue that, if young people are helped to manage and resolve their traumatic experiences, then they are less likely to be involved in further offending behaviour. Many young people themselves seem to report this dilemma themselves and will often state that they do not want to feel 'completely fine' about what they have done, as Luke did not. Most, however, want to be able to sleep through the night and to function during the day and, ultimately, an individualised approach to each case is needed.

Finally, the criminal justice system and prison itself has the potential to be traumatising for some young people. Young people, for example, frequently report experiences at arrest, a fear of attack or an actual attack from other young people in the prison, and experiences during control and restraint situations that either result in trauma-related symptoms or trigger symptoms from previous experiences.

Conclusion

In conclusion, many young people in the criminal justice system report symptoms that appear related to traumatic experiences, with a significant proportion presenting with post-traumatic stress disorder. Indeed, their behaviour – including, at least to some extent, their index offence – can often be understood in relation to the re-enactment of previous trauma and/or a 'fight, flight or freeze' response to the perception of a threatening situation. Furthermore, many young people will also have experienced early disruption in their attachment relationships and are likely to have underdeveloped abilities to tolerate and regulate their emotions. These traumatic experiences and symptoms may be further compounded by their offending behaviour and/or experiences within the criminal justice system itself and, as such, the original problems are compounded and the cycle of trauma and offending seems to be perpetuated.

Nevertheless, it would be argued that, on entering the juvenile secure estate, the young person has a window of opportunity. It is possible at least to assess the impact of past trauma and start to provide a framework for effective intervention, driven by a psychologically informed developmental approach and underpinned by models of attachment and trauma as applied to children and young people. A major focus of this intervention should be developing and supporting the skills, knowledge and emotional well-being of the people who provide the immediate care of the young people, be they parents, carers or professionals. Individual work for the young person should only form 'part' of the intervention.

These ideas are in no way intended to excuse the behaviour of young people who offend, nor to argue for an overly 'soft' approach to their treatment. Nor are they intended to suggest that experiencing trauma is 'the answer' to understanding the complexities of criminal behaviour. However, it is vital to support the criminal justice system in understanding the systemic and developmental impact of trauma and attachment disruption in terms of its hypothesised impact on young people and on their propensity to engage in offending behaviour. It is hoped that with this growing perspective, we can move forward in developing policy and treatments, driven by effective research, that move to prevent offending behaviour by addressing factors such as the effects of trauma as early as possible, rather than spending the majority of our time trying to intervene after the damage has been done.

References

Abram, K.M, Teplin, L.A., Charles, D.R., Longworth, S.L., McClelland, G.M. and Dulcan, M.K. (2004) 'Posttraumatic stress disorder and trauma in youths in juvenile detention', *Archives of General Psychiatry*, 61: 403–10.

APA (2000) *DSM IV-TR: Diagnostic and Statistical Manual of Mental Disorders – Text Revision.* 4th Edition. Washington, DC: American Psychiatric Association.

Beck, A.T. (1976) *Cognitive Therapy for the Emotional Disorders.* New York: International Universities Press.

Bloom, S.L. (1999) Trauma Theory Abbreviated. Available at: www.sanctuaryweb.com

Bowlby, J. (1988) *A Secure Base: Parent–Child Attachment and Healthy Human Development.* New York: Basic Books.

Breslau, N. (2002) 'Epidemiological studies of trauma, posttraumatic stress disorder, and other psychiatric disorders', *Canadian Journal of Psychiatry*, 47: 923–9.

Brewin, C.R., Andrews, B. and Valentine, J.D. (2000) 'Meta analysis of risk factors for post-traumatic stress disorder in trauma exposed adults', *Journal of Consulting and Clinical Psychology*, 68: 748–66.

Briere, J. (2002) 'Treating adult survivors of severe childhood abuse and neglect: Further development of an integrative model', in J.E.B. Myers, L. Berliner, J. Briere, T. Reid, and C. Jenny (eds), *The APSAC Handbook on Child Maltreatment.* 2nd edition. Newbury Park, CA: Sage.

Briere, J., and Runtz, M. (1989) 'The trauma symptom checklist (TSC-33): Early data on a new scale', *Journal of Interpersonal Violence*, 4: 151–63.

Briere, J. and Scott, C. (2006) *Principles of Trauma Therapy: A Guide to Symptoms, Evaluation, and Treatment.* Thousand Oaks, CA: Sage.

Clark, D.M. (1999) 'Anxiety disorders: why they persist and how to treat them', *Behaviour Research and Therapy*, **37**: S5–S27.

Cook, A., Spinazzola, J., Ford, J., Lanktree, C., Blaustein, M., Cloitre, M., DeRosa, R., Hubbard, R., Kagan, J., Mallah, K., Olafson, E. and van der Kolk, B.A. (2005) 'Complex trauma in children and adolescents', *Psychiatric Annals*, 35(5): 390–8.

Crighton, D.A. and Towl, G.J. (2008) *Psychology in Prisons.* 2nd edition. Oxford: Wiley Blackwell.

Davidson, P.R. and Parker, K.C.H (2001) 'Eye movement desensitisation and reprocessing (EMDR): A meta-analysis', *Journal of Consulting and Clinical Psychology*, 69: 305–16.

Foa, E.B. and Kozak, M.J. (1986) 'Emotional processing of fear: Exposure to corrective information' *Psychological Bulletin*, 99: 20–35.

Freud, S. (1914) 'Remembering, Repeating and Working-Through (Further Recommendations on the Technique of Psycho-Analysis II)', *The Standard Edition of the Complete Psychological Works of Sigmund Freud, Volume XII (1911–1913): The Case of Schreber, Papers on Technique and Other Works*, 145–56.

Freud, S. (1920). 'Beyond the Pleasure Principle'. *The Standard Edition of the Complete Psychological Works of Sigmund Freud, Volume XVIII (1920–1922): Beyond the Pleasure Principle, Group Psychology and Other Works*, 1–64.

Goff, A., Rose, E., Rose, S. and Purves, D. (2007) 'Does PTSD occur in sentenced prison populations? A systematic literature review', *Criminal Behaviour and Mental Health*, 17: 152–62.

Golding, K., Dent, H.R., Nissim, R. and Stott, E. (2006) *Thinking Psychologically about Children who are Looked After and Adopted: Space for Reflection*. Chichester: John Wiley & Sons.

Herman, J. (1992) *Trauma and Recovery*. New York: Basic Books.

Horowitz, M.J. and Becker, S.S. (1971) 'The compulsion to repeat trauma: Experimental study of intrusive thinking after stress', *The Journal of Nervous and Mental Disease*, 153: 32–40.

Koren, D., Norman, D., Cohen, A., Berman, J. and Klein, E. (2005) 'Increased PTSD risk with combat-related injury: A matched comparison study of injured and uninjured soldiers experiencing the same combat events', *American Journal of Psychiatry*, 162(2): 276–82.

Maier, S.F. and Seligman, M.E.P (1976) 'Learned helplessness: Theory and evidence', *Journal of Experimental Psychology*, 105: 3–46.

Meichenbaum, D.H. (1985) *Stress Inoculation Training*. New York: Pergamon.

NICE (2005) Post-traumatic stress disorder (PTSD): The management of PTSD in adults and children in primary and secondary care. Available online at: www.nice.org.uk/CG26

Ozer, E.J., Best, S.R., Lipsey, T.L. and Weiss, D.S. (2003) 'Predictors of posttraumatic stress disorder and symptoms in adults: A meta-analysis', *Psychological Bulletin*, 129(1): 52–73.

Pelcovitz, D., van der Kolk, B.A., Roth, S.H., Mandel, F., Kaplan, S. and Resick, P. (1997) 'Development of a criteria set and a structured interview for disorders of extreme stress', *Journal of traumatic stress*, 10: 3–16.

Perry, B.D. (2000) 'Traumatized children: How childhood trauma influences brain development', *The Journal of the California Alliance for the Mentally Ill*, 11(1): 48–51.

Piquero, A., Farrington, D. and Blumstein, A. (2007) *Key Issues in Criminal Career Research: New Analyses of the Cambridge Study in Delinquent Development*. Cambridge: Cambridge University Press.

Rogers, A. (1996) *A Shining Affliction: A Story of Harm and Healing in Psychotherapy*. New Jersey: Penguin.

Shapiro, F. (1989) 'Eye movement desensitization procedure: A new treatment for post-traumatic stress disorder', *Journal of Behavior Therapy and Experimental Psychiatry*, 20: 211–17.

Shapiro, F. (1996) 'Errors of context and review of eye movement desensitization and reprocessing research', *Journal of Behavior Therapy and Experimental Psychiatry*, 27: 313–17.

Shapiro, F. (2001) *Eye Movement Desensitization and Reprocessing: Basic Principles, Protocols and Procedures,* 2nd edition. New York: The Guilford Press.

Sunderland, M. (2006) *The Science of Parenting.* London: Dorling Kindersley.

Teicher, M.D. (2000) 'Wounds that time won't heal: The neurobiology of child abuse', *Cerebrum: The Dana Forum on brain science*, 2(4): 50–67.

UK Trauma Group (n.d) *Position Statement on Complex Post-Traumatic Stress Disorder*, Available at www.uktrauma.org.uk/cptsd.doc

van der Kolk, B.A. (1989) 'The compulsion to repeat the trauma: Re-enactment, revictimization, and masochism', *Psychiatric Clinics of North America*, 12(2): 389–411. Retrieved from www.cirp.org/library/psych/vanderkolk/

van der Kolk, B.A. (2005) 'Developmental trauma disorder: Toward a rational diagnosis for children with complex trauma histories', *Psychiatric Annals*, 35(5): 401–8.

Welch, K.L., and Beere, D.B. (2002) Eye movement desenisitisation and reprocessing: A treatment efficacy model', *Clinical Psychology and Psychotherapy*, 9: 165–76.

WHO (1992) *The ICD–10 Classification of Mental and Behavioural Disorders. Clinical Descriptions and Diagnostic Guidelines.* Geneva: World Health Organisation.

Wright, L., Borrill, J., Teers, R., and Cassidy, T. (2006) 'The mental health consequences of dealing with self-inflicted death in custody', *Counselling Psychology Quarterly*, 19(2): 165–80.

Chapter 8

Therapeutic practice with women in prisons and other secure settings

Jules Pearson

On 31 March 2009 there were 4,288 women in prison (Ministry of Justice 2010). The Prison Reform Trust (PRT 2009) reported that, in the past decade, the women's prison population has increased by 60 per cent. Women prisoners have been found to have high levels of mental health needs (HMCIP 2007; Corston 2007; PRT 2009). Her Majesty's Inspectorate of Prisons (HMCIP 2007) found that women were more likely than other prisoners to report mental health and drug problems. Others have found that a high proportion of women score above threshold on the GHQ-12, a screening questionnaire for psychological distress (see Liebling *et al.* 2005; Plugge *et al.* 2006; HMCIP 2007). Moreover, a high proportion of women in prison have harmed themselves in the past: 37 per cent of women have stated that they have attempted suicide in their lifetime (PRT 2009) and 16 per cent have reported that they have harmed themselves in the month before coming to prison (Plugge *et al.* 2006). While they are in prison self-harm continues to be a problem that women face: female prisoners constitute 6 per cent of the total prison population yet they account for 46 per cent of incidents of self-harm (PRT 2009). Outside prison, more men than women commit suicide but, once incarcerated, this situation is reversed (Corston 2007). Many women prisoners have also suffered disrupted and traumatic life experiences. The PRT (2009) reports that one in four women prisoners have spent time in local authority care, over half have reported domestic violence and one in three have reported sexual abuse.

Women prisoners are far more likely than men to be the primary carers of young children and this makes the experience of a prison sentence fundamentally different for women than men (Corston 2007). Due to the relatively small number of female prison places, women are more likely than men to be placed further away from home (Corston 2007), often at a considerable distance from their families and, significantly, from their children. It has been found that 66 per cent of women in prison have dependent children under the age of 18 and that only 5 per cent of children stay in their own house after their mothers are sent to prison (PRT 2009).

Women who have offended and who are suffering from a mental illness may be accommodated within secure hospital settings. In 2008, 447 of the 3,937 restricted 'mentally disordered offenders' were women (Ministry of Justice 2010).[1] This chapter explores the process of working therapeutically with women in prison and other secure settings. In particular it explores the complex dynamics often present in secure settings for women and offers practical suggestions for managing these dynamics.

Therapists, clinicians and activists who write about the subject of female violence and the concomitant dynamics (Welldon 1988; Mollon 1996; Pizzey 2003; Van Velsen 2003; Jeffcote and Watson 2004; Motz 2008) are able to name these dynamics, their toxicity, and the impact they have on the minds of those working in this area and with these dynamics. They describe how, for many women in this forensic cohort, such dynamics usually have their origins in histories of childhood neglect and trauma. A reluctance to name these issues is often due to a fear of 'demonising' women who have already been treated very badly. An essential point made by all these authors is that it is important to recognise that people who have been victimised may themselves become victimisers. Indeed, this is the very reason why many female offenders have come to be in forensic settings. Such acts often replicate past violations and traumatic experiences. These more threatening aspects of women's behaviour are hard to think about, both for the staff working with them, and for the women themselves, who often remain in states of trauma about their own abuse, unable to name these experiences, or their enactments of them with others. Tolerating these women's roles as both victim and perpetrator is a crucial part of the help that forensic services aim to provide. Not tolerating both roles polarises women as either poor victims or monsters, positions that can get enacted in the dynamics on a ward.

The importance of naming the dynamics of a forensic ward or service culture cannot be underestimated. Without such a process, a whole ward or service can unwittingly replicate aspects of abuse and neglect-filled histories. Such an idea is so difficult to imagine that most people, understandably, would rather not imagine how they may unconsciously represent painful aspects of a forensic patient's past. Indeed, this is the antithesis of why most people choose to work in the caring professions.

Yet this occurs because women in prisons and secure hospitals have experienced high levels of early abandonment, rejection, loss and abuse (DH 2002); some have also lost children, been rejected by family members and suffered extended periods of severe and enduring mental ill health (Jeffcote and Travers 2004). As a result they may also have expressed their distress about their past by carrying out desperate acts against themselves or against their own children and family members. As Jeffcote and Travers (2004) state, staff attempting to understand the meaning and function of the behaviours of women in forensic care need to see that such women have often been unable to process experiences of past abuse, and have a tendency to enact scenes from the past – both psychologically and physically – with those attempting to care for them. This is a complex but persistent aspect of forensic psychiatric care, and one that needs to be managed in a way that is not damaging for forensic patients nor for staff. In the first instance it is necessary, then, for mental health professionals to understand this dynamic and to be realistic about the ways in which clients can make use of the input being offered, as well as to be realistic about their progress through the forensic system.

The current chapter draws on the work of Jeffcote and Travers (2004), together with the clinical experience of the author in working with women with mental health problems in prisons and in medium- and low-secure psychiatric hospitals. The chapter provides some practical thinking around the management of what can feel like very complex dynamics, not only between staff and forensic patients, but also among the staff members caring for these patients. The main issues detailed in this chapter that arise from working with women in this field can be divided into three broad areas:

1 the internal worlds of female forensic patients;
2 the impact on the service dynamics; and
3 ways to respond to, rather than merely react to, the disturbing histories and current enactments of the past.

The aim of exploring these three areas is to understand some of the conceptual issues in a psychodynamic approach to therapeutic work. This chapter argues that one way to understand the underlying motivations of female offenders in psychiatric care is a psychodynamic approach, alongside some cognitive and behavioural approaches in the practical management of the issues arising.

Understanding the internal world of women in forensic settings

Histories of trauma and neglect and the effects on the minds of women

Some of the needs of women in forensic settings are different from those in general psychiatric settings. One of the main differences is that women are in forensic settings as a result of a criminal offence, which may often be seen as a physical enactment of past, traumatic, childhood experiences. Such acts may function as an attempt to expel or express these past unthinkable experiences, and the psychological effects on the individual, by giving them to someone else through an act of violence. As Motz (2008) says, 'what is too painful to be thought about may be enacted' (p. 2).

If an enactment is an understandable wish to get rid of, or to stop thinking about, the unthinkable, then staff are also likely not to want to think about the awful things that have happened to forensic patients. This can prevent staff from being able to recognise enactments going on around them. Given that the trauma experienced by these women is most likely to have occurred within a relationship or attachment, and often one that 'should' have been caring, then memories of trauma are likely to be triggered by attempts by professionals to establish a relationship of care. The sort of trauma referred to – that of childhood abuse – is qualitatively different from the trauma experienced in a car accident or a random attack on the street. It is an oversight to think that abusive trauma, experienced usually in the context of familial relationships, would not have implications for the way that a person will go on to relate to others who are caring for them in other contexts. Much of this abuse is likely to result in behaviours that fulfil the criteria for a personality disorder, usually a borderline personality disorder. However, the use of the term 'personality disorder' can often obscure what might be better termed an 'attachment disorder', which is the consequence of an abusive attachment. It is the abusive attachment that needs to be held in mind. Moreover, as Welldon (2008) states, victims are still thought to be women, and the perpetrators men, forgetting that the extreme abuse of anyone can lead to rare but appalling perversions of care by one who was previously a victim, and can go on to abuse others. If staff are unable to make a link between women's past abuse and their current offending, they will have difficulties in developing appropriate strategies for dealing with their risk of reoffending. It needs to be acknowledged that, when women have been subjected to abuse in childhood, they can feel preoccupied with memories of their own trauma, and for some it is only replacing their earlier persecution with offending that brings temporary relief from their own memories of victimisation (Motz 2008). As Motz (2008) says, this dynamic applies not only to sexual abuse, but also to physical and emotional abuse. When thinking specifically about maternal physical abuse in a review of studies, Motz (2008) concludes that:

> When women are violent, the aims or targets of their violence are more likely to be members of their family, including their children. Women are far less likely to be violent than men towards general members of the population, but when they are violent they target their own bodies and those of their children. It is a shocking statistic that so much violence is directed at children by the people into whose care they are entrusted. These findings of maternal abuse must challenge the myth of the all-nurturing, protective mother. (p. 75).

Disturbed attachment to care – the effect of past abuse on behaviour

Gorsuch (1999) writes about disturbed attachments, drawing on attachment theory (Bowlby 1969) in order to help us to understand what happens when attachment is disrupted in disturbing ways. She argues that where there is a history of severe parental abuse and maltreatment, a child will not have developed an appropriate response to obtain protection in the face of threat, since the protector and the threat are one and the same. Instead of developing a reasonably stable model of relationships and the care they can provide, the child is subject to constantly changing impulses towards the caregiver. In adulthood, these coexisting and incompatible forms of relating lead to sudden changes of mood and perception – the 'stable instability' that characterises borderline personality disorder (Higgit and Fonagy 1992). This oscillation is reflected in a flitting between two strategies to manage frightening feelings about care: (i) distancing, by being abusive or assaultative to staff, or using shocking methods of self-harm; and (ii) dependency, by presenting like a child with unmet needs, or with methods of self-harm that usually induce caring, rather than shock. Reluctance to care for women who are this disturbed in their way of relating to others is understandable. This is not to say that this reluctance is acceptable, but rather that the origins of these attitudes require exploration and understanding.

Gorsuch (1999) says that, if such women's disturbance can be understood as a disturbance of relationships, particularly relationships with significant and care-taking others, mental health professionals and prison staff will begin to see that one way or another they all become involved in intensely demanding, dependent and unstable relationships with the client group (as in case example 1). Staff will be subject to angry protest and punishment in the form of verbal and physical abuse and in the management of all levels of self-harming (Gorsuch 1999). To think that staff 'just need to respect, have positive regard towards and accept women' who have offended in disturbed and disturbing ways is unhelpful (Gorsuch 1999). Although this framework should always underpin the care of vulnerable groups, it may be insufficient as a sole means of intervention. Indeed, a model of pathology is needed to understand the level of these women's disturbance – disturbance that is an outcome of disturbing treatment from carers (Gorsuch 1999). 'Common sense' assumptions about how people 'normally' behave towards each other may be irrelevant to those whose hold on reality is fragile and fluctuating, and whose life experience has not been consistent with these 'normal' assumptions (Gorsuch 1999). Added to this, as Motz (2008) states, it is inevitable that trauma from childhood will be projected onto the whole network of people involved in their care, the understandable effect being one of triggering tremendous anxieties in staff. There is also considerable understandable resistance in staff to being associated in any way with women's abusers, and yet it is inevitable. Motz (2008) says that these feelings, having their origins in forensic patients, must be recognised and respected before a working therapeutic alliance can be made.

Case example I

Managing anger about having been abandoned by mother, by encouraging mothering behaviours in staff

Karen, a woman in her later 30s, had been in secure psychiatric care for two years. She had a diagnosis of borderline personality disorder. Her index offence was arson. She refused psychological intervention, and much of the psychological support was delivered through weekly nursing support groups. Problematic behaviours on the ward involved infrequent but serious assaults on staff. There was nothing to suggest that the assaults were driven by any psychotic process. Karen's relationships with staff were naturally strained as a result, and several nurses remarked that they found it very difficult to like her because of the assaults. When Karen became distressed she would sometimes ask female staff to brush her hair or to give her a hug. On other occasions she would try to hold hands with female staff. Some staff did as Karen requested; they reported that these acts helped them to manage their more negative feelings towards her because they felt that she was accepting care and support from them. However, it emerged that Karen's assaults on staff members often occurred in the context of her feeling let down by a female member of staff. Those behaviours that made the staff feel closer to her also created in Karen an expectation that she would be treated differently from other patients, more like a friend or family member. On those occasions when the reality of the professional relationship between them became clearer, for example when she was denied something she requested, she would assault that member of staff. Through opportunities for reflection during staff support groups, staff became more aware of their need to keep their professional boundaries in order to reduce their risk of being assaulted.

Problematic service dynamics

Both Motz (2008) and Adshead (1998) write about the idea that the hospital (or prison) can represent a functioning organisation or 'family' that needs to be attacked, where elements of revenge, deception and cruelty may well be part of the dynamic for those who have been abused within families as children. If this is not accepted as a basic premise of the ways in which forensic patients with such a history relate to others, the organisation can unwittingly become involved in enactments from the past. A common example in organisations caring for women who have been victims of secretive and deceptive abuse as a child involves the professionals within it being unconsciously made to experience what that child experienced – being silenced and made to feel helpless and hopeless. The woman is then able to rid herself of the experience of being let down and lied to by creating a situation where the victim part of herself is seen (the child), and the true and current source of danger in her as an adult (the offender) is disguised, and the staff treated as though they are the abuser (Motz 2008). For obvious reasons, this dynamic tends to be more prevalent in prisons, with a similar dynamic being present in secure units, with their culture of locked wards and most 'leaves' from the ward only being permissible once approved by the Ministry of Justice. When the staff try to help – usually moved by intense feelings of overidentification with the child part of the woman – they are sabotaged (because they are getting too close to naming the past), and instead made to feel the experience of being useless and humiliated (Motz 2008) – feelings that usually make the member of staff retreat.

The opposite can also happen. For example, in instances where women have committed serious acts of violence, including murder, the feelings evoked in the staff are so powerful that sometimes staff manage these feelings by taking a punitive approach – another form of over-involvement (Motz 2008). Motz (2008) states that this is more likely to occur if the offender does not report having psychotic symptoms, which would enable the staff to view her as 'mad' rather than 'bad'. (These dynamics are described in more detail below.) This may be an easier position for staff working in prisons, as the prevailing focus tends to be on criminal aspects of a person's presentation, compared to secure hospitals, where the main focus tends to be on mental health.

There seem to be two ways in which we as staff manage the 'awfulness' of what forensic women have experienced and have done (as mentioned earlier). The first is treating them as though they are totally responsible and able to control the more abusive aspects of their behaviour. At such times they are likely to be treated by some staff with little empathy or understanding. This dynamic is best understood as a way of women replicating their familiar experience of abusive attachments. It may also be in part the product of staff burnout in extremely demanding work. When this dynamic is present, staff members may describe such women as 'manipulative'. This amounts to underempathising with them, and to focusing primarily on the more criminogenic aspects of their histories. This could be seen as a defence against seeing the appalling histories of these women – against imagining the abuse that was inflicted upon them as children, and refusing to see them as victims because the abuse is unbearable to think about. As Cooper and Lousada (2005) state, 'the continual and perfectly understandable wish on the part of many staff to believe that what they are being presented with is *not* a [history] of child abuse […] is only human' (p. 160).

The second way of managing traumatic histories is not thinking about the abuse that women in forensic settings have committed, or which they are capable of committing again. Again, this dynamic is often the result of women presenting their needs in regressed and childlike ways. This way of behaving perhaps represents a wish to return to the beginning of life, probably to a time prior to their experiences of abuse. If the staff feel disturbed, as they might be expected to after hearing disturbing histories, and if staff are not supported in processing this information, they can easily respond to women with such histories as though they are totally unable to develop any control over their behaviour. In some cases, requests from women in forensic care, including clearly unboundaried requests, are treated as though they are totally reasonable and a part of 'service-user rights', with very little thought given to their function – that of keeping the unthinkable not thought about. For example, a woman might repeatedly ask for pregnancy tests because she believes she is pregnant; this could possibly be a functionally psychotic defence against her being separated from her baby since being admitted to a secure hospital; but when a test is done by the doctor, she is not found to be pregnant. When the patient thinks the doctor must be lying, she gives money to an inexperienced member of nursing staff to buy her a pregnancy test kit from the chemist, as she herself has no leave from the unit. The member of staff buys her a pregnancy test in the belief that this will relieve the patient's anxiety. This overempathising with forensic women (infantilising them) and focusing on the more psychiatric, and therefore less 'controllable', aspects of their presentations can be viewed as an understandable defence by staff against recognition of the violence of these women (see case example 2). Such women can only be seen as 'mad' and rarely 'bad'. Such a defence 'helps' to protect us from how we would feel about a woman who was, in fact, in her right mind when she committed a violent act. Such a defence is even more difficult to resist when someone presents as depressed and calm and talks only of experiences of being victimised (Motz 2008). When staff working in secure hospital wards or prisons infantilise perpetrators, it may become difficult for forensic patients to leave. Firstly, this may be because their risk is not being properly thought about, and they engage in care plans and probation orders in the community that so often lead to their failure and re-offending. Secondly, this may be because they have not had the best opportunity to develop rudimentary skills in self-soothing that allow for less problematic ways of relating with members of the public, housing officers, probation officers, or community mental health teams, without becoming abusive, assaultative or fleeing from care while on probation from prison or discharge from hospital.

Both ways of staff relating to forensic women, and of forensic women relating to staff, represent an attack on thinking where the outcome is collusion with a denial of what has happened or could happen – be it past abuse where the woman is the victim, or current abuse where the woman is the perpetrator (Motz 2008). These two areas of disavowal are particularly common in prisons and secure hospitals, and in themselves reflect the 'splitting' that is so often talked about within psychiatric services. Adshead (1998) writes well on this subject in psychiatric services, describing it as 'maladaptive caring'.

Case example 2

Staff unconsciously collude with a patient in her infantilisation, creating a blind spot for offending

Tracy, a woman in her early 20s, was arrested for a serious assault on another woman, by cutting her face with a small knife. She was brought straight to a secure psychiatric unit as it was immediately obvious that she had mental health problems. In spite of her age, she had a long psychiatric history of bipolar disorder, and became sexually vulnerable when unwell. She became the focus of attention on the ward for both patients and staff. She was too elated in mood most of the time to manage one-to-one psychological input, but she regularly managed to have one-to-one sessions with nursing staff, several times a day, during which she talked about her experience of childhood sexual abuse. The staff did not request any psychological input for her, as they felt that they were doing enough to support her with one-to-one sessions. They described her as charming, and felt sorry for her most of the time. Her day-to-day presentation made it difficult for staff to recall and think about her index offence, as she appeared to pose little risk on the ward. Her history of abuse led staff to focus on her victim status. This prevented the appropriate and very necessary regular assessment of risk. Tracy was prematurely recommended for escorted hospital leave, as 'the ward seemed to be making her feel low'. This enabled her to gain supervised access to the hospital shop. Two weeks after her escorted leave, a random search was made of the ward, in line with hospital procedure. During the search, a blade from a razor was found secreted in Tracy's pillow.

When asked where she had got it, she told staff she had stolen it from the hospital shop. She was unable to explain why she wanted the razor, but the fact that she had separated it from its original plastic handle suggested that she might have intended to use it as a weapon.

Helping staff to respond, rather than react, to disturbing histories and enactments of the past

Toxic, but essentially adaptive, ways of communicating distress can prompt in staff a compelling feeling of wanting to 'give it back' to female forensic patients, or to cut themselves off from them. It is rare for staff to hurt patients or prisoners physically, but acts of distancing themselves, of reducing therapeutic input or of not talking to clients after they have verbally or physically abused a staff member or after they have self-harmed, are all common but reactionary ways of managing the unprocessed trauma expressed or expelled by clients through these behaviours. The staff are largely unable to process these reactions without the assistance of a therapist, and it is effectively the therapist's job to help begin some of this processing for them. Where there develops an unconscious habit of 'not thinking', the role of clinical supervision and support external to the system becomes essential.

Making forensic wards and prison wings 'containing' and safe

Gorsuch (1999), Adshead (1998) and Petrie and Jeffcote (2004) all raise the importance of allowing the institution to become an attachment figure by offering consistent and reliable policies in day-to-day matters and in response to unexpected crises. This might, for example, involve establishing with each and every client how incidents of self-harm and violence will be dealt with and then involve responding to them accordingly. Petrie and Jeffcote (2004) put forward suggestions to help prevent crises on the ward, and to offer containment of both staff members' and patients' feelings of anxiety and threat. They specifically cover issues such as 'managing female staff and female patient/inmate relationships', reminding us that the staff needs to be as professional as possible in order to protect against overidentification between female workers and patients, which can so often emerge from prolonged periods of contact. Particular attention needs to be given to physical touch, which can so easily give mixed messages to patients about their relationships with staff. Within these sorts of relationships, Petrie and Jeffcote also note the need to avoid quasi-parental relationships which might create a need in the staff to 'repair the past' for the patient, which might reinforce a tendency to treat some patients like children, and which might generate unrealistic expectations of care from the patients (Petrie and Jeffcote 2004). Such a dynamic will inevitably push staff to operate outside their professional boundaries. Staff support groups are good places to bring these issues for discussion, or otherwise such practices will be pushed out of consciousness and no longer available for thinking and reflective practice.

Although the subject raised by Petrie and Jeffcote (2004) of 'gender mix and task assignment' may seem like an obvious one, the constant pressures on staffing often leave wards more likely to let male staff perform tasks that should always be done by female staff: observations inside female patients' bedrooms, observations in toilets, bathrooms or isolated areas, the administering of depot medication, searches of bedrooms, body search or personal searches, and supplying sanitary products. These can all make women feel threatened and leave the male staff member vulnerable to allegations of misconduct. Managers need to observe and be aware of attachments and behaviours from staff that are not consistent with safe, professional and therapeutic relationships, and address them. Yet this is a role managers often find difficult and awkward, and may avoid, and training and supervision are needed to support them in this aspect of their role (Petrie and Jeffcote 2004). Staff away days are useful for meeting this training need, which can be followed up with 'top up' supervision slots on wards or wings.

Lastly, with all the provision for regular staff, Petrie and Jeffcote (2004) note that it is easy to overlook new staff, especially those working bank shifts. They suggest that all new staff need an initial competency-based introduction to working with female forensic patients and prisoners. They argue that this should cover topics such as: responding to patients when they disclose personal information, managing sexualised conversations and inappropriate physical contact, judging appropriate contact between staff and patients, responding appropriately when patients attempt to find out personal information about staff, being aware of staff's behaviour towards one another, and presenting oneself as a professional person (see Petrie and Jeffcote 2004: 189–90).

Managing assaultative and self-harming behaviours

In order to safely manage female violence, it must be recognised and understood. Forensic organisations must guard against socially constructed stereotypes of women by recognising women's capacity for violence against people they are close to, as well as against themselves in the form of self-harm (Motz 2008). This requires moving to a middle ground of understanding, which incorporates both mental illness and attachment disorders, rather than a dichotomy. A focus on 'madness' locates women outside the realm of aggression and delinquency (Bushfield 1996) and may increase risks; it can have an effect on the ways in which all subsequent attacks on staff are understood and managed – or perhaps mismanaged by virtue of focusing solely on a mental illness explanation for the act.

Psychologists have long understood self-harm and assaults as tools of self-expression. They are ways of manipulating one's body, or the body of another, to reflect a psychological problem that is usually connected to trauma. It is essentially, then, a way of behaving to prevent thinking. In this sense self-harm may not be about attempting suicide, nor assault necessarily about trying to commit murder, but they may help to reduce the wish for suicide or murder. Many women who self-harm view their behaviour as self-preservative. This is perhaps why suicide attempts and assaults are increased when women are detained in secure settings where the means to self-harming, and access to substances that might dampen feelings of rage, are greatly reduced, and where anxiety is therefore likely to increase to levels that are totally unbearable without an outlet. The author has worked with women who have long histories of cutting themselves but who only attempted burning and self-strangulation in prison, because they had less access to 'sharps' and more access to lighters, shoelaces and belts. The function of self-harm may be different for each woman and within the same woman at different times and in different situations. One key function identified is the need to turn thoughts and memories, which cannot be processed or controlled, into a physical injury that can be controlled, or managed by intervention from others. The focus on the physical pain after the actual act can also function as a psychological distraction. Moreover, assaults on others can perform a similar function, where retaliatory assaults result in an injury that requires medical attention and temporarily keeps the victim of the retaliation from thinking about their reality.

Understanding the more specific reasons why a woman self-harms or assaults is the first stage in enabling her to find other less violent ways to articulate her distress and alleviate her pain. It can be useful to use a basic graded exposure model to less dangerous, less physically and psychologically damaging ways of managing distress. As part of the discourse around self-harm and assaultative behaviour, the author has found the greatest engagement from women when they are encouraged to think about these behaviours as related to addiction to alcohol and other substances. As many of these women also have such addictions, they relate to the comparison, admitting that self-harming and assaulting others may have a similar effect to that of substance abuse. A secondary therapeutic gain is that they are also thinking about the function of their substance abuse, without feeling that it is being challenged directly. Such use of comparisons in therapy can make thinking about these things less threatening, and help women to understand that the goal of therapy might not be to 'take away' their self-harming (a particular fear commonly vocalised by some women); the goal might instead be to help them to understand its function and development and to encourage them to think about ways in which they can downgrade their more serious methods of self-harming. Particularly for those who self-harm, the effect of this is often an increase in self-esteem, as some women admit to feeling embarrassed by having to resort to hurting themselves in order to feel better, wondering out loud 'what's wrong with me?' Being shown that there is a real function to their behaviour, and that their powerful attachment to it can be recognised as something as serious as an addiction, can have an empowering therapeutic effect and give some women the courage to explore alternative, less damaging ways of managing long-standing and acute levels of anxiety.

As well as the reduction of physical harm, attempts to explore the reasons for self-harm are also important. As a therapist, it can be helpful to think about the least difficult aspect of the patient's history, if and when she gives the therapist clues to it. By gently exploring what happened, and her experience of these things, the patient can learn that apparently intolerable psychic pain can be thought about, and that memories and feelings of despair do not necessarily require the urgent action of self-harm or assault (Motz 2008). By doing so, the therapist can offer the woman an experience of containment, and show her that she can bear to think about her history. The capacity to manage these powerful impulses and to put into words (to mentalise) these states of feeling, rather than to enact them, is central to this work (Bateman and Fonagy 2004).

When thinking about staff groups managing self-harm, as Motz (2008) states, these acts directed at the self also have indirect victims, such as the professionals who witness them and have to treat them. The failure to protect women from harming themselves can induce strong feelings of guilt. This commonly leads to two sets of behaviours in staff – rescuing or punishing – which are essentially ways of getting rid of feelings of guilt. On the one hand, a rescuing approach takes all control away from the woman, placing it in the carer who is expected to always be available and to see himself or herself as able to stop the patient from self-harming: 'as long as I'm on shift or available to them to give them a one-to-one, they won't self-harm'. On the other hand, the opposite approach, of 'punishing' the patient, puts all responsibility for the act of self-harm onto the patient, and is often aligned with a belief that 'she knows what she's doing' and is 'just attention-seeking'. In fact, women who self-harm in secure settings are often managing distress in the best way they know how. This may include 'proximity-seeking' through the attention of staff gained by self-harming acts, which may in turn prevent or reduce suicidal feelings. It is helpful to aim for an understanding of self-harm based on individual formulation that hopefully falls somewhere in between these two positions.

On managing self-harm on wards, Motz (2008) helpfully highlights research by Coid *et al.* (1992): women diagnosed with borderline personality disorder (BPD) tend to self-harm as a result of the intensity of their underlying symptoms of tension, depression, anxiety and anger, which build up during the day, without any particular external trigger. As a result, they are more likely to self-harm in the evening. This was not the case for those without such a diagnosis, for whom self-harm was triggered by external events. Those with BPD who experience depersonalisation and derealisation, particularly when they have a history of child abuse, may use self-harm to feel something, or to feel real again. Assaultative behaviour can also be understood in this way: those with BPD are more likely to assault others as a way of managing distressing feelings that have built up during the day, and those without such a diagnosis are more likely to assault others due to a specific incident.

Attempting to listen to the histories of women in forensic care

Once a basic and boundaried structure of care is in place, and not before, only then is it safe to think about one of the main tasks for forensic services for women: to provide safe opportunities for women to tell and think about their stories. This is a complicated and frightening task for both the women and their staff. When women do feel ready to start talking, they can do so in ways similar to verbal or physical abuse. For the listener, it can feel like being the recipient of something being expelled as they hear graphic details of past abuse, and in a way that may traumatise the listener. Sometimes the function of this is to shock and to keep the therapist at a distance. At other times, it might be an act of communication to help women make sense of some very disturbing, as yet unprocessed, experiences. In both instances, perhaps a basic response such as 'that sounds like a very frightening experience' is the beginning of something therapeutic – the naming of something that has previously been unnameable. Crucial to change is the capacity of these women to face their own destructive feelings and to experience feelings of dependency towards staff and others without collapsing (Kennedy 1997). This is something that is very difficult to do when the staff members are under extreme pressure from women in forensic care to retaliate verbally, or in some way to reject them. The effect of trying to manage these dynamics should not be underestimated for nursing and prison staff, whose core training is not in the processing of traumatic material. Working in such close proximity to these dynamics, and for protracted periods of time, means that this working relationship will involve being drawn into enactments of women's early traumatic experiences. Nursing staff especially need to be thought about and supported by the rest of the team through robust theoretical and practical frameworks of clinical management, as they often bear the main burden of this toxic material.

Conclusion

This chapter has primarily explored the polarised dynamic of care so commonly present in female forensic services – a dynamic unconsciously set up by forensic women as a way of managing the unbearable anxiety and disturbing thoughts that come from histories of unthinkable abuse, and a dynamic reflecting the 'splitting' that is so often talked about in women's forensic services. It is hoped that this chapter has shed some light on these dynamics by thinking about the internal worlds of these women, and about how their internal worlds affect the service dynamics in forensic settings. Therapists and all staff members working with women in their care want these women to receive the input that will help them to move on, and not to reoffend. It is equally important that the therapists and staff members are not traumatised by what they hear and experience on forensic wards and prison wings. Attending to their own feelings while looking after women in forensic care not only enables them to think in a way that assists them in providing appropriate therapeutic care; it also elicits the sort of thinking necessary for good-quality risk assessments. Being afforded the opportunity to express concerns about patients or prisoners in this way, and thereby to respond appropriately to the needs being communicated, is more likely to result in a psychological, rather than physical, containment of these needs (say, in one-to-one observations, seclusion, segregation, secure units and prison). In time, as forensic women learn to develop a form of self-containment, as modelled first by the staff, they will learn to develop less need for physical containment (secure units and prisons) in order to manage the very disturbing things that have happened to them. Only by looking after our feelings about the work we do as staff can we begin to help women in forensic settings to manage their feelings about what has happened in the past, and then to manage themselves in the community.

Note

1 These figures pertain only to 'restricted' patients: those patients that are subject to risk management by the Secretary of State for Justice (Ministry of Justice 2010).

References

Adshead, G. (1998) 'Psychiatric staff as attachment figures', *British Journal of Psychiatry*, 172: 64–9.

Bateman, A. and Fonagy, P. (2004) *Psychotherapy for Borderline Personality Disorder: Mentalization Based Treatment*. Oxford: Oxford University Press.

Bowlby, J. (1969) *Attachment and Loss, Vol 1: Attachment*. New York: Basic Books.

Bushfield, J. (1996) *Men, Women and Madness: Understanding Gender and Mental Disorder*. Basingstoke: Macmillan Press.

Coid, J., Wilkins, J., Coid, B. and Everitt, B. (1992) 'Self mutilation in female remanded prisoners II: a cluster analytic approach towards identification of a behavioural syndrome', *Criminal Behaviour and Mental Health*, 2: 1–14.

Cooper, A. and Lousada, J. (2005) *Borderline Welfare: Feeling and Fear of Feeling in Modern Welfare*. London: Karnac.

Corston J. (2007) *The Corston Report: A Review of Women with Particular Vulnerabilities in the Criminal Justice System.* London: Home Office.

DH (2002) *Women's Mental Health: Into the Mainstream, Strategic Development of Mental Health Care for Women* London: Department of Health.

Gorsuch, N. (1999) 'Disturbed female offenders: helping the "untreatable" ', *Journal of Forensic Psychiatry,* 10(1): 98–118.

Higgitt, A. and Fonagy, P. (1992) 'Psychotherapy in borderline and narcissistic personality disorder', *British Journal of Psychiatry,* 161: 23–43.

HMCIP (2007) *The Mental Health of Prisoners: A Thematic Review of the Care and Support of Prisoners with Mental Health Needs.* London: HM Inspectorate of Prisons.

Jeffcote, N. and Travers, R. (2004) 'Thinking about the needs of women in secure settings', in N. Jeffcote and T. Watson (eds), *Working Therapeutically with Women in Secure Mental Health Settings.* London: Jessica Kingsley Publishers.

Jeffcote, N. and Watson, T. (eds) (2004) *Working Therapeutically with Women in Secure Mental Health Settings.* London: Jessica Kingsley Publishers.

Kennedy, R. (1997) *Child Abuse, Psychotherapy and the Law.* London: Free Association Books.

Liebling, A., Tait, S., Durie, L., Stiles, A. and Harvey, J. (2005) *An Evaluation of the Safer Locals Programme.* Cambridge Institute of Criminology: Unpublished Report.

Ministry of Justice (2010) *Statistics of Mentally Disordered Offenders 2008 England and Wales. Ministry of Justice Statistics Bulletin.* London: Ministry of Justice.

Mollon, P. (1996) *Multiple Selves, Multiple Voices – Working with Trauma, Violation and Dissociation.* Chichester: John Wiley & Sons.

Motz, A. (2008) *The Psychology of Female Violence – Crimes against the body,* second edition. Abingdon: Routledge.

Petrie, L. and Jeffcote, N. (2004) 'Men, women and good practice', in N. Jeffcote and T. Watson (eds), *Working Therapeutically with Women in Secure Mental Health Settings.* London: Jessica Kingsley Publishers.

Pizzey, E. (2003) *The Women's Refuge Movement.* Lecture at North London Forensic Service, 6th International Conference: 'Women as victims and perpetrators of violence', Queen's College, Cambridge.

Plugge, E., Douglas, N. and Fitzpatrick, R. (2006) *The Health of Women in Prison Study.* Department of Public Health, University of Oxford. Available at: www.publichealth.ox.ac.uk/units/prison/2007-02-13.6702780065

PRT (2009) *Bromley Briefings Prison Factfile.* London: Prison Reform Trust.

Van Velsen, C. (2003) *Violent Women in Film and Literature.* Lecture at North London Forensic Service, 6th International Conference: 'Women as victims and perpetrators of violence', Queen's College, Cambridge.

Welldon, E.V. (1988) *Mother, Madonna, Whore.* New York: The Guilford Press.

Welldon, E.V. (2008) 'Foreword to first edition', in A. Motz *Psychology of Female Violence – Crimes against the body*, second edition. Abingdon: Routledge, pp. ix–xiv.

Chapter 9

Therapy with black and minority ethnic people in prisons and secure mental health settings: keeping race in mind

Frank Lowe and Jules Pearson

There was a culture within the Prison Service [...] to treat race relations as divorced from the basic operational requirements of prison work. There was a real tendency to ignore the holistic nature of race relations as something which affected every aspect of prison life. (Zahid Mubarak Inquiry 2006: 417, para. 51.14)

We heard that there is over-representation occurring in black people who fail to respond to treatment for schizophrenia. They tend to receive higher doses of anti-psychotic medication than white people with similar health problems. They are generally regarded by mental health staff as more aggressive, more alarming, more dangerous and more difficult to treat. Instead of being discharged back into the community they are more likely to remain as long-term in-patients. (David Bennett Inquiry 2003: 42)

This chapter will explore some of the mental health needs and issues for black and other minority ethnic (BME)[1] people in prison and secure mental health settings and will identify some of the key challenges facing therapists working with BME patients in these contexts. It puts forward the idea that the capacity to be curious and thoughtful about the experience and meaning of race, for both the patient and therapist, is critical to therapeutic effectiveness. Equally important is the ability to think about and work with the tensions, conflicts and issues within the triangular relationship of patient, therapist and forensic system.

Background and context

Black and minority ethnic people are significantly over-represented in British prisons and the forensic mental health system (Boast and Chesterman 1995; Shaw *et al.* 1999; Sharpley *et al.* 2001). Although BME people make up roughly 8 per cent of the UK's population, they make up 27 per cent of the prisoner population. This chapter will focus mainly on the black prisoners and patients in the forensic system as they are the largest minority group, making up 15 per cent of the prisoner population in the UK and 58 per cent of the BME forensic population. Annual statistics from the Ministry of Justice consistently show that black people are over-represented in almost all stages of the criminal justice system. They are seven times more likely than whites to be stopped and searched, three and a half times more likely to be arrested and five times more likely to be in prison (Ministry of Justice 2008).

The provision of appropriate mental health services for ethnic minority groups in Britain has become an area of considerable concern within both the NHS and forensic systems. This is important first because of the increasing ethnic diversity of the UK's population, second because of the over-representation of black people in psychiatric and forensic settings, and third because of repeated evidence that black people are the least satisfied of all groups with the psychiatric care they receive (Browne 1997; Butt 2001). The David Bennett Inquiry (2003) has also played an important role in highlighting some of the more significant problems with the treatment of black men in the forensic mental health system.

Black people's negative relationship to mental health services prior to this inquiry has been well documented (Fernando 1988, 1991, Fernando *et al.* 1998; Littlewood and Lipsedge 1981, 1988, 1997). They are more likely than white people to be admitted to psychiatric hospitals, more likely to be compulsorily detained there under the Mental Health Act 1983, more likely to be diagnosed as psychotic and less likely to receive psychological therapies (Keating *et al.* 2002; Sashidharan 2003; DH 2005; Williams *et al.* 2006). These are reasons likely to contribute greatly to the 'negative relationship'. Black people's dissatisfaction with psychiatric care is believed to be related to prejudicial assumptions and stereotypes within mental health services about black people, as well as to a failure to understand their cultural and social circumstances (CSIP 2006; Keating 2007). Keating *et al.* (2002) have shown that black people's negative experience of psychiatry has created a 'circle of fear'. They describe the circle of fear as involving a reluctance to ask for help when it might be needed. Consequently, untreated problems become crises, often leading to compulsory admission to hospital, thus reinforcing a fear of mental health services and so the circle of fear is perpetuated.

Delivering Race Equality (DRE) in mental health is a current government action plan which seeks to tackle these issues. So how are mental health services in prisons and secure mental settings implementing DRE, and how much are clinicians keeping race in mind in their practice in these settings? Given the high proportion of black people in prison and forensic psychiatric care, are the people working in these settings able to be thoughtful about race issues, and are they creating an environment where black prisoners are protected and appropriately cared for?

Before we explore these issues, it might be helpful to make it clear what we mean by the term 'race'. The classification of people into racial groups has a long and essentially racist history in western culture. Many erroneously believe that race is a scientific concept, but it is in fact a crude way of classifying people as a means to explain their status or access to power (Fernando 1991). In this chapter we use the term 'race' to refer to the continued classification of people into racial groups based on physical characteristics such as skin colour, using terms such as 'black' to define Africans and African-Caribbeans (British or otherwise) and 'white' to define Caucasians (British or otherwise). We accept that this is not ideal, but it is the currently accepted terminology for defining different racial groups.

Clinical assessments and psychological input for black and minority ethnic people in forensic settings

Given the concern that many of us have about stereotypical thinking, thoughtlessness and the failure to manage race issues in general clinical settings, the relevance of race increases considerably in forensic settings. For example a therapist might assess a black male patient who raped a woman while psychotic, or treat a young black man who has difficulties managing his angry feelings and is in a secure unit because he has stabbed another young black man during an argument while under the influence of cannabis. How will clinicians manage to think about cases with material that might trigger various stereotypes? What might these offenders think about their white, or indeed black, clinicians? What might these clinicians think about these offenders, and what does each party think that the other party thinks about them? This is a therapeutic minefield, and likely to have massive implications for trust and engagement and for the validity of clinicians' assessments and interventions. As Aitken (2000) outlines, forensic clinical psychologists and psychotherapists are an integral part of the interface between the medical and the legal systems. In such a role we are in a triangular relationship comprising patient/therapist/society (whether society is the public, criminal justice system, and so on), managing conflicting interests to a degree not seen in other settings.

The main challenge in treating black prisoners/patients is to engage in a process of self-development and professional development in order to become at least aware of the effects of racialised assumptions and practices in the forensic system (Aitken 2000). The first assumption identified by Aitken (2000) is problematising race. She highlights the stereotypes associated with people of African and Caribbean origin: an excess of family instability, criminality, irrationality, physicality, aggressiveness, dangerousness, over-sexualisation, substance misuse and a lack of intellectual capacity. How does a clinician address their own views about these stereotypes before completing a fair assessment of the risk of reoffending? How does the clinician think about a black patient's experience of having their intellectual functioning assessed so that they can perform in such a way that actually represents their best efforts? How does the clinician come to terms with the obvious cultural bias in some assessments of intellectual functioning, and reflect it in their interpretation of the scores? The clinician would first have to recognise the bias by reflecting on their thoughts about the individual, and be aware of the words they use to describe the individual they are assessing, both with colleagues and in their reports. Ndegwa (1998) points out that for some clinicians, being largely drawn from the middle classes, and in the main not attending multicultural or multiracial urban schools, nor growing up in racially mixed neighbourhoods, the first intimate contact with black and minority ethnic people may be in forensic settings, where judgements and decisions are being made about a person from a different race who are at their most vulnerable. The person being assessed could quite legitimately have a problem with this on a number of levels. One outcome is that they are unlikely to see psychiatry, psychology or psychotherapy as neutral or benign.

When dangerousness and risk are at the centre of our work in forensic settings, what factors are affecting our thinking around these issues in the face of so many potential triggers for unwitting stereotypical thinking? Fernando (1988) talks about the need for assessments to take in as much knowledge as possible about an individual's life circumstances. Although this sounds like a standard approach, he adds that these circumstances should be evaluated against a background of social conditions that must include experiences of racism. Contextual variables in the onset of aggression are likely to include repeated experiences of inequality, racism, homelessness and unemployment. Interpersonal variables include repeated experiences of conflict, provocation, hostility, stereotypes, prejudice and misunderstandings. We would add 'rejection'. Personal variables include repeated experiences of frustration, anger, imagined and real fears, psychological problems or illness, and family problems or illness. In analysing episodes of violence, Fernando (1998) talks about the importance of finding ways of understanding basic factors implicated in the genesis of aggression. Risk assessments of those with a mental illness also, Fernando argues, need to move away from an 'illness analysis' towards a real-life understanding of how repeated frustration, provocation, prejudice, stereotypes, family problems, homelessness and unemployment can all lead to violence in the context of a mental illness. The mental illness may not necessarily be the sole cause for aggression; it may be that it is the disinhibiting factor in the context of lifelong provocation. Fernando (1998) argues that the role of psychiatrists or psychologists in decision-making which involves the assessment of dangerousness, particularly when it leads to the deprivation of a person's liberty or rights or privileges, should be challenged by peers and other professionals, and the limitations of psychiatric and psychological assessments should be made explicit. Indeed, a service that meets the needs of BME prisoners and patients is one where stereotypes are recognised and challenged, not left untouched or not thought about.

To explore some of the mental health needs and issues for BME people, we will look at two forensic cases – the Zahid Mubarek Inquiry and the David Bennett Inquiry. These case examples illustrate some of the issues and challenges for BME people and therapists working with them in prisons and secure mental health settings. They also illustrate well the setting or context, and particularly the culture, which exists around race or culture, and how BME people are treated as a result. These two cases ended in the death of the person being discussed, but we have selected such cases because in our clinical experience, the discourse in BME cohorts (particularly black British people) in all forensic settings (secure hospitals, police cells and prison cells) contains genuine fears about safety. This suggests there are some very real fears about engaging with forensic services and with the therapy that forensic services offer. Such fears are based on actual incidents that have occurred, and which need to be thought about in the process of engagement.

Case example I

Zahid Mubarek – denial and thoughtlessness about racism in prison

The tragic death of Zahid Mubarek, who was killed by his cellmate in prison in March 2000, led to a public inquiry in April 2004. This provides the focus of our first case study. Zahid Mubarek was an Asian teenager with a drug addiction, serving a short sentence at HM Young Offender Institution (YOI) Feltham in March 2000 for a number of petty crimes. The day before he was due to be released from prison he was attacked and killed by Robert Stewart, with whom he had been sharing a cell for six weeks. Robert Stewart, a young white man, had strong racist views and a violent past. He was volatile, unpredictable and suspected of having mental health problems. He had two prominent tattoos on his forehead (a cross and the letters RIP). Why was someone like Robert Stewart put in a prison cell with Zahid Mubarek?

An internal Prison Service investigation (Butt 2000), a formal CRE investigation (2003) and an independent public inquiry into Zahid Mubarek's death (2006) all concluded that there had been collective organisational thoughtlessness about race in the Prison Service, which led to a tragic failure to provide proper care and protection for Zahid Mubarek. There had been no thought about the wisdom of putting Robert Stewart in a cell with Zahid Mubarek, even after a racist letter written by Robert Stewart had been intercepted. No thought was given to how Zahid Mubarek might feel about sharing a cell with Robert Stewart, or whether he might feel inhibited about asking to change cells.

The Zahid Mubarek Inquiry found that a small number of prison staff were overtly racist to prisoners and staff and that some BME officers would turn a blind eye to this racism, and sometimes even collude with it in order to fit in with their white colleagues (p. 419, para. 51.17). Racist attitudes and behaviour were common among prisoners, including BME ones. There was a wider, more subtle, racism in HM YOI Feltham which was manifested in the disproportionate number of BME prisoners whom officers restrained by force, or who were 'sent to segregation unit after fighting with a white prisoner, with the latter invariably remaining on the residential unit' (p. 414, para. 51.4).

The staff had little understanding of race relations, and although race relations training was mandatory, less than 30 per cent of the staff had received such training (p. 414, para. 51.6). HM YOI Feltham's management did not understand racial issues nor how to deal with them and lacked commitment to the promotion of good race relations. Race incidents and issues were not discussed in any depth, and no solutions or strategies were developed (p. 416, para. 51.10).

The report of the Zahid Mubarek Inquiry (2006) concluded that blindness to race existed both within and outside the Prison Service. It pointed out that although HM YOI Feltham's shortcomings in race relations were obvious, there was a culture within the Prison Service to treat race relations as divorced from basic operational requirements of prison work, and that the majority of staff continued to be in denial about the appalling state of race relations in the prison. This blindness, it found, was mirrored by Her Majesty's Chief Inspectorate of Prisons (HMCIP), which, while devastating in its condemnation of HM YOI Feltham's many failings, did not mention the problems with race relations anywhere in its report (p. 417, para. 51.14).

HMCIP (2005) published a thematic review of race within the Prison Service entitled *Parallel Worlds*. It described a lack of a shared understanding of race issues in prisons between black and white people. White managers and staff thought prisons operated in a broadly fair way, but BME staff and prisoners were less positive. In fact, BME prisoners consistently had the most negative perceptions of all, reporting poorer experiences across almost all aspects of prison life. This finding of a parallel world is not only applicable to prison settings or to prison staff, but also to secure mental health settings and mental health clinicians, where there can be insufficient consideration given to race in clinical practice. (The case of David 'Rocky' Bennett below further illustrates this.)

A Review of Race Equality in Prisons in 2008, five years after a CRE investigation into Zahid Mubarek's death, found that overt racism was far less likely to occur, but that concerns remained about covert or subtle structural racism. National monitoring data showed that the differential treatment of BME prisoners had not yet been fully addressed. The report stated that black prisoners in particular are consistently more likely to be on basic regime, to be in the segregation unit for discipline and to have force used against them. In almost all aspects of prison life, the perceptions of BME prisoners are still more negative than perceptions of their white counterparts. One of the most significant differences was that BME prisoners had more negative perceptions of their relationships with prison staff than did white prisoners (Ministry of Justice 2008). This is further supported by Cheliotis and Liebling's (2005) finding that perceived quality of race relations is significantly associated with prisoners' views of more general aspects of their treatment in prison, such as respect, humanity, fairness, safety and relationships with staff.

Case example 2

David 'Rocky' Bennett Inquiry – race and cultural blindness in secure hospitals

This case is a good illustration of a race-blind approach to care and treatment in the forensic system, and its devastating consequences on the life of a vulnerable patient.

David Bennett was a British African-Caribbean man who was being treated for schizophrenia for 18 years before his death in October 1998 in a medium-secure unit in Norwich. On the evening of his death he had been involved in an incident with another patient who was white. During that incident each man struck out at the other, with further assaults between them that could be described as a fight. During these assaults Bennett was also repeatedly racially abused by the other patient (pp. 16–17). After this incident the staff moved Bennett to another ward because they felt his mental state was fragile and therefore appropriate for the more acute ward. They did not consider it appropriate to transfer the white patient to the acute ward, as his mental state was not in question. Despite Bennett saying, 'I don't know why it's me that's going,' and being told, 'Well, you need to,' he responded well and moved to the other ward without any incident. While on the acute ward Bennett was told that he would be staying the night on the ward, to which he responded, 'Yep, yep, OK.' When he asked about the other patient he was told, 'No, he will be staying where he is'; in other words, he was not moved. Bennett immediately punched the nurse three times in the face (p. 17). He seemingly did so because he thought that he was being treated less favourably than the white patient who had racially abused him. Consequently, four or five nurses attempted to restrain him and after a prolonged struggle of almost half an hour, he died.

The consultant psychiatrist responsible for David Bennett's overall treatment at the clinic never discussed the issue of race with him because she did not feel it was an issue. She did not see that the fact that he was either the only black man, or possibly one of two or three on the ward, might have an effect on his mood or aggression. A psychologist thought that David Bennett was not well enough at the time for psychological intervention. She reported that initially he was friendly, but that after she told him that she was a psychologist and suggested that they should talk, he always refused. He later told her that she was a spy from Peterborough Football Club. The psychologist did not consider whether Bennett's response might have had anything to do with his or her race.

One of David Bennett's nurses remembered him having once said, 'Don't you know I am black? Why do you treat me like everybody else?' The nurse had replied, 'Well, you are no different to everybody. I do not see you as different from anybody else.'

The inquiry found no evidence of deliberate racism by mental health staff towards David Bennett, but concluded that insufficient attention had been paid to his ethnic, cultural, social and religious needs, and that this seriously diminished the quality of his life in the medium-secure unit. In 1993, David Bennett had written a letter to the head of nursing saying that the fact that the clinic had no African staff was appalling, and that there should be at least two black people in the medical or social work staff, 'for the obvious reasons of security and contentment for all concerned'.

The evidence given in the Inquiry led those writing the report to conclude that racism affects its victims. They surmised that the victim is bound to feel acutely sensitive, and frequently has the desire to retaliate, particularly if his perception is that no action may be taken to prevent racist abuse. Where victims are mentally ill and subjected to racist abuse, they are likely to have greater difficulty in dealing with it. It is also often mistakenly believed that racism only occurs if it is conscious and deliberate. The Inquiry concluded that mental health practitioners did not recognise that a patient's needs include cultural, social and spiritual needs. This is a common deficiency in mental health clinical practice and is a form of institutional racism. The Inquiry made a total of 22 recommendations, which included the stipulation that all clinical staff should receive training in cultural awareness and sensitivity, and in tackling overt and covert racism and institutional racism.

Training in cultural awareness, competency and sensitivity is now a mandatory part of training for all clinical staff in the NHS. Although there has been ministerial acknowledgement of institutional racism in mental health services, it is our experience that race still baffles some staff, thereby making it difficult for mental health services to make a commitment to address it. Often there is little, if any, meaningful guidance or policy from managers and senior staff that translates into day-to-day practice in the management of issues around race and culture. It is our sense that many services have taken up the importance of recording incidents of racial abuse between patients. However, some services are still struggling with thinking about what sanctions to apply when it occurs, almost as if they have forgotten that racist abuse is a criminal offence. Also, there does not yet seem to be service-wide consistency about displaying signs and policies outlining how racist abuse will be managed.

All psychiatric settings now have to keep a record of restraints and seclusions, but not all are consistently recording ethnicity. The 'Count Me In' Census (2005) – a national census of inpatients in mental health hospitals and facilities in England and Wales – looked at a number of aspects of inpatient psychiatric care. It was found that the rate of control and restraint among men from the 'Black Caribbean group' was 29 per cent higher than the average rate for all inpatients (Healthcare Commission 2005).

Discussion of case examples 1 and 2

Although there is more acknowledgement of the effects of racist abuse on patients' day-to-day well-being, there is not yet open discussion of the long-term effects of racism on an individual's mental health, including the effects on his or her relationship to himself or herself and to others, in the formulation of mental illness. Nor is there much in the way of thinking about how BME patients experience hospital, socially and psychologically. Pertinently, the case examples resulted in the death of a prisoner and an inpatient. These are well documented and publicised events. How such events are carried in the minds of our BME patients needs to be thought about by therapists, and possibly also with our patients, when attempting to engage them in psychological therapy.

In short, there has been considerable progress with the basics, especially the more practical aspects of the recommendations, but more thinking is needed in the area of managing racism in day-to-day incidents. Further attention also needs to be given to thinking about race in the patient–clinician relationship, and its implications for the care and treatment the patient might need.

The tragic deaths of Zahid Mubarek and David Bennett demonstrate that although race is an obvious issue in prisons and secure mental health settings, there is little real thinking about the impact of race on assessment and treatment, and on the quality of the lives of black inmates or patients. The David Bennett Inquiry demonstrated that mental health practitioners could not recognise that a patient's needs include their cultural and spiritual needs.

There is immense resistance within many organisations and occupational cultures to think seriously about race in service delivery. Jack Straw's view, expressed in response to the Stephen Lawrence Inquiry report, comes to mind: 'In my view, any long-established, white dominated organization is liable to have procedures, practices and cultures, that exclude or disadvantage non-white people'(Straw, in *Hansard*, 24 February 1999: col. 391).

Thinking about psychological input for black people

In thinking about the preceding cases in more depth, there is some helpful literature on therapy with people from BME groups, but it is limited, and more so when referring to therapy with BME groups in the forensic system. A collection of papers from Moodley and Palmer (2006) on *Race, Culture and Psychotherapy: Critical Perspectives in Multicultural Practice* provides the most up-to-date literature in this area. The sort of thinking that is demonstrated in our summary of these papers, we believe, provides a context and a place to start, with a subject that can so often cause considerable anxiety in institutions.

Moodley and Palmer (2006) highlight an obvious absence of thinking about notions of race in the world of psychotherapy. One of the papers in their book raises the importance of readdressing this problem, as race is an important organiser of experience for black people (Yi 2006), and particularly in countries where they are seen as a minority group. Not addressing race in therapy means doing disservice to a large number of patients, and particularly in settings where black and minority ethnic people are over-represented. On reviewing the dearth of literature on this subject, there seems to be a general discomfort with talking about 'race'. When there is an attempt to address difference, it tends to take the more comfortable position of exploring 'cultural' issues.

The exotic position and cultural blindness

Moodley and Palmer's book highlights two problems with focusing exclusively on culture: (i) becoming fixated by culture, to the exclusion of race – what Halsey and Patel (2003) call 'the exotic position'; and (ii) attempting culture-free therapy, which excludes race in a different way – what Halsey and Patel (2003) call 'the colour-blind position'. The latter position seems the most common in the literature to date. Morgan (1998) explains why: it is as if we are trying to swallow up a difficult subject and lose it in a generality of difference. This has the appearance of good therapeutic practice, for it seems to be seeing the individual and not the category. Morgan names the difficult subject 'racism', and admits how very hard it is for all of us to think about it. Ignoring the difference is more comfortable, but it is a denial – a defence against a complex array of emotions that includes anxiety, fear, guilt, shame and envy. No wonder we do our best to avoid the subject (Morgan 1998).

Helpful criticism of the culturalist therapeutic approach (exoticising the patient) comes from Dalal (2006). He gives a powerful hypothetical example of the various possible reactions to a black man versus an elderly white woman knocking at someone's door, showing us that such reactions have little to do with 'culture'. The person having a negative reaction to the black man is unlikely to be helped by 'diversity training', where they might learn about the food preferences or religious beliefs of black men in the UK. Translated into race in the therapy room, Dalal says that by using the 'culture' approach one needs to ask what purpose is being served by making the differentiation about culture, rather than about race.

The following case example paraphrased from Dalal shows us how the two usual approaches to culture (fixation with/exclusion of culture) do not quite work: a black group member ('Winston') had given very little of himself in the two years since joining the group. He missed a session, and on his return told the group that he had needed to be with his partner as she had just had a miscarriage. While sympathetic, the other group members were aggrieved because they had had no idea that his partner had been pregnant for some months. When they challenged him as to why he had kept this significant life event to himself, he replied that it was not his intention to hide anything; the reason for his reticence was that in his culture one kept this sort of thing in the family. When the group challenges Winston his defence is to play the 'culture card', to close the door on any further exploration. The group falls silent because of the unspoken injunction to 'respect cultural difference', leaving them nowhere to go. But there are other cultures present in the room. The culture of psychotherapy encourages people to be open in their communication on all sorts of levels. Winston's 'hiddenness' is therefore seen as something needing interpreting and deconstructing. What is taking place here is a cultural conflict. According to the ethics generated by the psychoanalytical cultural system, 'respecting' Winston's cultural difference would be to abandon him to his fortress of solitude. But neither would it be ethical to try and break down Winston's defences forcefully, because presumably the defences are there for a reason. Dalal says there is also the question of how true Winston's claim is that the conventions of his culture prohibit certain things being spoken about. It would certainly be helpful to know about the conventions of that culture (perhaps 'diversity training' would help here), as it would give the therapist grounds for challenging Winston's defensive use of a cultural convention. However, even if the convention is true, not everyone from that cultural background would follow the convention in the same way and to the same degree. Dalal concludes that none of us resides in a culture-free zone, and it is not enough to simply respect cultural differences; rather, what is required is a critical engagement with the differences, with some change in thinking occurring in both parties as a consequence.

More racial than cultural

Other literature prefers to focus more centrally on the issue of 'race', as it is this aspect of a person that usually leads to experiences of being devalued, and to subsequent self-devaluation. Being aware of this is more significant than, or at the very least equal to, awareness of cultural differences affecting diet, dress or religious beliefs. Experiences of racism have long been ones that many people from BME groups in the mental health system want to talk about (Wilson and Francis 1997). Bhugra and Bhui (2006) say that if a patient is not able to feel believed or understood about these aspects of their life, even if the therapist believes they are not significant, an insensitive disavowal of them will lead to therapeutic barriers. A therapist's own knowledge and continual self-awareness are important factors in preventing personal reactions affecting therapeutic efficacy. The psychodynamic trainings in particular attend to this, but racial attitudes may never be properly scrutinised in the therapist's personal analysis, or in the training programmes of the training organisations (Bhugra and Bhui 2006). One of the current authors' experience of training in the UK as a clinical psychologist was of lectures on the subject of race (usually just ethnicity), being separated from other lectures exploring the intra-psychic worlds of patients with borderline personality disorder, depression, psychosis and so on. The predominant lectures made little reference to how these illnesses, for BME groups, might in any way be linked to their, and others', experience of their 'race'.

Conspiracies of silence

One of the more prolific writers on the subject of race in therapy, Dorothy Evans Holmes, examines racial transferential reactions in psychoanalysis and psychotherapy (Holmes 1992; 2006). For her, not addressing race in all its reality-bound aspects is equivalent to ignoring the elephant in the room. Due to the issue of over-representation of BME groups, particularly black men, in the forensic system, we would suggest that in no service more than forensic services does the 'elephant' need acknowledging. Holmes explains that racial issues carry burdens beyond ordinary countertransferences. Her view is that didactic learning and supervision are necessary tools in gaining mastery as a therapist with respect to race. But she says that this alone is not adequate, that only a therapist's own therapy being attuned to racial meanings can help them to master their own racially related issues, and for therapists of all races and ethnicities. She goes on to say that unless this sort of exploration is entered into, we are more likely to yield to conspiracies of silence with our patients around race. Representations of race within each of us need deciphering. Access to racially influenced constructions of others is not always to hand because we are all so strongly motivated to hide them (Holmes 2006). Holmes (2006) describes two key things that BME people often need in therapy. The first is the realisation that the lived reality of race demands that people from BME groups are often invalidated. The therapist must convey this realisation because in experiencing oneself as invalid one cannot conceptualise oneself, and if one cannot conceptualise oneself, one cannot begin to take up what is being thought about in therapy. The second is that the therapist must be able to help the patient to mentalise what has been constructed around race, externally and internally – that is, the painfully limited and limiting experience of self via others, and of being given low value and expectation.

Not talking about difference too soon

Yi (2006) highlights the importance of not explaining away mental health problems as exclusively due to the effects of racism, thereby neglecting their personal or individual meaning. Not that we, or any of the authors in this book, seem to be doing this. However, there is a danger of racial minority therapists, who are usually more cognisant of race and the impact of race on therapy than white therapists, raising the issue of race with patients regardless of their patient's individual position on it. This is echoed by Tang and Gardner (2006) who believe that there are times in therapy when highlighting differences forecloses on the potential space where the patient is able to use fantasy to feel connected or even similar to their therapist, where the illusion of similarity is vital to the therapeutic work. If this is true, then there are many considerations that go into the decision about whether to make racial differences, or similarities, explicit in the work – the when and how. How can we engage with such important considerations if we have had so little practice in thinking about race in the first place?

Trying not to be defensive about racism

Focusing on what the patient brings to sessions, Liggan and Kay (2006) talk convincingly of the potential damage that can be done when BME patients' expression of their difficulties pertaining to race is not legitimised by the therapist as an important focus for treatment, but is interpreted as a defensive attempt to avoid painful inner conflict. Liggan and Kay (2006) highlight the importance of treating such disclosures as central to therapeutic work. However, they acknowledge that it seems to be difficult for us as therapists, both BME and non-BME, to examine openly and critically how our own unconscious biases and perceptions adversely affect and limit our treatment of BME patients. Altman (2006) goes further. He argues that we are all socialised to be racist, and to take for granted the discriminatory practices of our society, profession, or employer. He says, however, that we need not be a prisoner of the language and concepts within which we have been trained to think and experience; we have the capacity to reflect on preconceptions, even those ingrained during our early 'socialisation'. What Altman suggests is that we should *expect* to find racism in our countertransference, and in our thoughts and feelings generally, and that reflection on our countertransference is essential if we wish to deal with race in our therapeutic work. He advocates that as clinicians we become familiar with our racist feelings and attitudes. If not we will mistake our 'goodwill' and good intentions as non-racism, and miss all that needs to be attended to in the transference and countertransference. Altman has the view that it is safer to take the attitude that racism is always there and that vigilance in our practice is required. Lowe (2008) uses some very helpful clinical examples to help us think about the difficult subject of black and white object relations within the historical context of colonialism and slavery. He shows how this history has produced a tendency in black–white relationships for the white to control, or attempt to control the black and how this impacts on our relationships in the here and now, both inside and outside the therapy room.

Conclusion

This chapter has explored some of the mental health needs and issues for black and minority ethnic people in prisons and secure mental health settings. It has identified some of the key challenges facing therapists working with prisoners and patients in these contexts. The capacity to be curious and thoughtful about the experience and meaning of race, for both the patient and therapist, has been highlighted as critical to therapeutic effectiveness with black people. Thinking about race is difficult for so many of us, and yet it is an important factor in our unconscious, and at times conscious, expectations of others' behaviour, and consequently in our treatment of them. Attempts at thinking about race have often been skewed in the direction of focusing only on cultural factors, reflecting a defence against the anxiety that 'race' engenders. In conversation with our peers, we have heard it said that there is little, if any, guidance or meaningful policy on racial awareness from managers and senior staff. There is a fair amount of basic principles, but this is sometimes difficult to translate into day-to-day practice. We hope that this chapter has equipped the reader with a sense that differences, racial and cultural, can be engaged with and at the very least thought about, so that difference for both parties either side of the racial or cultural divide is neither fixated upon nor ignored.

Thinking about these things, like anything, requires practice, and practice will undoubtedly involve making mistakes. Given the current anxiety about 'getting it wrong' following inquiries into the deaths of Stephen Lawrence, Zahid Mubarek and David Bennett, some have described the attention to issues of race as 'political correctness'. We would suggest that this is an understandable, yet unhelpful, defence against thinking about an area that can be fraught with difficulties – indeed, who can bear to think that such difficulties could ever lead to the death of someone in custody or in hospital? Since these public inquiries some progress has been made in the practical treatment of black and minority ethnic members of the public, prisoners and patients. Further, in psychiatric settings all seclusions and restraints of patients now have to be recorded, including the ethnicity of the person being restrained or secluded and the reasons for doing so. Again, however, there continues to be an absence of a forum for exploring the reasons why black patients are over-represented in such practices while they are in psychiatric care.

It is our hope that this chapter has highlighted some of the thinking in the literature that we believe is helpful in considering how these problems can be approached. This is necessary for a large number of patients in forensic settings, for whom parts of their experience have not been thought about at all; that is their experience of their 'race'. Given our responsibility as therapists in forensic settings, and our assessments of prisoners and patients likely to determine the length of their detention, it is essential that attention is paid to the issue of race and its influence on our thinking, treatment recommendations and interventions.

Note

1 In this chapter, the term black and minority ethnic people is used to refer primarily to people from African, African-Caribbean, Asian and mixed-parentage backgrounds. We recognise that there are significant differences between and within minority ethnic groups; however, people from black and minority ethnic communities are more likely to live in deprived areas, to experience racial discrimination and social exclusion regardless of age, sex and place of residence.

References

Aitken, G. (2000) 'Clinical psychology in a cold climate: Towards culturally appropriate services', in J. Batsleer and B. Humphries (eds), *Welfare, Exclusion and Political Agency*. Abingdon: Routledge, pp. 79–101.

Altman, N. (2006) 'Black and White thinking: a psychoanalyst considers race', in R. Moodley and S. Palmer (eds), *Race, Culture and Psychotherapy*. Abingdon: Routledge, pp. 139–49.

Bhugra, D. and Bhui, K.S. (2006) 'Psychotherapy across the cultural divide', in R. Moodley and S. Palmer (eds), *Race, Culture and Psychotherapy*. London: Routledge, pp. 46–58.

Boast, N. and Chesterman, P. (1995) 'Black people and secure psychiatric facilities: Patterns of processing and the role of stereotypes', *British Journal of Criminology*, 35: 218–35.

Browne, D. (1997) *Black People and Sectioning*. London: Little Rock Publishing.

Butt, J. (2001) *Ethnicity and Mental Health Service Provision*. West Midlands: NHS Executive.

Butt, T. (2000) *Report of the Prison Service Internal Inquiry*. See www.zahidmubarekinquiry.org.uk/

Cheliotis, L.K. and Liebling, A. (2005) 'Race matters in British prisons: Towards a research agenda', *British Journal of Criminology*, 45: 1–32.

CRE (2003) *Racial Equality in Prisons: A Formal Investigation by the Commission of Race Equality into HM Prison Service of England and Wales*. London: Commission for Racial Equality.

CSIP (2006) *10 High Impact Changes for Mental Health Services*. Colchester: Care Services Improvement Partnership.

Dalal, F. (2006) 'Culturalism in multicultural psychotherapy', in R. Moodley and S. Palmer (eds) *Race, Culture and Psychotherapy*. Abingdon: Routledge, pp. 36–45.

DH (2005) *Delivering Race Equality in Mental Health Care: An Action Plan for Reform Inside and Outside Services and the Government's Response to the Independent Inquiry into the Death of David Bennett*. London: Department of Health.

Fernando, S. (1988) *Race and Culture in Psychiatry*. London: Routledge.

Fernando, S. (1991) *Mental Health, Race and Culture*. London: Macmillan/MIND.

Fernando, S. (1998) 'Part 1: Background', in S. Fernando, D. Ndegwa and M. Wilson (eds), *Forensic Psychiatry, Race and Culture*. London: Routledge.

Halsey, R. and Patel, M. (2003) 'The perils of race and culture for clinical psychology trainees: the missionary position in the 21st century', *Clinical Psychology*, 28: 29–32.

Healthcare Commission (2005) *'Count Me In': Results of a National Census of Inpatients in Mental Health Hospitals and Facilities in England and Wales*. London: Healthcare Commission.

HMCIP (2005) *Parallel Worlds: A Thematic Review of Race Relations in Prisons*. London: HM Inspectorate of Prisons.

Holmes, D.E. (1992) 'Race and transference in psychoanalysis and psychotherapy', *International Journal of Psychoanalysis*, 73(1): 1–11.

Holmes, D.E. (2006) 'Racial transference reactions in psychoanalytic treatment: an update', in R. Moodley and S. Palmer (eds), *Race, Culture and Psychotherapy*. Abingdon: Routledge, pp. 61–73.

Keating, F. (2007) *African and Caribbean Men and Mental Health. Better Health Briefing No. 5*. London: Race Equality Foundation.

Keating, F., Robertson, D., McCulloch, A. and Francis, E. (2002) *Breaking the Circles of Fear: A Review of the Relationship between Mental Health Services and African and Caribbean communities*. London: Sainsbury Centre for Mental Health.

Liggan, D.Y. and Kay, J. (2006) 'Race in the room: issues in the dynamic psychotherapy of African-Americans', in R. Moodley and S. Palmer (eds), *Race, Culture and Psychotherapy*. Abingdon: Routledge, pp. 100–16.

Littlewood, R. and Lipsedge, M. (1988) 'Community-initiated research: a study of psychiatrists' conceptualizations of "cannabis psychosis"', *Psychiatric Bulletin*, 12: 486-8.

Littlewood, R. and Lipsedge, M. (1997) *Aliens and Alienists*. London: Routledge.

Littlewood, R. and Lipsedge, M. (1981) 'Psychiatric illness among British Afro-Caribbeans', *British Medical Journal*, 296: 950–1.

Lowe, F. (2008) 'Colonial object relations: Going underground Black–White relationships', *British Journal of Psychotherapy*, 24(1): 20–33.

Ministry of Justice (2008) *Race Review 2008: Implementing Race Equality in Prisons – Five Years On*. London: NOMS.

Moodley, R. and Palmer, S. (2006) 'Race, culture and other multiple constructions: an absent presence in psychotherapy', in R. Moodley and S. Palmer (eds), *Race, Culture and Psychotherapy*. Abingdon: Routledge, pp. 11–26.

Morgan, H. (1998) 'Between fear and blindness: the white therapist and the black patient', *British Journal of Psychotherapy*, 34(3): 48–61.

Ndegwa, D. (1998) 'Part 2: Clinical Issues', in S. Fernando, D. Ndegwa and M. Wilson (eds), *Forensic Psychiatry, Race and Culture*. London: Routledge.

Report of the Zahid Mubarek Inquiry, Volume 1 (2006) London: The Stationery Office. Available at: www.zahidmubarekinquiry.org.uk/

Sashidharan, S.P. (2003) *Inside Outside: Improving Mental Health Services for Black and Minority Ethnic Communities in England*. Leeds: Department of Health.

SHA (2003) *Independent Inquiry into the Death of David Bennett*. Cambridge: Norfolk, Suffolk and Cambridgeshire Strategic Heath Authority.

Sharpley, M., Hutchinson, G., McKenzie, K. and Murray, R.M. (2001) 'Understanding the excess of psychosis among the African-Caribbean population in England', *British Journal of Psychiatry*, 178: 60–8.

Shaw, J., Davides, J. and Morey, H. (1999) *Secure Needs Assessment in the North-West – Summary Findings*. Report to NHS Executive, NW Regional Office: Manchester.

Straw, J. (1999) *House of Commons Hansard Debates for 24 February 1999*. London: Her Majesty's Stationery Office.

Tang, N.M. and Gardner, J. (2006) 'Interpretation of race in the transference: perspectives of similarity and difference in the patient/therapist dyad', in R. Moodley and S. Palmer (eds), *Race, Culture and Psychotherapy*. Abingdon: Routledge, pp. 89–99.

Williams, S., Wilson, A., Myrie, L. and Collymore, M.A. (2006) *Report of the community-led Research Project focusing on the Mental Health Needs of African and African-Caribbean Women*. Available at: www.mentalhealthequalities. org.uk/silo/files/the-mental-health-service-needs-of-african-and-african-caribbean-women.pdf

Wilson, M. and Francis, J. (1997) *Raised Voices: African-Caribbean and African users' views and experiences of Mental Health Services in England and Wales*. London: MIND.

Yi, K.Y. (2006) 'Transference and race: and intersubjective conceptualization', in R. Moodley and S. Palmer (eds), *Race, Culture and Psychotherapy*. Abingdon: Routledge, pp. 74–88.

Chapter 10

The role of therapeutic communities in forensic settings: developments, research and adaptations

Richard Shuker and John Shine

Introduction

In this chapter we will be outlining the work of democratic therapeutic communities in forensic settings. Descriptions of forensic therapeutic communities (TCs) such as HMP Grendon have been well publicised and widely cited during the past 20 years (for example, Genders and Player 1995; Cullen *et al.* 1997; Shine and Morris 2000). However, the past decade has seen important developments in the clinical practices of forensic TCs, linked to research, accreditation, audit and peer review systems. The enhanced legitimacy of forensic TCs linked to these developments has been influential in the opening of several new units, some with important adaptations to the classic TC model. Our purpose in this chapter is to outline the TC model as it is practised in forensic settings, to summarise recent changes and to present the challenges for the further development of this treatment approach.

Origins and background to therapeutic community practice

Democratic TCs originate from a model of social psychiatry which emphasises the rehabilitative role of patient involvement and responsibility. The defining components are communal living and therapy groups which allow patients to explore and challenge one another's behaviour. They have provided a rehabilitative service in the Prison Service for half a century. Deriving from the concept of a Quaker 'retreat', they arose from a belief that a supportive and constructive environment could ameliorate psychological distress, and later emerged after the Second World War as a treatment for traumatised servicemen, with a social therapeutic approach that has been used to empower and support the vulnerable and psychologically distressed.

Adopting TC principles and practices to meet the needs of anti-social and aggressive offenders seemed in some respects unlikely to succeed. Those with neurotic disorders or traumatised through their experience of combat require a supportive, safe and psychologically nurturing environment in order to resolve psychological distress. The assumption that equivalent practices would translate to meet the needs of men with histories of chronic maladjustment and abuse, who have displayed enduring patterns of exploitative, tough-minded and abusive behaviour, without the protective role afforded by an experience of stable or secure attachment, may have been based more on hope than empirically informed judgement.

When Grendon, the first TC in the Prison Service, was opened its remit was to act as an experimental prison with the aim of meeting the needs of psychologically disturbed prisoners. Clinically it adopted a medical model with a medical superintendent in charge rather than a prison governor, and this continued until the mid 1980s. The model of Grendon TC was based to a large extent on the principles of Rappaport (1960) who argued that the right type of community could deal with the problems that society has created and identified principles of democracy, communalism, permissiveness and reality confrontation as forming the basis of the treatment approach. Interlinked with these governing principles were a set of therapeutic practices emphasising the prisoners' involvement in the running of communities. Processes such as shared decision making, open communication, the flattening of the treatment 'hierarchy', staff and prisoners being jointly accountable to each other, and therapeutic groups and full community meetings, were established as the central pillars of the clinical programme.

This approach presented a number of problems within forensic settings. First, beyond promoting self-esteem, well-being and personal accountability, it was unclear how far therapeutic communities could adapt their practice to address not only psychological needs but also the deep-rooted anti-social beliefs, attitudes and patterns of behaviour associated with criminality. Second, the extent to which the goals of treatment were sufficiently articulated was unclear: were TCs to provide a means to make disruptive prisoners conform or were long-term clinical and behavioural changes to be expected? Third, it was not clear whether the practice in TCs represented a treatment model based on psychological principles, or whether it provided a supportive, humane, attractive environment where prisoners would feel more contented and less inclined to misbehave. Finally, the questions of whether or not disturbed, psychopathic offenders would undermine and exploit the opportunities of a TC, and whether certain personality traits associated with a sense of entitlement, control and interpersonal exploitation could be exacerbated, remained unaddressed.

Therapeutic communities and interventions for offenders

Until the early 1990s approaches to intervention in the Prison Service remained rather unstructured and uncoordinated. Since its opening in 1962, the TC at HMP Grendon had provided the most intensive and consistent intervention for offenders. In the following decade two other units were set up – one in the Scottish Prison Service at Barlinnie and one inside HMP Wormwood Scrubs. The opening of the unit at Barlinnie was timely in that it coincided with a highly influential meta-analytic study which concluded that interventions aimed at reducing risk of offender recidivism were, by and large, ineffectual (Martinson 1974). This study, and the accompanying pessimism it evoked, was highly significant in terms of its impact on rehabilitation practice in forensic settings. As enthusiasm for the concept of rehabilitation declined, the 'justice' or 'just deserts' model of imprisonment, in which treatment played no part in an offender's sentence, became more influential (Bottoms 1998). Interestingly the TC interventions at Grendon, Barlinnie and the Max Glatt Unit inside HMP Wormwood Scrubs did survive during this time, perhaps indicating the strengths and resilience of the TC.

Changes in policy and developments in clinical practice occurred swiftly, upon a revaluation of Martinson's work which suggested that, if certain psychological techniques were used, and if the specific lifestyle, behavioural, and attitudinal deficits associated with criminal behaviour were addressed, then consistent and meaningful reductions in recidivism could be achieved. Although Barlinnie and eventually the Max Glatt Centre were shut down, treatment at Grendon continued more or less untouched and unrefined during this period. However, with the rebirth of interventions for offenders, TCs faced a significant challenge to their practice. While it had continued without articulating a psychological 'model of change' and with many of its treatment principles being loosely based on psychodynamic modes of treatment, Grendon now risked being placed at the periphery of mainstream interventions, and at the margin of what were considered empirically defensible, and evidence-based, forms of practice. In particular, it became incumbent for the establishment to demonstrate that the treatment model gave sufficient attention to the 'criminogenic needs' (risk factors linked to offending) of the residents. Defining adequately how this was to be achieved was more than just an academic exercise; failure to do so could result in prisoners who had completed substantial periods in therapy being advised that they needed to complete treatment elsewhere because key risk factors had not been addressed. This was particularly the case for long-term and life-sentenced prisoners.

The challenge for TCs was to explain and articulate what psychological techniques and methods their practice was based on and, to demonstrate that its psychological methods were those proven to be effective in reducing recidivism (as opposed to controlling and containing difficult prisoners). With the emerging 'what works' consensus the only psychological methods given any real legitimacy and respect were those based on social learning and cognitive behavioural principles (Andrews and Bonta 1994). The position reached was that it was largely behavioural, cognitive and attitudinal deficits, as well as vocational or educational deficits, which were the 'risk factors' associated with criminal behaviour. Furthermore it had become widely accepted that the most effective way to rectify these deficits was to employ cognitive behavioural treatment methods, linked to enhanced education and vocational training and supported through aftercare linked to community resettlement and integration (Andrews 1995).

A further difficulty for TCs was that they were not regarded as meeting another critical feature of effective interventions, treatment 'responsivity'; that is, the treatment methods adopted needed to be those which offenders were most likely to engage in, and those which were most likely to help offenders to learn new skills. The absence of these features – structure, multicomponent methods, role play, skills 'training' – and the lack of what was seen as sufficient evidence to support TCs as an effective treatment method, led to them being marginalised outside mainstream forensic interventions in the Prison Service.

It is only within the past five years that TCs have been adequately defined, modified (slightly) and researched to the extent that they now hold the same degree of acceptance and legitimacy as those interventions underpinned by conventional cognitive behavioural methods. The achievement of TCs jointly receiving 'accreditation status' – formal recognition within the Prison Service of their efficacy – was only achieved six years after they originally made their submission.

The development of a treatment model

Shine and Morris (2000) developed a 'multi factorial' (p. 201) model of treatment for forensic TCs based on three domains of therapeutic work: attachments (childhood memories, scripts or schemas linked to important developmental experiences), criminal behaviour (offending history) and behaviour on the unit (interpersonal style, behavioural patterns, demonstration of anti-social characteristics, etc.). It was proposed that dynamic risk factors could be addressed within this model through the framework of offence parallelling behaviour (OPB) (Jones 2004). The central notion of OPB is that behaviour within the community will have parallels with, or mirror, the behaviours observed in the offending cycle. The rigorous 'culture of enquiry' which operates within the openness of a TC allows any offence-paralleling behaviours to be closely and thoroughly explored (Genders and Player 1995). This theoretical approach adopted by all democratic TCs has been developed in a manual (Home Office 2007) which explores the psychological theories which underpin the practice of TCs.

In the environment of a TC, this model suggested that new behaviours could be practised and risk formulations made and revised as offending patterns emerged and new pro-social behaviours were practised. Shuker (2010) argues that therapeutic communities provide a framework for integrated practice, where cognitive, behavioural and psychodynamic approaches are able to operate alongside each other within one overriding programme.

Within TCs a number of defining characteristics are present which provide the arena for integrated intervention.

Therapeutic alliance

The clinical structures and treatment practices in TCs provide a clinical environment where the engagement of prisoners and the staff team is its defining feature. The practices centre on enhancing the role and contribution of prison staff to the treatment process and underpin one of the core components of clinical practice, the collaborative therapeutic alliance. Features including giving staff a clear and central role as group facilitators and having a 'flattening of hierarchy' within the staff team which supports shared decision-making, are established parts of the multidisciplinary team's work. Specific clinical processes also promote the engagement of the prisoners, and clinical activities such as prisoners chairing wing meetings or having meaningful community responsibilities enhance their involvement and engagement. Embedded in this is a degree of risk-taking. During activities such as prisoner-chaired wing meetings, at which community members can be held accountable for the behaviour, and democratised decision-making, during which prisoners are able to suggest and vote upon sanctions, the prisoners are expected to resolve their own conflicts and disputes and to make important decisions about affecting community life which the staff will only exceptionally veto. It is these practices which bring about a strong attachment to the treatment process.

Opportunities to learn new skills

A central feature of a TC, which has been coined as the 'living, learning experience', is that different disciplines within the regime are all recognised as playing an essential part in the acquisition of new skills. Areas such as work, education, leisure and therapy are seen as important in promoting the development of skills and as important components of the treatment process. While this may be the aim of other clinical programmes, the climate of TCs allows effective integration by affording opportunities for collaboration and debate and emphasising the principle that TCs comprise a variety of clinical activities. Furthermore, this climate also presents opportunities for OPBs which occur within or outside formal treatment sessions to be fed back into the therapeutic work. For example, a confrontation occurring during work or a failure to sustain a commitment to attend an education class can become the focus of exploration during the therapy sessions.

Structured and consistent treatment process

Consistency, structure and an emphasis on maintaining treatment boundaries also typify the practice in TCs; they are important components of intervention whether applied to offenders (Lipsey

1995), people with personality disorders (Waldinger and Gunderson 1989) or non-offenders. The emphasis on community boundaries, supported by a clear constitution emphasising pro-social behaviour, is a central operating principle of TCs, where members can be immediately accountable for transgressing rules.

Therapeutic communities and evidence-based practice

Although therapeutic techniques associated with cognitive behavioural principles did form a central part of TC practice, for example, learning more adaptive behaviours and beliefs within a pro-social environment (Genders and Player 1995), they did not include the learning methods such as role play, practice, modelling, rehearsal, structured learning and multiple teaching methods which were regarded as those relevant to the needs of offenders. The task for TCs was to adapt their practices and adequately incorporate these methods (Home Office 2007).

This presented a challenge for TCs and raised questions about the limitations of their approach and specifically whether only certain types of offenders should be selected for treatment. Before TCs described their treatment model, and gave a formulation of what treatment targets would be addressed, there was limited emphasis on identifying which offenders would be likely to benefit from therapy. While insight and motivation were specified as being necessary, the question of who was likely to respond to a psychotherapeutic approach (Andrews 1995) was not addressed. There was a reluctance to match those selected for treatment with defined therapeutic goals and to acknowledge the relevance of levels of risk and of treatment need when assessing suitability for treatment; there was also a lack of clarity about which personality factors would not respond to TC treatment: all this led to an overinclusive approach. It represented some different conceptual positions; from a clinical mental health perspective it was considered that in principle most people could, in some respects, benefit from treatment, whereas the psychological 'evidence-based' approach in forensic practice emphasised the need for a rigorous assessment and selection process. The questions of who TCs should select for treatment, and what outcome measures TCs have focused upon in answering this question, will now be considered.

TCs, research and treatment outcomes

A notable feature within TC practice has been that the energy and commitment put into maintaining and delivering this treatment ethos has not been matched by the same effort to evaluate the effectiveness of its practice. Rutter and Tyrer (2003) suggest that the 'culture of enquiry' needs to become a 'culture of research' within TCs for forensic, personality-disordered populations. Recent meta-analytical reviews into the efficacy of TCs with severe personality-disordered populations and substance misusers concluded that 'therapeutic communities have not produced the amount or quality of research literature as might be expected' (Lees *et al.* 2004: 291). Inadequate definition of what constitutes a TC, a lack of control groups, failure to specify clear outcome measures, limited definition of what constitutes treatment 'completion', and failure to separate completers from non-completers have all limited the quality of research. Rutter and Tyrer (2003) also concluded that there has been no proper evaluation of the efficacy of the democratic TCs; they suggest that the obstacles cited by TC practitioners against adopting a randomised control methodology (RCT) could be, and need to be, overcome. They argue that in doing so the quality of the research evidence provided will allow 'opinion and dogma [to] be replaced by facts and recommendations based on empirical findings' (p. 301).

Despite the need for more and better quality research in order, as Lees *et al.* (2004) put it, 'to counter the charge that there is not a proven case that therapeutic communities are effective' (p. 292), it is possible to draw a number of tentative conclusions about the efficacy of TCs and the role they have as a forensic intervention. Within forensic TCs perhaps the most rigorous research has been conducted within hierarchical TCs for substance misusers. These 'concept' TCs have a more clearly delineated structure, which differentiates newcomers from senior members, and adopt a more explicit emphasis and treatment model focusing on addictive behaviour. The consistent finding has been that TCs with an aftercare component have achieved significant reductions in reconviction (Lipton 2002). While reconviction studies have been completed within forensic democratic TCs these tend to be relatively small in scale, and while some modest reduction in reconviction has been reported by some authors (Taylor 2000) it has not been replicated by others (Newton, under review). Likewise, McMurran (2002) states that TCs have not established an evidence base against which any claims about effectiveness in recidivism can be substantiated, although more recently there has been evidence from hierarchical drugs TCs (McMurran 2007).

In contrast Warren *et al.* (2003) cite therapeutic communities as having the 'most promising evidence' in the treatment of severe personality disorder; they conclude that 'the therapeutic community ethos could be used as a dominant approach and structure [...] of new regimes [...] and could include other treatments targeting specific aspects of methodology' (Warren *et al.* 2003: 5). A meta-analysis involving a systematic literature review of international research into the effectiveness of TCs in treating people with personality and other mental disorders in secure and non-secure psychiatric settings indicated positive findings with respect to TCs and the treatment of personality disorder (Lees *et al.* 1999). However, as noted by Warren *et al.* (2003) there remain difficulties in drawing conclusions from this analysis because of the heterogeneous nature of the participants and the broad range of outcome measures. They conclude that while TCs did largely demonstrate a range of positive outcomes, including better institutional adjustment, improvements in mental health, reductions in self-harm and substance misuse, and fewer anti-authority and anti-social attitudes, the implications for practice are limited by the quality of the research evidence.

Research and prison-based TCs

Research on reconviction from prison-based TCs, while at best producing inconclusive results about their impact on recidivism, has consistently demonstrated that the people who participate in intervention do demonstrate psychological, attitudinal, interpersonal and behavioural changes. The improvements consistently found in psychological well-being, self-esteem and personal distress have been paralleled in improvements in criminogenic factors such as anti-social attitudes, hostility and impulsivity (Newton 1998; Shine 2000). This mirrors findings with personality-disordered patients in non-secure settings (Chiesa and Fonagy 2000; Warren *et al.* 2003) where reductions in psychological distress, anxiety, impulsivity and self-harm are routine post-treatment outcomes. In a recent study Shuker and Newton (2008) confirmed reliable and clinically significant improvements in mental health and reductions in criminogenic risk in a prison-based TC. They found that, while offenders demonstrated improvements in mental health-related needs relatively early in treatment, significant reductions in risk tended to occur only in those who remained in treatment for one year or more. Research into the efficacy of TCs has also demonstrated improved prison behaviour: Lees *et al.* (1999)

reported fewer assaults and serious incidents than were expected and Newton (2006) found significant improvements in behaviour which were sustained following transfer from a TC to mainstream prisons. Newton (2006) also demonstrated significant reductions in self-harm and drug use during intervention in a TC, and highlighted that the majority of those participating in TC intervention for over 18 months were assessed as making significant progress on meeting treatment targets.

TCs and responsivity: which offender groups benefit from treatment?

TCs have traditionally been advocated as an intervention to meet the need of high-risk, personality-disordered and disturbed prisoners. While some authors (Marshall 1997) have drawn rather tentative conclusions about their efficacy with this population, research to support this practice, especially with regard to reductions in recidivism, remains equivocal. Evidence does suggest that prisoners with high levels of psychological need and risk can be contained and managed effectively within the clinical environment presented by the TC (Shine 2000; Manning 2005). However, research has also demonstrated that, whether looking at engagement in treatment (Hobson et al. 2000), length of stay (Shuker et al. 2007) or reductions in recidivism (Newton 2010), higher-risk offenders do less well than their lower-risk counterparts. Studies have also shown that the offenders who are more likely to engage in, benefit from and remain in treatment are those who are more intelligent, introverted and less psychologically tough-minded (more empathic, less hostile, impulsive, domineering, Shine 2001). So too are those with lower levels of risk, who have previously completed prison programmes, have a good sense of problem recognition and demonstrate good institutional conduct (Shuker and Newberry 2010).

This presents a potential conflict for forensic TCs. While the high-risk, more disturbed populations can be managed effectively, if engagement in treatment leading to reductions in risk is the desired treatment outcome, then there is limited evidence to support selecting this population for treatment. There are also additional risks in attempting to work with high-need, psychologically disturbed or psychopathic offenders in a TC. Particular personality traits such as superficiality, self-entitlement and grandiosity and tendencies to deceive, mislead and exploit are those which have the potential to undermine and destabilise the treatment process, and misuse the responsibilities and opportunities presented.

Treatment dosage and sequencing

Perhaps one of the most consistent findings in research on TCs has been the relationship between time, treatment and clinical improvement. The North American literature on the prison-based TCs for addiction has found a consistent association between the length of stay and treatment outcomes, and this finding has also consistently been replicated in forensic TCs across a broad range of outcomes (Marshall 1997; Newton 1998; Shuker and Newton 2008).

Research has indicated that TCs are unlikely to be effective at reducing recidivism as a stand-alone intervention without adequate throughcare or aftercare (Lipton 2002). Indeed, the question of what TCs can be realistically expected to achieve has also been subject to some debate. Genders and Player (2004) suggested that the unique role of the TC is their 'humanitarian role' and it is this that forms the 'essence of the rehabilitative task' (p. 264). If TCs are to become more centrally recognised as a forensic intervention, they need to be clear about their strengths, where they lie in the sequencing of interventions and the role they have in this sequence.

Their role in the treatment of personality disorder has traditionally been well recognised: TCs provide a safe environment, promote collaborative alliances, reduce psychological distress and help to address mistrustful attitudes. For personality disordered offenders, intervention in a TC may be a useful means of promoting 'treatment readiness' prior to focusing on criminogenic factors. However, while this may be the case for offenders with personality disturbance, for other offenders it appears that TCs may only be effective where precipitated by prior behavioural and attitudinal changes which serve more adequately to equip participants to engage. Shuker *et al.* (2007) found that previous completion of an accredited intervention, a heightened sense of problem recognition and recent improvements in prison behaviour (expected treatment goals of prison programmes) were factors associated with TC treatment completion. The implications are that structured cognitive behavioural programmes may make offenders more 'ready' to engage effectively in a TC and, in the majority of cases, more likely to complete and benefit from that treatment.

Future challenges

Despite the challenges posed by changes in penal policy since Grendon opened 50 years ago (Newell 2000), forensic TCs continue to provide therapy for some of the most disturbed and dangerous men in the Prison Service. Indeed, the past decade has seen the opening of a second 200-bed therapeutic community prison (HMP Dovegate) together with a number of smaller TC wings inside larger prisons. All these institutions are accredited as effective interventions in reducing reoffending by the Correctional Services Accreditation Panel and they must meet strict audit criteria to maintain this status. In addition, they are 'peer reviewed' on an annual basis by staff and patients from other therapeutic communities. Nevertheless, as with all interventions, TCs continue to face questions and challenges about their work.

Cost-effectiveness

In contrast to cuts in public spending affecting the Health Service, which tend to attract public outcry and intense media interest, reductions in spending in prison rehabilitation receive relatively little attention. Perhaps the reason for this is because the recipients of those reductions, prisoners and offenders, are seen as less 'deserving' of public sympathy and therefore of appropriate levels of funding and political interest (Jones 2006). Given the economic climate at the time of writing, NOMS has been required to look at ways of reducing overall cost and improving efficiency. This applies to all establishments including those providing therapy based interventions. The key aim is to maximise efficiencies by reducing overheads and administration costs so that frontline services are protected and prioritised and the standards expected to deliver therapeutic based programmes are maintained. As outlined above, there is evidence that forensic TCs such as HMP Grendon are effective in reducing rates of aggressive behaviour and self-harm, and in improving levels of self-esteem and personal distress; there is also some evidence of reductions in recidivism, if prisoners complete therapy. Nevertheless, this counts for little unless the evidence is robust enough to withstand independent scrutiny. In the authors' view, independent research comparing treatment in TCs in prisons and in hospitals specialising in the treatment of personality disorders would help to clarify the cost-effectiveness of forensic TCs in prisons and should be undertaken as a matter of priority. Such research should consider outcome measures linked to the psychological health of prisoners, as well as criminogenic factors, as forensic TCs in prisons may be providing cost-effective alternatives to similar personality-disorder units in the NHS.

Provision for the range of psychopathology

Most of the prisoners admitted to forensic TCs are assessed as meeting the diagnostic criteria for personality disorder. For these clients, treatment has always focused on much more than criminogenic risk factors, but on a wide range of psychopathology that may interact with known risk factors for reoffending. This can be either through a 'functional link' between personality disorder and offending,[1] or through complex ways that are, as yet, poorly understood. It is well established that there are high levels of co-morbidity between Axis I and Axis II disorders (Coid *et al.* 2006).[2] Many prisoners with anti-social or borderline personality disorders – the most common PDs in prison (Singleton *et al.* 1998) – suffer from disorders such as clinical depression, generalised and specific anxiety disorders, obsessive compulsive disorder (OCD), panic disorder, specific phobia, social phobia and so on. The provision of treatment for these disorders is currently undergoing major changes with the advent of the national programme for Improving Access to Psychological Therapies (IAPT) initiative.[3] Only therapies recognised by the National Institute for Health and Clinical Excellence (NICE) are currently used in this programme, which is set to fundamentally change future provision of psychological therapies for those suffering from mental disorders in the UK.

One of the features of the NICE guidance is the increasing specificity of recommended forms of treatment according to the type of disorder treated. For example, although cognitive behaviour therapy (CBT) is the main form of psychological therapy currently recommended for Axis I disorders, specific types of interventions are recommended for particular disorders, based on either better quality of evidence, evidence of differential superiority, and/or cost-effectiveness. For example, at the time of writing, CBT plus behavioural activation is recommended for the treatment of depression, exposure and response prevention for OCD, exposure-based CBT or EMDR for post-traumatic stress disorder, and so on.

In addition, the (then Labour) UK Government published the draft NHS Constitution which set out what patients, staff and the public could expect from the NHS in future.[4] The draft NHS Constitution recommends that patients have a right to evidence-based treatment, unless there are exceptional reasons why it should not be offered. Democratic TCs are not mentioned in any of the recommended NICE treatments for Axis I disorders. This raises questions as to how the treatment of TCs, which is largely group-based, can deal with the wide range of co-morbid clinical and criminogenic needs of its clients, particularly when clients have a right to expect evidence-based treatment (as recommended by NICE). One approach might be to conduct research trials to assess whether or how the usual treatment in TCs is effective for co-morbid Axis I disorders. A second approach might be to consider whether specific forms of intervention could be offered within this model to deal with the wide range of psychopathology presented by the clients, without compromising the treatment integrity of the TC.

Adaptation of the TC model

There have been recent developments in models of treatment that incorporate concepts from TCs into their practice and therapeutic approaches which define themselves as TCs but with adaptations to the classic model.

Livesley (2001) recommends that, in order to deal with the wide range of psychopathology presented by personality-disordered clients, a range of specific interventions, rather than reliance on one approach, should be offered. One such intervention he recommends is prescribed medication. Pharmacological interventions have always had an uneasy place within the TC model, with some institutions – in the past including HMP Grendon and the Henderson Hospital – banning them altogether and insisting that patients who request medication leave the institution; others, such as the Cassel Hospital, offer pharmacological treatments for their patients. A paper by Cartwright and Gordon (2007) outlines differences in practice among TCs and argues that medication could be utilised more often in TCs in order to promote readiness for treatment with specific problems in areas such as emotional dysregulation (a major feature of borderline PD) and deviant sexual arousal. However, they add important advice to help avoid potential problems, such as splitting dynamics between medical staff and other members of the MDT, through a process of consultation and discussion in clinical decision-making.

Similarly, the provision of individual-based therapy, alongside group-based intervention, has historically presented difficulties for TCs, in a tension between the needs of the individual and the group-based approach. As with pharmacological treatments, TCs have responded in different ways: some, such as the Cassel Hospital, offer individual therapy; others insist that all but the most extreme problems are dealt with in a group. Interestingly, there is very little research on whether, in fact, the provision of individual therapy is detrimental or beneficial to patients in TCs or to the integrity of the TC model. Research on Axis I disorders has provided compelling evidence of the benefits of mainly individual-based CBT.[5] Clinicians need to be careful of promoting therapies on the basis of clinical lore and intuition, however strongly held. For example, the condition of social phobia was, for obvious reasons, until very recently considered best treated through group interventions. However, randomised control trials of group-based CBT versus individual-based CBT (the recommended NICE treatment for this condition) have shown, in fact, that individual-based CBT is superior in clinical outcomes to group CBT (Stangier *et al.* 2003). This is a finding that is in many respects counter-intuitive. The optimal TC model in terms of established evidence of TC efficacy has yet to be shown. In some recent models of adapted therapeutic communities (Shine 2010), the provision of individual approaches to patients with complex problems has been incorporated into the treatment model in areas such as CBT for Axis I disorders, offence-focused work and longer-term dynamic therapy.

Finally, it is important to note that aspects of the approach of TCs have also grown within treatment models that do not define themselves as TCs. For example, in all the units that are part of the dangerous and severe personality disorder (DSPD) programme,[6] community meetings, traditionally a central part of the TC model, play a role in treatment. While these are sometimes more akin to 'business meetings' where patients present grievances to be addressed through minuted action points, there is an increasing interest in developing them to support a 'culture of enquiry' or a forum to practice skills learnt on programmes. The authors have received several enquiries both from staff in the pilots interested in expanding this part of their treatment model, and from prison management keen to transfer the collaborative nature of TC prisoner–staff relationships into mainstream penal establishments. This indicates that therapy models are becoming increasingly aware that a 'one size fits all' approach is not best suited to working with complex cases and therapeutic integration offers more potential for managing and treating severe personality disorder. The model of a TC, with its emphasis on holistic ways of working and its planned environment based on psychological principles, has an important role to play in treating patients with severe personality disorders.

Conclusion

In this chapter we have outlined how forensic TCs originated in the treatment of neurotic disorders and were adapted for offenders. In the past decade they have developed to become accredited interventions in the Prison Service, which offer an important resource for the management and treatment of disturbed and dangerous prisoners. We have summarised research on outcomes and highlighted some of the essential questions that, in our view, TCs need to address in order to continue to survive and flourish. Finally, we have touched on some recent adaptations of the classic TC model that have been introduced in order to deal with client groups with complex needs and to deal with the problem of attrition. However, interesting though research and theoretical models are, we would like to encourage readers of this volume who are curious, or sceptical about TCs, to visit a forensic therapeutic community for themselves. In our view it offers an opportunity for powerful experiential learning that is difficult to convey adequately through words alone.

Notes

1 See   www.dspdprogramme.gov.uk/media/pdfs/High_Secure_Services_ for_Men.pdf
2 Axis I disorders are mainly disorders of mood, while Axis II are mainly personality disorders.
3 See www.iapt.nhs.uk/
4 See www.dh.gov.uk/en/Healthcare/NHSConstitution/index.htm
5 See   www.cabinetoffice.gov.uk/media/cabinetoffice/strategy/assets/mh_ clark.pdf
6 See www.dspdprogramme.gov.uk/ The DSPD programme is a joint initiative between the Ministry of Justice and the National Health Service to develop and deliver mental health services for people whose dangerousness is linked to their personality disorder. Currently there are four high-secure sites in prisons and NHS sites providing up to 300 beds and 75 places in medium-secure and community sites.

References

Andrews, D.A. (1995) 'The psychology of criminal conduct and effective treatment', in J. McGuire (ed.), *What Works: Reducing Reoffending*. Chichester: John Wiley & Sons.

Andrews, D.A. and Bonta, J. (1994) *The Psychology of Criminal Conduct*. Cincinatti, OH: Anderson.

Bottoms, A. (1998) 'Five puzzles in von Hirsch's Theory of punishment', in A.J. Ashworth and M. Wasik (eds), *Fundamentals of Sentencing Theory: Essays in Honour of Andrew von Hirsch*. Oxford: Oxford University Press, pp. 53–100.

Cartwright, J. and Gordon, H. (2007) 'Beyond the "quick fix": The role of medication in readiness for psychological treatment of severe personality disorder', *Issues in Forensic Psychology*, 7: 55–61.

Chiesa, M. and Fonagy, P. (2000) 'Cassell personality disorder study: Methodology and treatment effects', *British Journal of Psychiatry*, 176: 485–91.

Coid, J., Tyrer, P. and Roberts, A. (2006) 'Prevalence and correlates of personality disorder in Great Britain', *British Journal of Psychiatry*, 188: 423–31.

Cullen, E., Jones, L., Woodward, R. (eds) (1997) *Therapeutic Communities for Offenders*. Chichester: John Wiley & Sons.

Genders, E. and Player, E. (1995) *Grendon: A Study of a Therapeutic Prison*. Oxford: Clarendon Press.

Genders, E. and Player, E. (2004) 'Grendon: A therapeutic community in prison', in J. Lees, N. Manning, D. Menzies and N. Morant (eds), *A Culture of Enquiry: Research Evidence and the Therapeutic Community*. London: Jessica Kingsley.

Haigh, R. (1999) 'The quintessence of a therapeutic environment: five universal qualities', in P. Campling and R. Haigh (eds), *Therapeutic Communities: Past, Present and Future*. London: Jessica Kingsley.

Hobson, J., Shine, J. and Roberts, R. (2000) 'How psychopaths behave in a prison therapeutic community', *Psychology, Crime and Law*, 6: 103–19.

Home Office (2007) *Democratic Therapeutic Communities Training Manual*, available at: www.dspdprogramme.co.uk

Jones, D. (ed.) (2006) *Humane Prisons*. Abingdon: Radcliffe Publishing.

Jones, L. (2004) 'Offence paralleling behaviour as a framework for assessment and intervention with offenders', in A. Needs and G. Towl (eds), *Applying Psychology to Forensic Practice*. Malder, MA: Blackwell.

Lees, J., Manning, N. and Rawlings, B. (1999) *Therapeutic Community Effectiveness: A Systematic International Review of Therapeutic Community Treatment for People with Personality Disorders and Mentally Disordered Offenders. CRD Report 17*. York: NHS Centre for Reviews and Dissemination.

Lees, J., Manning, N. and Rawlings, B. (2004) 'A culture of enquiry: Research evidence and the therapeutic community', *Psychiatric Quarterly*, 75(3): 279–94.

Lipsey, M.W. (1995) 'What do we learn from 400 studies on the effectiveness of treatment with juvenile delinquents?', in J. McGuire (ed.), *What Works: Reducing Re-offending: Guidelines from Research and Practice*. Chichester: John Wiley & Sons.

Lipton, D.S. (2002) 'Therapeutic community treatment programming in corrections', in C.R. Hollin (ed.), *Handbook of Offender Assessment and Treatment*. Chichester: John Wiley & Sons, pp. 155–79.

Livesley, J. (ed.) (2001) *Handbook on Personality Disorder: Theory, Research and Treatment*. New York: The Guilford Press.

Manning, N. (2005) *The Therapeutic Movement: Charisma and Routinisation*. Abingdon: Routledge.

Marshall, P. (1997) *A Reconviction study of HMP Grendon Therapeutic Community. Research Findings 53*. London: Home Office Research and Statistics Directorate.

Martinson, R. (1974) 'What works – questions and answers about prison reform', *Public Interest*, 35: 22–54.

McMurran, M. (2002) 'Offenders with personality disorders' in C.R. Hollin (ed.), *Handbook of Offender Assessment and Treatment*, pp. 467–80. Chichester: John Wiley & Sons.

McMurran, M. (2007) 'What works in substance misuse treatments for offenders?', *Criminal Behaviour and Mental Health*, 17: 225–33

Newell, T. (2000) 'Foreword', in J. Shine (ed.), *A Compilation of Grendon Research*. Available from: Psychology Department, HMP Grendon, Grendon Underwood, Aylesbury, HP18 0TL, pp. 23–35.

Newton, M. (under review) 'Reconviction after treatment in a prison-based therapeutic community', *Journal of Forensic Psychiatry and Psychology*.

Newton, M. (1998) 'Changes in measures of personality, hostility and locus of control during residence in a prison therapeutic community', *Legal and Criminological Psychology*, 3: 209–23.

Newton, M. (2006) 'Evaluating Grendon as a prison: research into quality of life at Grendon', *Prison Service Journal*, 165: 18–22.

Newton, M. (2010) 'Changes in prison offending among residents of a prison-based therapeutic community', in R. Shuker and E. Sullivan (eds), *Grendon and the Emergence of Forensic Therapeutic Communities: Developments in Research and Practice*. Chichester: Wiley Blackwell.

Rappaport, R.N. (1960) *Community as Doctor*. London: Tavistock.

Rutter, D. and Tyrer, P. (2003) 'The value of therapeutic communities in the treatment of personality disorder: A suitable place for treatment?', *Journal of Psychiatric Practice*, 9(4): 291–302

Shine, J. (ed.) (2000) *A Compilation of Grendon Research*. Available from: Psychology Department, HMP Grendon, Grendon Underwood, Aylesbury, HP18 0TL.

Shine, J. (2001) 'Characteristics of inmates admitted to Grendon therapeutic prison and their relationships to length of stay', *International Journal of Offender Therapy and Comparative Criminology*, 45(2): 252–63.

Shine, J. (2010) 'Towards a social analytical therapy', in R. Shuker and E. Sullivan (eds), *Grendon and the Emergence of Forensic Therapeutic Communities: Developments in Research and Practice*. Chichester: Wiley Blackwell.

Shine, J. and Morris, M. (2000) 'Addressing criminogenic needs in a prison therapeutic community', *Therapeutic Communities*, 21(3): 197–219.

Shuker, R. (2010) 'Personality disorder: Using therapeutic communities as an integrative approach to address risk', in R. Shuker and E. Sullivan (eds), *Grendon and the Emergence of Forensic Therapeutic Communities: Developments in Research and Practice*. Chichester: Wiley Blackwell.

Shuker, R., Falshaw, L. and Newton, M. (2007) 'Risk and treatment readiness: The impact of historical and psychosocial variables on treatment completion', in R. Shuker and E. Sullivan (eds), *Issues in Forensic Psychology: Readiness for Treatment*, 7: 87–97. Leicester: The British Psychological Society.

Shuker, R. and Newberry, M. (2010) 'Changes in interpersonal relating following therapeutic community treatment at HMP Grendon', in R. Shuker and E. Sullivan (eds), *Grendon and the Emergence of Forensic Therapeutic Communities: Developments in Research and Practice*. Chichester: Wiley Blackwell.

Shuker, R. and Newton, M. (2008) 'Treatment outcome following intervention in a prison-based therapeutic community: a study of the relationship between reduction in criminogenic risk and improved psychological well-being', *The British Journal of Forensic Practice*, 10(3): 33–44.

Singleton, N., Meltzer, H., Gatward, R., Coid, J. and Deasy, D. (1998) *Psychiatric Morbidity among Prisoners*. London: Office for National Statistics.

Stangier, U., Heidenreich, T., Peitz, M., Lauterbach, W. and Clark, D.M. (2003) 'Cognitive therapy for social phobia: individual versus group treatment', *Behaviour Research and Therapy*, 41(9): 991–1007.

Taylor, R. (2000) *A Seven-Year Reconviction Study of Grendon Therapeutic Community Research Findings*. London: Home Office Research and Statistics Directorate.

Waldinger, R.J. and Gunderson, J.G. (1989) *Effective Psychotherapy with Borderline Patients: Case Studies*. Arlington, VA: American Psychiatric Publishing.

Warren, F., Preedy-Frayes, K., McGauley, G., Pickering, A., Norton, K., Gedees, J.R. and Dolan, B. (2003) *Review of Treatments for Personality Disorder*. Home Office Online Report 30/03. London: Home Office.

Chapter 11

Therapy and offending behaviour programmes

Danny Clark

Introduction

Accredited offending behaviour programmes (OBPs) are now the main means by which psychologically-based interventions intended to reduce reoffending are delivered in prisons in England and Wales. In the financial year 2007–8 over 34,000 offenders completed OBPs. A large percentage of the psychological resources available to the National Offender Management Service (NOMS) is devoted to them. However, the accredited programme approach has been criticised on a number of counts (Mair 2004 and SCMH 2008). Although more individual psychological therapy is now being offered in prisons, through the introduction of prison mental health in-reach teams (MHIRTs), one of the main accusations against OBPs is that the predominance of structured offending behaviour programmes has led to all other aspects of individual therapy and counselling being devalued as a means of rehabilitation, in the eyes of both prison staff and prisoners. This chapter presents a brief history of OBPs and describes how the accredited OBPs gained pre-eminence, and why other psychotherapeutic approaches are now influencing the direction and development of structured programmes once more.

Early psychological interventions with offenders

In Britain, as in most westernised societies, there is a very long history of correctional interventions based on psychological concepts.

Psychologists were first appointed to posts in prisons in 1947, and, although initially involved in assessing 'convicts', they quickly became involved in therapy. From the 1960s onwards, in Europe and North America, more overtly psychologically-based interventions were introduced as elements of prison regimes. Originally, most of these were distinctly psychotherapeutic in nature and specifically orientated to 'treating' criminal behaviour.

There was an overenthusiasm for these therapies and there were unsubstantiated claims about their benefits. The idea of the offender and of criminality as being treatable permeated popular culture, as was evident in many crime films and television dramas of the post-war era, where once the criminal was apprehended some righteous character would express the view that they 'really needed, or might actually receive, help'. In reality, the treatments offered were limited and varied greatly in their content, quality and theoretical basis, if indeed they had any such basis. Most were based on general psychotherapeutic techniques which had been applied to non-offender groups and could loosely be termed psychodynamic in orientation. They included counselling, intensive casework, psychotherapy, therapeutic milieux and various forms of group work. In general they were very verbal and introspective, for they had originally been applied to populations suffering from neurosis. Many were unstructured and had fairly vague aims, such as improving self-esteem, self-actualisation, personal growth or just insight into oneself. The range was limited only by the imagination of practitioners and the security requirements of the establishment.

Interventions were applied by various types of professionals – psychologists, psychiatrists, therapists, probation officers, welfare workers, voluntary workers and custodial staff – in various settings. Usually the therapies were voluntary, offered as an extra for offenders who were willing to participate. The rationale for most of these programmes was that the traditional punishment of offenders, especially imprisonment, only reinforced criminality and increased problems for the delinquent; therefore, any form of therapy was better than nothing. In spite of these obvious limitations, many theorists and practitioners were extremely optimistic about what might be achieved. Unfortunately, very little proper evaluation occurred, and when it did occur it was usually at a fairly superficial level. The reviews of evaluation studies which were completed, produced very unsatisfactory results (Robinson 1971; Brody 1976).

The reaction to this exponential development of psychotherapeutic programmes without any substantiated benefits, such as a reduction in recidivism, was inevitable. In the face of continually spiralling crime rates many politicians and administrators became cynical about the role of therapy in rehabilitation and embraced the doctrine that 'nothing works' (Martinson 1974) and the abandonment of all treatment. Many policy-makers accepted the position of Robinson (1971) who argued, from a review of contemporary research, that the criminal remained much the same however one treated him.

Another difficulty for psychological interventions first noted at this time was that therapists frequently seemed to be unwilling to address their clients' most important problem, namely their criminal behaviour. Johnson (1977), reviewing the literature concerning behaviour modification interventions in correctional settings, concluded that therapy had demonstrated that it could change prisoners' behaviour in many ways but not that it could rehabilitate them. He believed that this was because actual criminal behaviour was never targeted. Emery and Marhollin (1977) showed that interventions were applied in a way to produce only first order change and that most interventions concentrated on aims such as raising self-esteem, improving social skills or coping with stress, changes which did not generalise to the problem of criminal behaviour. They inferred that this was because of lack of individual focus and follow-up sessions. They suggested that a functional analysis of each individual is essential to make interventions work. The situation improved very little over the next 10 years. Fisher and Towl (1989) stated in an Introduction to an evaluation of an offending behaviour course that, 'There is reluctance on the part of specialist staff (i.e. psychologists) working in prisons to tackle offending behaviour directly' (p. 2). It was often easier to deal with prisoners' other problems, albeit perhaps in the hope that there might be an indirect impact on criminal behaviour.

By the time the present author began working in prisons in 1978, 'nothing works' was the prevailing paradigm among prison staff of all types and grades. It appeared that the rehabilitative effort, at least with adult offenders, had reached an all-time low. Prison policy at the time did not have the high political visibility it does today and was primarily focused on containment. In this atmosphere it was very difficult for the sort of unstructured and unproven psychotherapeutic interventions which had existed in earlier years to survive. Many prison psychologists redirected their attention away from working directly with offenders and towards working with prison management, to which they felt they were able to make a greater and more valued contribution. They became involved in staff selection and training, monitoring the prison environment, and evaluating prison policy. Other staff groups who in earlier times had counselled offenders were also reviewing their roles. The Probation Service's presence in prisons was, as ever, under pressure, with posts extremely difficult to fill; and the role of Assistant Governor, which had been relatively undefined – and often a resource enthusiastically committed to offenders' rehabilitation – disappeared in the unified grading structure introduced by the initiative known as Fresh-Start.

Of course, psychotherapeutic work did not disappear entirely. Individual psychologists continued to provide counselling for individual offenders in many circumstances. Usually, though, the objective was not to reduce offending but rather to assist offenders with coping with the pains of imprisonment. During his first two or three years of working in prisons the author spent much of his time counselling offenders who were suffering from anxiety and reactive depression due to their circumstances. The prevention of suicide and self-harm was always a priority, and managing offenders who were deemed to be disruptive to the regime was also an essential task. It is rather surprising, then, to note that, despite the lack of support for rehabilitative work at this time, when McGurk *et al.* (1987) edited *Applying Psychology to Imprisonment* to mark 40 years of prison psychology, around a third of the book was about psychological interventions aimed at aspects of offending. Granted, many of the studies related to young offenders and some represented the behaviour modification tradition. However, the published studies represented only the tip of the iceberg of psychologists' work with offenders, essentially a sub-sample of work that practitioners were prepared to submit, and that the editors considered suitable for publication.

Applying Psychology to Imprisonment also contained a seminal chapter by David Thornton which re-evaluated the work of Martinson and reviewed the original studies. Thornton (1987) showed that of the 231 studies originally gathered by Martinson, only 38 met the stringent criteria of using recidivism as an outcome variable, of assigning subjects randomly, or of matching processes to treatment and non-treatment groups, and were thus classified as methodologically acceptable. Most of these studies (34 out of 38) involved a comparison of an experimental group exposed to what might loosely be described as psychotherapy and a control group treated in the normal way, while the others (four out of 38) focused on halfway houses and vocational training. Thornton argued that this gave Martinson's work a much narrower significance than had often been supposed. It revealed the dearth of well-researched intervention studies at the time and showed that Martinson's findings related to interventions which were predominantly verbal and which relied on the relationships developed between offenders and staff. Thornton (1987) indicated that these treatments are completely different in nature from behaviour therapies, vocational skills training and cognitive behavioural programmes. He argued that there was no basis for judging the effectiveness of these other kinds of treatment from the 34 studies using psychotherapy. Moreover, Thornton demonstrated that, of those 34 studies, 16 showed a positive advantage for the treated group, one showed a disadvantage and 17 showed no significant differences. Thus almost 50 per cent of studies did show a treatment effect. Thornton concluded that the catalogue of studies reported by Martinson might properly be read as indicating that psychological therapy can have positive effects on recidivism, or indicating that no conclusion can yet be drawn, but not as showing that nothing works.

The development of offending behaviour programmes

Evidence that something did work was building up elsewhere. Between 1985 and 2000 a series of reviews using meta-analytic techniques was published demonstrating that some interventions did reduce offending behaviour (Garrett 1985; Gendreau and Ross 1987; Gendreau 1990; Andrews 1995; Lipton *et al.* 2000; McGuire 1995; Nuttall *et al.* 1998; Izzo and Ross 1990; Sherman *et al.* 1997). Cumulatively these reviews incorporated findings from more than 2,000 primary studies and allowed a clear consensus to develop among researchers about the aspects of work with offenders likely to contribute to success in reducing rates of offending. McGuire (2000: 98) summarises the conclusions as follows:

- The contents of effective interventions are clearly conceptualised, theoretically driven and empirically based and are more likely to involve the application of cognitive-behavioural models than other forms of treatment.

- Effective interventions incorporate an assessment of risk of reoffending which allows allocation of individuals to different levels of service according to their likely future risk.

- There is a focus on aspects of individuals' lives which are conducive to or supportive of offence acts (e.g. patterns of social interaction, skills deficits, and anti-social attitudes) in effective interventions.

- The methods used in effective interventions, and the manner of interaction between staff and offenders, are designed to reflect the learning styles of the majority of offenders.

- The integrity of interventions is maintained in that they are delivered by enthusiastic, empathic, and appropriately trained staff. They are adequately resourced. Practitioners engaged in the intervention adhere to pre-decided methodological principles in undertaking their work.

The findings from the meta-analytic studies became the body of evidence known as the 'what works' research and began to inform the work of prison psychologists in Britain during the 1980s. One of the earliest examples was the use of anger management techniques based on the work of Novaco (McDougall *et al.* 1987). Anger management programmes addressed offending behaviour and also dealt with the frustrations and tensions generated by the prison. They could be evaluated against such outcomes as a reduction in prison disciplinary adjudications and improved institutional behaviour. McDougall *et al.* (1987) were able to demonstrate the efficacy of such programmes against these outcomes at one young offender institution. Anger management programmes benefited from high face validity with prison staff and management because they dealt with the immediate problem of volatile offenders disrupting prison regimes. Once there was a modicum of evidence to suggest that they were effective, they quickly spread across the prison estate and became a regular component of the prison psychologist's repertoire.

In many ways anger management programmes were the ideal intervention for prisons. In assessing the effectiveness, there were none of the confounding variables associated with reintegration, nor did the researchers need to wait two years after prisoners were released to gather data; there was tangible evidence of offenders remaining calm and stable on the prison wings. However, the success rate, although statistically significant, was not outstanding and relapse was common. It is important to note, though, that, the prisoners who failed were usually subject to other measures, which reduced their visibility, such as segregation or transfer, whereas successes remained highly visible on normal location.

Another innovation in anger management programmes was the use of prison officers as therapists. This had many benefits: it allied the delivery of psychological interventions with the wider interests of prison staff, in terms of job enhancement; it mined a rich seam of knowledge and experience about prisoners' behaviour which could be used in sessions; it created programme champions who were able to ensure that the work was not stymied by other pressures in the prison; and it greatly increased the chances that the programmes would be successful, by creating wing mentors for programme graduates and spreading the message of emotional control techniques to other members of staff.

The downsides to involving prison officers as therapists, of course, was that the majority did not have any clinical or counselling experience, or any prior knowledge of psychological theory. And although prison officers could develop a good rapport and a mentoring relationship with prisoners, there was always a tension in the dual role of being a group worker and custody officer; the presence of uniformed staff definitely impacted on the level of disclosure and openness of participants. But the most significant side effects of this innovation were a resulting simplification of the social learning models which underpinned the treatment and a move from a psychotherapeutic approach to one which was primarily psycho-educational. The courses became very structured: in order to ensure that they were delivered properly, they had clear objectives and clear boundaries for the problems which would be dealt with; issues such as the early causes and development of maladaptive behaviour were not dealt with in any detail. These programmes did not promise to deliver a greater insight into the prisoners' past behaviour, but rather provided a way of helping them to learn new skills which would be advantageous in dealing with frustrating and confrontational situations during their sentence and in the future.

Not all programmes developed at this time were concerned with anger management. The fledgling work with sex offenders that would become the basis of the national Sex Offender Treatment Programme (SOTP) was beginning in two or three establishments. These programmes were always offence-focused and based on the premise that offenders needed to understand the background to their offending by developing an individual functional analysis of their offending, within a cognitive behavioural framework.

There were also programmes which addressed a specific range of difficulties which had been identified as common to many offenders. One example of these was a short intervention developed by the author (Clark 1993). The intervention programme was only 16 hours long; it was to be used within the constraints of a high-security prison; and it was aimed at improving cognitive skills among long-term prisoners. Research has established that an array of cognitive skills deficits, such as poor problem-solving, a lack of impulse control, egocentric thinking, an external locus of control and a lack of consequential or critical thinking were associated with offending behaviour (Clark 2000). This programme drew heavily on earlier programmes and on research demonstrating methods of improving cognitive skills, but was unique in that it was intended not only to encourage the development of cognitive skills which would reduce offending, but also to assist prisoners with the problems they encountered in their current custodial environment. It focused on material relevant to long-term prisoners who had little previous custodial experience; they were individuals who lacked resilience and personal resources, had difficulty coping with life, had problems coping with imprisonment and would find resettlement difficult.

Offenders assessed as requiring the course were randomly allocated to the course or an alternative more traditional course of stress management and progressive relaxation which was already running in the establishment. Those who completed the cognitive skills course were found to have improved on psychometric measures of impulsivity, locus of control, problem solving, abstract and critical reasoning. They also showed improved attitudes to staff and other prisoners. The control group did not show any such gains. Staff using behavioural checklists assessed prisoners who completed the course as improving on how well they dealt with problems, coping with imprisonment, impulse control and relationships with others. The gains made were still evident when the sample was followed up six months after the course.

This short course appeared remarkably effective within the confines of the prison. It was delivered by a small group of enthusiastic psychologically-trained staff, who were closely involved in its development, and the participants were volunteers who were motivated to change. Involved staff and motivated offenders are now known to improve the effectiveness of programmes. However, the programme did not have any impact on measures of empathy nor did it reduce anti-social attitudes. It was also found that there was deterioration in the observed behaviour of the 13 prisoners who failed to complete the course, as judged by the behavioural checklists. Further investigation revealed that those who dropped out could be identified by the pre-course measures as those with the most extreme cognitive deficits. This indicated that the programme was probably not delivered with sufficient intensity and not suitable for everyone – especially not for offenders who had a very high level of risk and need.

The programme was revised and extended with additional material on empathy and moral development and became the Thinking Skills Programme which was implemented across a number of prison establishments in 1994. After further review in 1996 the course was reorganised, and additional sessions were added to improve the development of social skills and to challenge cognitive distortions. In this format it became the National Enhanced Thinking Skills (ETS) programme which has been the mainstay of OBPs for offenders who do not have complex needs for the past 15 years.

ETS was not the only offending behaviour programme introduced or developed in British prisons around that time. Various programmes for cognitive skills, anger management and sex offender treatment sprang up at various prisons in response to the new enthusiasm for treatment – among them, the Canadian programme Reasoning and Rehabilitation, and a programme authored by James McGuire, a precursor of the Think First programme. In an attempt to bring a coordinated and strategic approach to programme development and implementation the Prison Service set up the offending behaviour programmes unit (OBPU). This small team was initially tasked with coordinating sex offender treatment programmes, but that remit was swiftly extended to cognitive skills programmes and then interventions for violent offenders, including anger management.

The standardisation and accreditation of programmes

The remit of the OBPU was to develop a range of ways to address the risk and needs of specific subsections of the prison population. The OBPU was also responsible for training prison staff to deliver programmes and for supporting and advising prisons on implementation. It soon became clear that merely providing training and support was not enough to ensure effective delivery. There were numerous ways that programmes were undermined, ranging from a lack of priority and resourcing by prison managers to well-intended but inappropriate modifications by facilitators. In order to reduce the risks to programme integrity, a process of accreditation and audit was established.

At first, two small expert panels were set up in 1996 to advise the OBPU on the design and delivery of sex offender treatment programmes and general offending programmes respectively. The panels included independent experts and representatives of the Prison Service; they operated in a relatively informal way, working closely with those responsible for the design and delivery of programmes. In 1999 they were replaced by a new, more formally constituted non-departmental public body, which became known as the Correctional Services Accreditation Panel (CSAP). The CSAP members were appointed on the basis of open competition and their remit was expanded to include programmes delivered in the community. CSAP had two main functions: to accredit 'gold standard interventions' against an agreed set of criteria and to scrutinise the auditing of programmes.

The accreditation criteria used by CSAP have changed relatively little over time. Maguire *et al.* (2009) noted that the criteria reflect the main principles of effective interventions suggested by the results of meta-analyses and that they strongly favour cognitive behavioural methods. However, the panel's experience is that the criteria could be adapted to the assessment of interventions based on quite different principles (such as therapeutic communities or 12-step drug programmes). The 10 accreditation criteria are as follows:[1]

- *Clear model of change*: There should be an explicit model to explain how the programme is intended to bring about relevant change in offenders.

- *Selection of offenders*: The types of offenders for whom the programme is intended and the methods to select them should be specified.

- *Targeting a range of dynamic risk factors*: It should be described how the programme addresses the dynamic risk factors associated with reoffending.

- *Effective methods*: Evidence should be provided to show that the treatment methods used are likely to have an impact on the targeted risk factors.

- *Skills oriented*: It should be shown how the programme will facilitate the learning of skills that will assist participants to avoid criminal activity.

- *Intensity, sequencing and duration*: The frequency and number of treatment sessions should be matched to the degree of treatment needs typical for most participants in the programme.

- *Engagement and motivation*: The programme should be structured to maximise the engagement of participants and sustain their motivation.

243

- *Continuity of programmes and services*: There should be clear links between the programme and the overall management of the offender both during a prison sentence and in the context of community supervision.

- *Maintaining integrity*: There should be in-built mechanisms which monitor operations and enable service delivery to be adjusted where necessary.

- *Ongoing evaluation*: There should be an outline of how a programme will be evaluated so that its effectiveness can be analysed.

Maguire *et al.* (2009) describe the official remit of the CSAP in authorising procedures for audits of programme delivery and in receiving an annual assessment of the quality of actual programmes. The main objectives are to ensure: that senior managers are supplying the necessary resources to run programmes properly; that programme and treatment managers are adequately supervising delivery and supporting staff; and that facilitators are maintaining programme 'integrity' and avoiding 'drift'. Prison audits use a combination of psychologists, who assess the quality of delivery, principally through the video monitoring of facilitators running sessions, and prison governors, who focus on management. Audit instruments were designed in consultation with CSAP and marks are awarded to sites under headings such as 'institutional support', 'committed leadership', 'programme management', 'quality of programme delivery' and 'continuity and resettlement'. The results of the audits are reported to CSAP on an annual basis for scrutiny and approval. Maguire *et al.* (2009) state that, 'the programme audits have made an important contribution, in particular by regularly pressing prison managers to resource programmes adequately and by firmly repeating messages to practitioners at all levels about the importance of high quality delivery' (p. 9).

However, not everyone was enamoured of the joint approaches of accreditation and audit. Maguire *et al.* (2009) note that, 'There was considerable disagreement about the accreditation criteria adopted, and those who disagree may become resistant or attempt to undermine the process' (p. 4). It is certainly the case that if accreditation is empirically based, it is bound to favour interventions which are more easily replicable, rather than those therapies which adopt a more individually tailored approach; indeed, the Canadian equivalent of CSAP made replicability into a discrete criterion for accreditation. The process of obtaining accreditation also requires programme developers to manualise their treatment; and apart from objecting to the workload that involved, some authors are fundamentally opposed to this approach (as is discussed below). Undoubtedly, accreditation can become an obstacle to innovation and creativity, unless a process of review and change management exists. The CSAP has also expressed concerns that accreditation becomes an end in itself and displaces the onus on to programme developers to demonstrate the effectiveness of their interventions thorough commissioning good-quality research into outcomes.

While most people recognise that accrediting design is not sufficient on its own, and that quality assurance is important, the audit process has been accused of being overbearing, time-consuming and non-supportive. A major criticism is that the assessment for quality assurance by video-monitoring restricts a facilitator's options to deliver programmes responsively to participants. It has been suggested that audit requires too much effort to be expended on monitoring to the detriment of delivery and removes the focus on longer-term outcomes.

Evaluation and outcomes of programmes

The first national evaluation of the impact of cognitive skills programmes produced encouraging results in reduced reconviction (Friendship *et al.* 2002). However, two further evaluations of the same programmes were much less positive: Cann *et al.* (2003) found no significant differences between programme participants and a comparison group, and Falshaw *et al.* (2003) found significant benefits for programme completers only. On the other hand, international evidence from various systematic reviews and meta-analyses of a large number of studies continues to support the effectiveness of these programmes in reducing reoffending (Aos *et al.* 2006; Lipsey and Landenberger 2006). A recent briefing paper from the Ministry of Justice summarises the evidence as follows:

> [A] recent international review found that, on average, cognitive behavioural programmes for general offenders reduced recidivism by four percentage points: positive effects of programmes are associated with treatment of higher risk offenders, and high quality treatment implementation. The evidence from research in England and Wales on the effectiveness of OPBs is mixed, and these findings may be due to implementation failure or the

research designs used which makes it difficult to attribute the outcomes directly to the impact of the intervention (OMSAS 2009: 45).

The quantitative studies demonstrated that OBPs in prisons were not working as had been hoped. Clarke *et al.* (2004) set out to obtain a subjective understanding of 'what works' by conducting 113 interviews with offenders and members of staff from six prisons. The study sought a full understanding of what constitutes effective practice by exploring what social and institutional factors enabled prisoners to use the treatment programmes successfully, and how prison and resettlement contexts can encourage or inhibit them in that. The offender interviewees comprised both programme graduates who had successfully completed a cognitive skills programme and 'reconvicted' graduates (that is, those who had completed a programme but had been reconvicted and had returned to prison). In addition, interviews were conducted with people who had been released from prison after completing a cognitive skills programme and had not yet reoffended. Clarke *et al.* (2004) found that there was a general recognition that the programmes made a contribution to behaviour adjustment: prison staff reported a perceptible improvement in the attitudes and behaviour of programme participants; offender interviewees regarded their newly-acquired thinking skills as having a positive impact on the ways in which they approached other people and social situations. However, few of them identified desistance from reoffending as a direct consequence of the programme. Interestingly, the 'reconvicted' graduates appeared anxious to attribute their reoffending to extraneous factors such as resettlement difficulties and addiction problems rather than to the failure of the programme. It was also found that those who had not reoffended acknowledged that they had benefited from supportive influences such as resettlement and acquiring employment, but also recognised the need to apply their cognitive skills in daily life. There was a widespread acceptance among this group that the programme had worked for them because they had reached a stage in their lives at which they realised that they genuinely wanted to change. Clarke *et al.* (2004) concluded that, 'The motivation of individual programme participants was a key factor in explaining the treatment impact and outcomes of cognitive skills programmes. Motivation for programme participation and individual change are influenced by a complex combination of the individual's characteristics, the institutional context in which programmes are delivered and how the individual engages with the programme' (p. 64).

The importance of motivating offenders was always well understood by programme developers, and concepts such as the cycle of change were well established. However, there was a tendency among programme developers at this stage to assume that motivational work would be done before attending the programme, by referring agents such as personal officers or by treatment managers. It was only with the introduction of programmes such as the Focus on Resettlement (FOR)[2] and other interventions that were explicitly motivational that this motivational work became the norm.

Back to basics

The evaluation studies above made it clear that OBPs were not working effectively and did not provide the promised results. Clarke *et al.* (2004) thought that institutional factors were affecting the efficacy of OBPs; Briggs and Turner (2003) identified a range of organisational factors contributing to non-completion. McMurran and McCulloch (2005), when examining programme attrition, identified several contributory factors including: having to work in a group; the irrelevance of programme content to the offender's own needs; the chance to attend coming at the wrong time; and inappropriate 'pitching' of the programme (some offenders found the programme insufficiently stimulating, and others too demanding). A widely expressed view was that the rapid expansion of OBPs and the inadequate skills and poor retention of facilitators were limiting their success.

Andrews *et al.* (1990) identified four principles which they claim are the key characteristics of effective intervention: the 'risk principle', which states that treatment resources must be matched to the level of risk posed by the offender; the 'need principle', which states that interventions must address offenders' criminogenic needs; the 'responsivity principle', which asserts that effective treatment and the way it is delivered must take account of all aspects of the offender's characteristics, including their personality traits, learning styles, cultural diversity and levels of motivation; and 'professional discretion', which implies practitioners have a duty to revise treatment if an offender's unique characteristics and situation are not adequately taken into account by the first three principles.

OBPs have attempted to adhere to the first two principles but have tended to overlook the third and fourth principles and to replace them with a fifth principle of programme integrity, which has not always been to the benefit of programmes or of offenders. It is possible that in the drive to ensure consistency of treatment, and to provide treatment on a large scale, OBPs may have become too structured and facilitators too regimented in their delivery. The CSAP recognises this problem and Maguire *et al.* (2009) argue that 'unless interventions are delivered as designed and in a mindful and responsive style, much of the value of even the best designed programme is likely to be lost' (p. 8). Evidence from psychotherapy in general shows that relationship and interactional factors are at least as relevant for the outcome as the type and design of the programme (Orlinsky *et al.* 1994). Drozd and Goldfried (1996) argue that manualised treatment may be able to specify the principles of effective therapeutic process but does not guarantee the development of a therapeutic alliance.

Some experts have argued against the whole concept of manualisation. Laws and Marshall (2003), writing about sex offender treatment, argue that for the most part treatment manuals were rare or non-existent until the more recent advent of behavioural and subsequently cognitive behavioural programmes. Marshall (2009) states that early behaviour therapists were determined to specify what they did in sufficient detail so that their treatment could be replicated by others; this led to the creation of manuals and to a focus on procedures, in part because they were the elements of treatment that were easiest to specify. He reports that surveys of clinicians have shown that approximately 50 per cent of therapists essentially ignore the use of manuals and that one third even expressed uncertainty about what constituted a manual. Marshall quotes many research sources to explain that, in order to maintain fidelity, therapists feel obliged to take the manual into the treatment room. But he is emphatic that most clinicians declare that they dislike manualised interventions because their use impedes the development of the therapeutic relationship by distracting both the therapist and client. In addition, therapists object to the restrictions imposed by a manual that does not allow them the flexibility to respond to the unique characteristics of clients; and it could be argued that clients too might feel that an approach that does not take into account their unique features is less likely to be effective.

However, an entirely different view is taken by Mann (2009). She describes how general psychotherapy research literature comparing manualised therapy as opposed to individualised therapy has produced mixed results, but notes that the balance of findings seems to point to the superiority of the manualised approach; she claims that in the correctional programming literature, the evidence leads to a similar conclusion. Mann states that the major commentators on the body of knowledge known as 'what works' always include 'printed/taped manuals' in their lists of essential ingredients for an effective correctional programme. Mann quotes a study by Webster *et al.* (2005) where the researchers were able to compare two interventions, and because both interventions were manualised, the researchers were confident that they were isolating the effect of a specific exercise in their comparison. Mann concludes that manualisation increases the likelihood that a therapist will deliver a psychological treatment in line with evidence-based practice and will remain faithful to the principles that research has established to be most consistently linked to successful outcomes.

The current author would concur with Mann's view that structured programmes are better and that OBPs have demonstrated their worth as the most practical means of addressing anti-social attitudes, thinking and behaviour on the scale necessary to make a difference. However, he would also agree with the opinion of Hollin (2009) that:

structured treatment such as Accredited Programmes should only ever be delivered by therapists who are mindful facilitators, and who are supervised in terms of their therapeutic alliance as well as their adherence to the manual. Otherwise manualised treatment will be ineffective, and might prove detrimental if delivered by untrained and unguided therapists. Therefore, therapists need to be trained in the skills of therapeutic style as well as therapy content. (p. 128)

The therapeutic relationship between practitioners and offenders is increasingly seen as playing an important part in treatment outcomes. Harris (2007) notes that the importance of the therapeutic alliance in clinical treatment was highlighted in a meta-analysis of 79 studies by Martin *et al.* (2000). Marshall *et al.* (2003) found that positive treatment outcomes were associated with a range of behaviours by therapists, including empathy, emotional responsiveness, a warm interpersonal style, acceptance and support, genuineness, respect, the use of open-ended questions, directiveness, encouragement of the client to participate, self-confidence, moderate levels of self-disclosure, flexibility, the use of humour, and a non-confrontational style. Keijsers *et al.* (2000) found two clusters of therapist behaviour associated with positive outcomes in cognitive behavioural treatment. The first cluster related to Rogerian values such as empathy, warmth, positive regard for clients, and genuineness; the second cluster was linked with the establishment of a good therapeutic alliance with the client.

Ward and Brown (2004) have criticised the risk–needs approach to treatment because it fails adequately to link risk management with new constructive ways of living, and because it provides little motivation and encouragement to offenders to change. They argue that offender rehabilitation should focus on giving offenders the necessary capabilities to secure important social and personal goods in an acceptable and pro-social way, rather than focusing simply on the reduction and management of risk. In other words, Ward and Brown (2004) suggest that in order to reduce offending one needs to give individuals the necessary conditions to lead better lives. The 'Good Lives' approach in cognitive behaviour therapy has seen a shift away from focusing on problems and deficits towards building positive adaptive functioning (Harris 2007).

Finally, Ward and Nee (2009) argue that a lack of attention occurs to emotional functioning in offender rehabilitation, whereas emotions function to integrate and motivate action and to influence the way in which the environment is perceived. Day (2009) reviewed the limited research and concluded that there are grounds for considering emotional states as important dynamic risk factors that should be addressed as part of any psychological intervention. He notes that CBT often targets emotional change, but that the treatment process tends to emphasise the modification of dysfunctional thoughts. In this way they promote antecedent-focused and response-focused affective regulation skills. Day (2009) suggests that for some offenders on some occasions a more acceptance-based approach – which taught clients to feel emotions and to notice the presence of thoughts without reacting to them – might be as helpful as the usual approach of challenging and changing thinking to reduce levels of emotional arousal. Day (2009) concludes that, from a therapeutic perspective, the way in which an individual understands and accounts for his or her experiences is clearly important. Offenders who are emotionally inhibited will find it difficult to engage in any therapeutic activity; exploring clients' own theories of emotional regulation is clinically useful. Day (2009) suggests that interventions that explicitly aim to increase emotional awareness, such as experiential therapies, may have a role to play in the treatment of offenders.

Improving offending behaviour programmes

To summarise, there are consistent findings from research that indicate that structured programmes which adhere to the risk, need and responsivity principles (RNR) do produce the greatest benefits in reduced reoffending. Of these three principles, responsivity is probably the most difficult to define and operationalise; it is likely that it will be in the search for a means to increase responsivity that the approaches of structured programmes and dynamic psychotherapy will converge. Marshall (2009) suggests that a more psychotherapeutic approach with sex offenders would have several advantages, such as enhancing responsivity and introducing new therapeutic elements that would enhance treatment, and would have the overall effect of increasing the effectiveness of interventions to reduce sexual offending. It might be that approaches which are effective in engaging sex offenders could be applicable with other types of offenders. This is already happening to some extent, for example, in the introduction of a new thinking skills programme by NOMS in all prisons and probation trusts. This programme represents a significant move in this direction with its focus on engaging and motivating offenders and its opportunities for individual work. Harris (2007), writing in the theory manual for the new thinking skills programme, suggests that the risk–needs approach is usefully complemented by a greater emphasis on other aspects of offenders' lives, such as focusing on the wider needs, goals and ambitions of offenders (e.g. Ward 2002), and considering a desistance approach (e.g. Farrall 2002). The desistance approach highlights how the success of any intervention rests upon offenders being able to integrate or reintegrate into society; it is mirrored by wider innovations in cognitive behaviour therapy.

Harris (2007) describes how these points have been built into the new thinking skills programme:

- The programme adopts a style of facilitation that is respectful, non-judgemental, curious, warm, supportive, collaborative, genuine, and that is directive without being confrontational.

- The programme assessment supports engagement and establishes a collaborative working alliance by being transparent, evolving, highlighting strengths as well as needs, and informing goal setting.

- The programme acknowledges the participants' right to choose their own actions while maintaining a clear focus on promoting participants' acceptance of responsibility for the consequences of these choices.

- The programme emphasises that participants are experts in their own lives, and have an explicit goal of building on strengths.

- Programme facilitation explicitly focuses on establishing a collaborative alliance between programme staff and participants, and between group participants.

- The layout of manuals and manual content should contribute to enhancing facilitators' skills and treatment styles.

- The recruitment and training of staff focuses on identifying, developing and monitoring effective facilitation skills and treatment styles.

Another innovation of the new programme is that individual sessions are interspersed with group work modules. They are designed to enable facilitators to better understand the participant and for the participant to develop their own understanding of themselves. This sets the tone of collaborative, transparent and respectful working and emphasises that the participant is the expert in their own life. The new programme has been provisionally accredited by the CSAP and piloted in both prisons and probation; once fully accredited, it will be implemented across NOMS and replace ETS and all other cognitive skills programmes. This is a major project of renewal for NOMS, which will involve reassessing and retraining over 900 facilitators.

One view of the history of OBPs might be that we have come full cycle. In the beginning programmes were broadly psychotherapeutic and unfocused; because they lacked impact, practitioners moved to highly-structured skills-based interventions; now that the early positive results of this approach have proved difficult to reproduce, they are returning to a less-structured model. Such a view, however, would negate the vast amount of knowledge and evidence which has accumulated over the past 30 years. We are now far better informed and take a more evidence-based approach to psychological interventions to reduce offending than at any time in the past. The OBPs are changing in the light of this knowledge, incorporating many recent advances from wider clinical psychology and psychotherapy, while remaining true to the principles exemplified in the CSAP criteria. This would seem to be a balanced approach to development. There are still many challenges remaining, one of the greatest being to recruit, develop and support facilitators who are competent and confident to deliver this service, in sufficient numbers to really make a measurable impact on reoffending. It is on this area that one would hope to see attention paid in the future.

Notes

1 See any of CSAP's annual reports from 2003 to 2009 published by the Ministry of Justice.
2 Focus on Resettlement (2004) is a short motivational programme developed by T3 Associates Toronto and licensed by NOMS which aims to motivate offenders to seek assistance with their problems after release from prison.

References

Andrews, D.A. (1995) 'The psychology of criminal conduct and effective treatment', in J. McGuire (ed.), *What Works: Reducing Reoffending*. Chichester: John Wiley & Sons.

Andrews, D.A., Zinger, I., Hoge, R.D., Bonta, J., Gendreau, P. and Cullen, F.T. (1990) 'Does correctional treatment work? A clinically relevant and psychologically informed meta-analysis', *Criminology*, 28: 369–404.

Aos, S., Miller, M. and Drake, E. (2006) *Evidence-based Adult Correction Programs: What Works and What Does Not*. Olympia, D.C.: Washington State Institute for Public Policy.

Briggs, S. and Turner, R. (2003) *Barriers to Starting Programmes: Second Phase Report*. West Yorkshire: National Probation Service.

Brody, S. (1976) *The Effectiveness of Sentencing: A Review of the Literature*. London: HMSO.

Cann, J., Falshaw, L., Nugent, F. and Friendship, C. (2003) *Understanding What Works: Accredited Cognitive Skills Programmes for Adult Men and Young Offenders*. Home Office Research Findings 226. London: Home Office.

Clark, D.A. (1993) *Implementation of a Cognitive Skills Programme for Long-Term Prisoners. Proceedings of the Prison Psychology Conference, Bristol 1993*. London: Home Office.

Clark, D.A. (2000) *Theory Manual for Enhanced Thinking Skills Programme*. Prepared for Joint Prison/Probation Accreditation Panel. London: Home Office.

Clarke, A., Simmonds, R. and Wydall, S. (2004) *Delivering Cognitive Skills Programmes in Prison: A Qualitative Study*. Home Office Findings 242. London: Home Office.

Day, A. (2009) 'Offender emotion and self-regulation: Implications for offender rehabilitation programming', *Psychology, Crime and Law*, 15: 119–30.

Drozd, J.F. and Goldfried, M.R. (1996) 'A critical evaluation of the state-of-the-art in psychotherapy outcome research', *Psychotherapy*, 33: 171–80.

Emery, R.E. and Marhollin D. II. (1977) 'An applied analysis of delinquency: the irreverancy of relevant behaviour', *American Psychologist*, 77: 860–73.

Falshaw, L., Friendship, C., Travers, R. and Nugent, F. (2003) *Searching for 'What Works': An Evaluation of Cognitive Skills Programmes*. Home Office Research Findings 206. London: Home Office.

Farrall, S. (2002) *Rethinking What Works with Offenders. Probation, Social Context and Desistence from Crime*. Cullompton: Willan Publishing.

Fisher, J.F. and Towl, G. (1989) *The Offending Behaviour Course at HMP Highpoint. DPS report II. No. 174*. London: Home Office Prison Department.

Friendship, C., Blud, L., Erikson, M. and Travers, R. (2002) *An Evaluation of Cognitive Behavioural Treatment for Prisoners*. Home Office Research Findings 161. London: Home Office.

Garrett, C.J. (1985) 'Effects of residential treatment in adjudicated delinquents', *Journal of Research in Crime and Delinquency*, 22(4): 287–308.

Gendreau, P. (1990) 'Introduction', *Criminal Justice and Behavior*, 17: 4–5.

Gendreau, P. and Ross, R.R. (1987) 'Ramifications of rehabilitation evidence from the 1980s', *Justice Quarterly*, 4: 349–408.

Harris, D. (2007) *The New Cognitive Skills Theory Manual*. London: Ministry of Justice/NOMS Interventions and Substance Misuse Group.

Hollin, C.R. and Palmer, E.J. (eds) (2006) *Offending Behaviour Programmes: Development, Application and Controversies*. Chichester: John Wiley & Sons.

Hollin, C.R. (2009) 'Treatment manuals; the good, the bad, and the useful', *Journal of Sexual Aggression*, 15(2): 121–31.

Izzo, R.L. and Ross, R.R. (1990) 'Meta-analysis of rehabilitation programs for juvenile delinquents', *Criminal Justice and Behaviour*, 171: 134.

Johnson, V.S. (1977) 'Behaviour modification in the correctional setting', *Criminal Justice and Behaviour*, 4(4): 397–432.

Keijsers, G.P.J., Schaap, C.P.D.R. and Hoogduin, C.A.L. (2000) 'The impact of interpersonal patient and therapist behavior on outcome in cognitive-behavioral therapy: A review of empirical studies', *Behavior Modification*, 24(2): 264–97.

Laws, D.R. and Marshall, W.L. (2003) 'A brief history of behavioural and cognitive-behavioral approaches to sexual offender treatment: Part 1. Early developments', *Sexual Abuse: A Journal of Research and Treatment*, 15: 75–92.

Lipsey, M. and Landenberger, N. (2006) 'Cognitive-behavioral interventions', in B. Welsh and D. Farrington (eds), *Preventing Crime: What Works for Children, Offenders, Victims, and Places*. Berlin: Springer Verlag.

Lipton, D.S., Thornton, D.M., McGuire J., Porporino, F.J. and Hollin C.R. (2000) 'Programme accreditation and correctional treatment', *Substance Use and Misuse*, 35: 1705–34.

Maguire, M., Grubin, D., Lösel, F. and Raynor, P. (2009) '"What Works" and the Correctional Services Accreditation Panel: Taking stock from an inside perspective', awaiting publication in *Criminology and Criminal Justice*.

Mair, G. (2004) 'The origins of what works in England and Wales: A house built on sand?', in G. Mair (ed.), *What Matters in Probation*. Cullompton: Willan Publishing, pp. 12–33.

Mann, R.E. (2009) 'Sex offender treatment: the case for manualisation', *Journal of Sexual Aggression*, 15(2): 121–31.

Marshall, W.L., Fernandez, Y.M., Serran, G.A., Mulloy, R., Thornton, D., Mann, R.E. and Anderson, D. (2003) 'Process variables in the treatment of sexual offenders: A review of the relevant literature', *Aggression and Violent Behviour*, 8(2): 205–34.

Marshall, W.L. (2009) 'Manualisation: A blessing or a curse?', *Journal of Sexual Aggression*, 15(2): 109–21.

Martin, D.J., Garske, J.P. and Davis, M.K. (2000) 'Relation of the therapeutic alliance with outcome and other variables: A meta-analytic review', *Journal of Consulting and Clinical Psychology*, 68(3): 438–50.

Martinson R. (1974) 'What works – questions and answers about prison reform', *Public Interest*, 35: 22–54.

McDougall, C., Thomas, M. and Wilson, J. (1987) 'Cognitive anger control', in B.J. McGurk, D.M. Thornton and M. Williams (eds), *Applying Psychology to Imprisonment*. London: HMSO.

McGuire, J. (ed.) (1995) *What Works: Reducing Re-offending*. Chichester: John Wiley & Sons.

McGuire, J. (2000) *Cognitive Behavioural Approaches: An Introduction to Theory and Research*. London: HM Inspectorate of Probation.

McGurk, B., Thornton, D.M and Williams, M. (eds) (1987) *Applying Psychology to Imprisonment*. London: HMSO.

McMurran, M. and McCulloch, A. (2005) *Why Don't Offenders Complete Treatment? Prisoners' Reasons for Non-Completion of a Cognitive Skills Programme*. London: Report to HM Prison Service.

Nuttall, C.P., Goldblatt, P. and Lewis, C. (1998) *Reducing Reoffending: An Assessment of Research Evidence of Ways of Dealing with Offending Behaviour*. London: Home Office.

OMSAS (2009) *Evidence Digest Volume 1*. London: Ministry of Justice.

Orlinsky, D.E., Grawe, K. and Parks, B.K. (1994) 'Process and outcome in psychotherapy – noch einmal', in A. Bergin and S. Garfield (eds), *Handbook of Psychotherapy and Behavior Change*, 4th edition. New York: Wiley.

Robinson, J. (1971) 'The effectiveness of correctional programmes', *Crime and Delinquency*, 1: 67–80.

SCMH (2008) *A Review of the Use of Offending Behaviour Programmes for People with Mental Health Problems*. London: Sainsbury Centre for Mental Health.

Sherman, L.W., Gottfredson, D., Mackenzie, D.L., Eck, J., Rueter, P. and Bushway, S. (1997) *Preventing Crime: What Works, What Doesn't and What Looks Promising*. Washington, DC: National Institute of Justice.

Thornton, D.M. (1987) 'Treatment effects on recidivism: a reappraisal of the nothing works doctrine', in B.J. McGurk, D.M. Thornton and M. Williams (eds), *Applying Psychology to Imprisonment*. London: HMSO.

Ward, T. (2002) 'The management of risk and the design of good lives', *Australian Psychologist*, 37(3): 172–9.

Ward, T. and Brown, M. (2004). 'The good lives model and conceptual issues in offender rehabilitation', *Psychology, Crime, & Law*, 10: 243–57.

Ward, T. and Nee, C. (2009) 'Surfaces and depths: Evaluating the theoretical assumptions of cognitive skills programmes', *Psychology, Crime and Law*, 15: 165–82.

Webster, S.D., Bowers, L.E., Mann, R.E. and Marshall, W.L. (2005) 'Developing empathy in sexual offenders: The value of offence re-enactments', *Sexual Abuse: A Journal of Research and Treatment*, 17: 63–77.

Wilson, G.T. (1996) 'Manual-based treatments: The clinical application of research findings', *Behaviour, Research and Therapy*, 34: 295–314.

Index

Added to a page number 'f' denotes a figure, 't' denotes a table and 'n' denotes notes.

disorders 172, 179, 180–1
figures 186
in prison environment 56–9
styles 51–3
attachment anxiety 56, 61
attachment theory 50–3, 180
relevance to adult offenders 53–5,
68
attachment-based psychodynamic
therapy 48–68
case example 62–5
endings 66
importance of clinical supervision
66–7
key theoretical concepts 49–53
markers of progress 65–6
attendance, therapy sessions 94
automatic thoughts 77
see also negative automatic
thoughts
avoidance snag 118f
Axis I disorders 227, 228, 229, 230n
Axis II disorders 227, 230n

Barlinnie 41, 217
Bateson, Gregory 131, 135, 136
Beck, Aaron 75–6, 78
behaviour modification interventions
236
behavioural repetition 152
behaviour(s)
appraisal of events 81–2
effects of past abuse on 180–1
maladaptive 53
TCs and improvement in 224
understanding in terms of
systems 130–1
beliefs 76, 77, 88, 107, 131, 160, 216
Bennett, David 202–4
bilateral stimulation 160
bipolar disorder 3
black and minority ethnic people
background and context 196–7
terminology 211n
black and minority ethnic prisoners

31, 195–211
case examples
denial and thoughtlessness
about racism 200–2
discussion of 204–5
race-blind approach to care
and treatment 202–4
clinical assessments and
psychological input for 197–
200
likelihood of receiving mental
health services 36–7
literature on therapy with 205–10
mental health difficulties, young
offenders 73
blocked psychological maturation 88
borderline personality disorder 8,
179, 180, 190, 227
Bowlby, John 50
brain 153
brain development 153, 154
bullying 5, 103, 162
bureaucracy xxvi

Campbell, David 131
Canada, prison reforms 41
Cannon, Walter 151
captions, use of 125
CARAT services 35
carceral clawback 40, 41
care
and attachment style 51–2
continuity of 29, 30, 35–6
'good enough' 154
maladaptive 185
race-blind approach to 202–4
see also day care; equivalent care;
mental health care
care planning 34–5
care programme approach (CPA)
30, 35
care-control balance 21
carer-custodian balance 133, 137
'caring for others trap' 117f
case formulation 78

emotional inhibition 250
emotional numbing 152
emotional regulation 6, 154, 172
emotional responses, validation of
    62
emotional states, as dynamic risk
    factors 250
emotions, circularity of 138–9
empathy 53, 54, 62, 154, 183, 241,
    242
enactment, of past abuse 178
ending of therapy 66, 93, 110
engineering concepts, in psychology
    131
England and Wales
    national census of inpatients 204
    offending behaviour programmes
        234
    prisons
        numbers 2
        therapeutic approaches 8
    rate of imprisonment 2
    young offenders
        increased use of custody 72
        numbers in custody 102
        secure settings 72, 73
Enhanced Thinking Skills (ETS) 242,
    252
entry period 5–6
environments see prison
    environment; safe environments
equivalent care xxiii–xxiv, 1, 37–9
ethical considerations
    cognitive analytic therapy 125–6
    working with trauma 170–2
ethnic minorities see black and
    minority ethnic people
evidence-based practice 82–4, 221
evidence-based treatments 78–9, 159,
    228
exits, developing, in CAT 120–2
exotic position 206
explicit memory 55
exposure technique 160
eye movements, in EMDR 159–60

family, prison/hospital as
    representation of 182–3
family contact 7
family system, understanding
    mental illness in terms of 131
family therapists 134
family therapy 96, 133–4, 136–7
family work 134
family work team (FWT) 134–5
feedback loops 139
feedback mechanisms 131
feelings 77, 81–2
female prisoners 176–92
    as both victims and perpetrators
        177
    CBT with 9
    effect of past abuse on behaviour
        180–1
    effects of trauma on minds of
        179–80
    high levels of mental health
        needs 176
    and MHIRTs 36
    mother and baby units 57
    narrative therapy 9
    negative life experiences 178
    numbers 176
    percentage with psychological
        distress 4
    prevalence of mental disorders 27
    as primary carers of young
        children 176–7
    susceptibility to pains of
        imprisonment 27–8
    working with
        anger management, case
            example 181–2
        collusion with patient's
            infantilisation 185–6
        listening to traumatic histories
            190–1
        making a containing and safe
            environment 186–7
        managing assaultative and
            self-harming behaviours
            188–90

individual-based therapy 228–9
infant-caregiver interaction 50, 51, 153–4
infantilisation 184, 185–6
infants, paranoid/schizoid position 49–50
information processing, biased 76–7
information sharing 19, 36, 97
insecure attachment 54
insecure-ambivalent attachment 51
insecure-avoidant attachment 51
institutional racism 203
institutionalisation 75
integrated interventions 161, 219–21
integrated working, need for 42
integrity, in OBPs 247–8
intelligence quotient (IQ) 73
intensive casework 235
inter-prison transfers 94
interactional factors, relevance for outcomes 248
internal conflict, unconscious 49
internal thought 108
internal working models 50, 154
interpersonal therapy 9
interrelationships 50
interventive interviewing 139
isolation 5, 62

just deserts 217

key performance indicators xxvi
Klein, Melanie 49

Labour manifesto (2001) 104
language, capacity for 108
learned helplessness 151
letters, in CAT 109–10
life transitions, young people 74–5
'living, learning experience' 220
locus of control 8, 241
loss 56
low-trust environments 19, 77

maladaptive behaviours 53
maladaptive caring 185

male prisoners
  percentage with psychological distress 4
  prevalence of mental disorders 27
male staff, vulnerability to allegations of misconduct 187
manualisation xxvi, 248–9
mastery 151, 161
maternal abuse 180
Maturana, Humberto 136
Max Glatt unit 41, 217
memory, and trauma 55, 152, 159
mental disorders
  early life experiences 76
  not explaining as due to racism 208–9
  prevalence among prisoners 26–8
  prevalence among young offenders 28, 73–4
  understanding in terms of family system 131
Mental Health Act (1983) 196
mental health care
  improving 1, 31–2
  race equality 197
  see also primary mental health care
mental health in-reach teams (MHIRTs)
  attitudes of prison staff 31–2, 39
  context of 26–31
  difficulty in meeting expectations 42
  equivalent care 37–9
  introduction and remit 1, 11
  realities 31–7
    barriers and challenges 32–3
    improving mental health care 31–2
    meeting the needs of diverse groups 36–7
    mission creep and primary mental health care 33–4, 42
    practical issues 34–5
    working with other agencies 35–6